MEDJUGORJE
THE FIRST SEVEN DAYS

The Events That Took Place from June 24 to July 3, 1981

Author: Darko Pavičić

Translator: Miljenko Musa

Editors: Stella Mar Films (stellamar.org), Christy Bock

Graphic Design and Equipment: LM Design

Photographs: Siniša Hančić, Mijo Gabrić, Foto Djani

Special Thanks: Fr. Leon Pereira, Mary Manning, Sean Bloomfield, Miljenko Musa and Cimela Kidonakis

Published by Catholic Shop LLC and Filip & Darko Pavičić

Catholic Shop LLC - 317 Riveredge Blvd, Suite 102
Cocoa, FL 32922 USA - CatholicShop.com

Filip & Darko Pavičić - Pavičić izdvaštvo i publicistika
Istarska 45b - Zagreb, Croatia

Printed in the USA

ISBN *978-1-954438-03-3*

Darko Pavičić

MEDJUGORJE
THE FIRST SEVEN DAYS

The Events That Took Place from June 24 to July 3, 1981

2021

CONTENTS

INTRODUCTION

The first seven days

WHY?

In May 2017, the respected Vaticanist Andrea Tornielli disclosed on his blog "Vatican Insider" the findings of the Holy See's international commission investigating the events in Medjugorje. After this, I began investigating the first seven days of the apparitions, which, as Tornielli publicized, may become the basis for the official recognition of the Medjugorje phenomenon. Immediately, many questioned the reason for focusing on only seven days, as opposed to the subsequent events. Specifically, whether it was related to the symbolism of the number seven as a perfect biblical number (the same number of days in which God created the world, according to the Book of Genesis)?

Tornielli reported that the commission gave a positive opinion regarding the authenticity of the first apparitions between June 24 and July 3, 1981; thirteen members of the commission voted in favor of recognizing the supernatural nature of the first seven apparitions, one voted against, and one was undecided. According to Tornielli, the group also determined that the young visionaries were psychologically normal; that the apparitions caught them by surprise; and that none of what they had seen was influenced by either the parish Franciscans or anyone else from their surroundings. Moreover, despite police detention and interrogation, the visionaries did not abandon their statements—even under death threats. Tornielli added that the commission also rejected the hypothesis that the apparitions were of a demonic origin. Cardinal Camillo Ruini led the commission.

In May 2017, Pope Francis reported that he had received the results from Cardinal Ruini at the end of 2013 or the beginning of 2014.

"The commission was made up of good theologians, bishops, and cardinals—good, good, good people," he said. "The Ruini report was very, very good. Then, there were some doubts at the Congregation for the Doctrine of the Faith, and the Congregation judged it appropriate to send each member of the *feria quarta*[1] meeting the entire documentation, even the things that seemed contrary to the Ruini report. I was notified about this; I recall that it was late on a Saturday evening. It didn't seem right to me; it was like putting the Ruini report up for auction—sorry for this word—a report which had been done very well. On Sunday morning, the Prefect of the Congregation for the Doctrine of the Faith received a letter from me, in which I asked him to tell them that, instead of sending their opinions to the *feria quarta,* they should send them to me personally."

1 Latin for Wednesday

The commission divided their findings into two parts, and Tornielli discusses the "second phase [of the apparitions]," which refers to the time after July 3. It was about this time that they expressed some doubts. Specifically, the commission noted conflict between the local bishop and the Franciscans, as well as the fact that the apparitions were pre-announced and tailored individually for each visionary.

"These visions continued, despite the youngsters having said they would end, though that has actually never happened," Tornielli wrote. "There is then the issue of the 'secrets' of a somewhat apocalyptic flavor, which the visionaries claim the apparitions revealed to them."

Tornielli added that, in the second stage, the commission voted in two phases. First, they considered the spiritual fruits of Medjugorje while leaving aside the conduct of the visionaries. On this point, three members and three experts said there were positive outcomes; four members and three experts said they were mixed with mostly positive effects; and the remaining three experts claimed there were both positive and negative effects. Next, the members of the commission reviewed the conduct of the visionaries. To this end, twelve members declined to give an opinion, while two other members voted against declaring the apparitions authentic. The commission also noted that the Medjugorje visionaries have not had any intense spiritual accompaniment and that, for quite some time, they have not been acting as a group but, rather, separately by themselves. As a result, Tornielli explained that the Ruini commission concluded and suggested that the Pope lift the ban on organized pilgrimages because—as it is well-known—priests were not allowed to organize pilgrimages to Medjugorje and could only provide spiritual accompaniment. The commission also suggested that the parish of Medjugorje be put under the direct control of the Holy See and become a so-called pontifical shrine.

"This decision is based on pastoral reasons: the care of millions of pilgrims, avoiding the formation of 'parallel churches,' and transparency on financial issues," Tornielli wrote. "But all this would not imply the recognition of the supernatural nature of the apparitions."

Consequently, on February 11, 2017—the feast of Our Lady of Lourdes—Pope Francis appointed Polish Archbishop of Warsaw-Prague, Monsignor Henryk Hoser, as his special envoy to Medjugorje. Then, one year later, Pope Francis appointed him Apostolic Visitor for Medjugorje, specifically for the purpose of improving pastoral care.

So, that is why this book is titled "Medjugorje – The First Seven Days," with the subtitle "The Events That Took Place from June 24 until July 3, 1981." As such, it covers almost all of the events that were recorded in those days—everything that was written and published about the first days: my interviews with the primary individuals of that period, as well as audio tracks of conversations that the pastor, Father Jozo, had with the visionaries. Here, for the first time and gathered in one place, is all the trepidation of that moment. All the doubts and fears, the faith, the determination, and the drama of this celestial intervention that has made a lasting impression upon the time in which we live.

HOW?

This book is a classic journalistic piece. It is based on documents that were produced during the first few days, as well as the result of research and conversations with the visionaries and everyone who participated in those early days. Herein, I use the statements, reflections, and memories of different groups of witnesses of those times. The first group consists of the six visionaries, with whom I spoke:

Ivan Dragičević is the son of Zlata and Stanko and was born on May 25, 1965, in Bijakovići (one of five villages in the Parish of Medjugorje). After finishing high school, Ivan become a caterer. He still has daily apparitions, and Our Lady has confided nine secrets to him so far, as well as a prayer intention to pray for young people and priests. Our Lady also asked him to establish a prayer group. In his youth, Ivan felt called to the priesthood and attended seminary in both Visoko and Dubrovnik. But, feeling misunderstood, he left. In 1989, in Medjugorje, he met American Laureen Murphy, whom he married in 1994. They have four children: Kristina Marija (1995), Mikela (2000), Daniel (2001), and Matthew (2008). They live in Boston, Massachusetts, as well as in Medjugorje.

Vicka Ivanković-Mijatović, the daughter of Zlata and Pero, was born in Bijakovići on September 3, 1964. She has seven brothers and sisters and is a textile technician by training. Our Lady has confided nine secrets to Vicka so far, in addition to a prayer intention to pray for the sick. Vicka still has daily apparitions, and Our Lady dictated her life story to her, which Vicka wrote in three notebooks. She will publish it when Our Lady gives her permission. In January 2002, Vicka married Mario Mijatović and they have two children: Marija-Sofia (2003) and Ante (2005). They live in Krehin Gradac, which is not far from Medjugorje.

Marija Pavlović-Lunetti is the daughter of Iva and Filip. Born on April 1, 1965, in Bijakovići, Marija went to hairdressing school in Mostar. She still has daily apparitions, and Our Lady has entrusted nine secrets to her. Through Marija, Our Lady conveys a message to the parish and to the world on the 25th of each month. Her prayer intention is to pray for consecrated religious and for the souls in purgatory. She married Italian Paolo Lunetti in 1993, and they have four sons: Michele Maria (1994), Francesco Maria (1994), Marco Maria (1998), and Giovanni Maria (2002). They live in Monza near Milan, as well as in Medjugorje.

Mirjana Dragičević-Soldo, the daughter of Milena and Jozo, was born on March 18, 1965 in Sarajevo, where she finished high school and studied agriculture. Mirjana had daily apparitions until December 25, 1982, when Our Lady entrusted her with the tenth and final secret and said that she would appear to Mirjana only once a year, on March 18. However, from August 2, 1987, until March 2, 2020, Mirjana had apparitions on the second day of each month. Her prayer intention is to pray for unbelievers—that is, as Our Lady says, for those who have not yet come to know the love of God. She married Marko Soldo in 1989 and they have two daughters: Marija (1990) and Veronika (1994). They live in Bijakovići.

Jakov Čolo is the son of Jaka and Ante. Although he was born in Sarajevo on March 6, 1971, Jakov has lived in Bijakovići since childhood. After high school, he trained as a locksmith and helped the Franciscans in the parish office in Medjugorje. Today, he runs the charity "Mary's Hands." Our Lady appeared to Jakov daily until September 12, 1998, when he received the tenth and final secret: She promised him that he would have one apparition each year for the rest of his life—every Christmas Day. Jakov's mission is to pray for the sick. In 1993, he married Annalisa Barozzi, an Italian from Asola near Mantova, whom he met while working in Italy. The couple has three children: Arijanna Maria (1995), David Emmanuel (1996), and Myriam (1999). They live in Bijakovići, but often reside in Italy as well.

Ivanka Ivanković-Elez, the daughter of Jagoda and Ivan, was born on June 21, 1966, in Bijakovići. She has an older brother and a sister. At the time of the first apparitions, Ivanka attended an economics high school in Mostar, but withdrew soon after. She was the first to see Our Lady and had daily apparitions until May 7, 1985, when Our Lady entrusted her with the tenth secret. At that time, she told Ivanka that she would receive apparitions once a year on June 25—the anniversary of the apparitions. Ivanka's task is to pray for families. In December 1986, she married Rajko Elez and they have three children: daughter Kristina (1987) and sons Josip (1990) and Ivan (1994). They live in Miletina, in the parish of Medjugorje.

The second group of witnesses consists of individuals who were closest to the visionaries. These are people who were with them daily—especially during the first days and years—and who shared the same fate with them. In addition to their families, these included two priests: **Father Jozo Zovko**—the pastor of Medjugorje, who was sentenced by communist authorities to three and a half years imprisonment—and his chaplain, **Father Zrinko Čuvalo**. Also included are neighbors, such as **Marinko Ivanković** and his wife, **Draga** and **Ivan Ivanković**, who were with the visionaries daily and were persecuted by police. Ivan was sentenced to three months in prison for openly testifying in front of a gathering of factory workers that he saw the cross rotating on Cross Mountain.

The third group of witnesses includes people who were with the visionaries or near them occasionally and who directly followed the events in those first days and months. One of them is **Grgo Kozina**, a radio and recording enthusiast, who made the first audio recordings of the apparitions. He was on Apparition Hill daily, watching the visionaries and carefully recording everything.

In preparation for this book, I spoke with most of the individuals who are still alive. I also used written sources from police inspector Ivan Turudić and Dr. Darinka Glamuzina. This book also incorporates audio recordings of the first conversations between then-pastor Father Jozo Zovko and the visionaries. The children spoke in their local dialect and excitedly recounted what they had experienced, which offers a special dynamic and authenticity to the accounts. As such, I have rendered these conversations literally.

WHERE?

On an evening walk on our first night in Nazareth in Israel, I said to my wife, "Lift your head and look at the sky, please."

"Why?" she asked, looking at the starry sky.

"You see, Mary watched the same sky above Nazareth every evening," I replied. "Everything else around us has changed; only that view has remained the same."

That night, we looked wide-eyed at the same sky that was, long ago, watched by Mary, Joseph, and Jesus.

Much has changed in Medjugorje from the first days of the apparitions until the creation of this book. For instance, in the beginning, the environment changed as small farmhouses were replaced—first by pilgrimage guesthouses and later by large hotels. Then, the people changed. The visionaries—who were children in 1981—are now adults with their own adult children. Nevertheless, the sky above Medjugorje remains the same. It is the same sky with the same constellations as could be seen on the night of June 24, 1981—the evening the first visionaries saw a beautiful woman in white on Crnica, a hill overlooking the Medjugorje village of Bijakovići. That night, love in their hearts overcame fear, grace overflowed, and their lives became testimonies to the whole world.

All of these years—even as this book was being produced and, certainly, as you are reading this—Medjugorje has been a place in the world where the sky broke through to Earth and to man, and where it continues to do so day after day. In this place, Heaven opened and literally descended to Earth; Heaven and Earth merged in an invisible, transcendent point in the most mystical way that, even to this day, cannot be fully comprehended or rationalized. One can only choose to believe or not to believe, just as it was under the Nazareth sky 2,000 years ago.

However, as this book is being produced, this is not crucial. As a journalist and publicist who has been writing exclusively on religion and religious topics for 30 years, my challenge was to collect and process—specifically, to document—material that Cardinal Ruini's commission judged to be authentic so that the very first days of the apparitions could be incorporated into the foundations of official church acknowledgement. From the perspective of the sky above Medjugorje, it does not matter when this will happen, or even if it will ever happen. Why? Simply because the visible and tangible Church, which heals the world through the power of her sacraments, lives in Medjugorje.

Still, those first days are important for understanding everything that happened afterward. That's because every day carried within it the symbolism of condensed times and events that, over the years, revealed itself from that core as it was unraveled from the tangle of events. (This will become more apparent in the pages that follow.) Namely, the first days reveal all of the incredible things that happened at the moment that Heaven broke through to Earth—from the choice of visionaries to the pastor's absence from Medjugorje and the exclusively oral transmission of everything that happened during those first days because lightning had damaged the post office and telephone lines. Yet, from the very first days, thousands of people were attracted to these events, despite the fact that they were persecuted by the police and communist authorities. And the apparitions that began then have continued to this day, even up until the publication of this book.

The first days of the apparitions firmly demonstrate to us that every time we visit Medjugorje or are there for the first time, we should still look up into the sky above Medjugorje — the starry one above Podbrdo. That is the same sky yesterday, today, and tomorrow. This is the sky under which time and history, people and destinies, man and his faith—have changed.

Darko Pavičić

THE FIRST DAY – JUNE 24

We saw Our Lady

One October afternoon, I set out on foot from the center of Medjugorje toward the home of Marinko Ivanković in Podbrdo, where he and his wife, Draga, provide accommodations for pilgrims. Along the way, I meet various sizes of groups of pilgrims who are going to and from Apparition Hill. Often, they have rosaries in their hands, which is a common sight in Medjugorje; nowhere else in the world will you see people walking along the street praying the rosary, as well as entering shops and restaurants or walking while praying.

But, in those first years in Medjugorje, there were no restaurants and shops—and certainly no hotels and guest houses. So, when passing through these streets and paths, I try to picture those times—humble houses; yards and gardens with vines and tobacco; the faces of people who never dreamed that something like this would happen to them, and that their village—rather remote in the small region of Herzegovina—would become such a spiritual hub for millions of people from all over the world.

Questions about the first days of the apparitions—during which so many incredible, surprising, and amazing events occurred—flood my mind as I walk toward the house of Marinko, the immediate neighbor of the visionaries. How is it possible that the Blessed Virgin Mary, the mother of our Lord Jesus Christ, appeared precisely then and in those days, at this place, to the most ordinary children walking along the rocky ground? Why did she choose them and not others? Was it actually Our Lady, someone else, or the children's imagination? What did a grown man like Marinko think when he heard such an incredible story come from a child's mouth?

. . .

Because he was with the visionaries practically all day, Marinko was one of the most important individuals in the first days of the apparitions in Medjugorje. He accompanied them every day to the place of apparitions on Podbrdo and back, gave them rides, guarded them, and conversed with them. In fact, besides their parents, Marinko was among the few adults near the children who, every day beginning June 24, 1981, met Our Lady in Bijakovići in Medjugorje.

"Dado, where's Marinko?" I asked Darko Ivanković, the younger son of Draga and Marinko, who was distilling *rakija*[2] with his friends in the yard beside the house.

"He's in the house," Darko said. "I'll go get him now. And you, come to the barbecue later. Our custom here is such: to invite people to a barbecue when the *rakija* is being distilled."

2 Grape brandy

We climbed the terrace toward the entrance, where I warmly greeted his immobile mother, Draga, who was sitting in her wheelchair.

Marinko Ivanković is a tanned man of firm build, about 70 years old, with an emphatic, clear gaze and a strong handshake.

"I remember everything as if it were yesterday," he said as we sat on chairs in their dining room.

In 1981, Marinko worked as a car mechanic at the Auto Repair Center in Mostar. Every day, he drove to work in Mostar, about twenty kilometers (12 miles) away, and also regularly drove neighbors to work or children to school. That morning, on the second day of the apparitions, June 25, Marinko went to Mostar with Draga. They also took with them Vicka Ivanković and Marija Pavlović—girls who lived in the immediate neighborhood—who went to Mostar for summer school.

"Every morning, at five o'clock in the summer, I went to work," Marinko said. "I had a Volkswagen minivan. In those days, there was no traffic or cars, so my van was filled with neighbors who worked in Mostar; about fifteen would gather. On that morning, Vicka and Marija went with me for a summer-school class in Mostar, and when we passed the church, Marija said, 'Marinko, last night we saw Our Lady!'"

"Marija, what are you playing at, with God and Our Lady? Is that what your mother taught you?!" Marinko recalled saying to the girl sternly and with a sharp look.

"It wasn't me. Vicka saw," Marija replied. Vicka was sitting behind Marinko, on a seat next to his wife.

"Vicka, is it true?" Marinko asked in a loud voice.

"I did," she affirmed, which is a typical way to respond in their dialect.

"Tell us what you saw and where you saw it!" Marinko practically commanded her.

Vicka, a little confused, began her story. In the afternoon, the day before, Marija's younger sister Milka, who had been sent by her mother to bring a flock of sheep home, met two girls from the neighborhood, Mirjana and Ivanka, at the foot of Podbrdo. The two had seen a beautiful woman whom they immediately thought was the Blessed Virgin Mary.

"Walking ahead, about hundred meters (110 yards) from where the Cenacolo Community is today, Ivanka looked at the hill and said to Mirjana, 'Look at Our Lady on the hill,'" Marinko recounted of Vicka's testimony. "At that moment, Mirjana hit her on the shoulder and said, 'You are stupid. You are playing with God and Our Lady.'"

Ivanka was the first to see Our Lady, and then Mirjana. After that, they set out toward the village and met Vicka, who had fled at first. Then, after meeting two boys (both named Ivan), Vicka returned with the other children, who were fearfully watching the bright appearance of a woman on Podbrdo.

"Marinko, when I saw Our Lady, I was so scared," Vicka recounted to her neighbor that morning on the way to Mostar. "I had flip flops on my feet; I ran home and I lost them. I went to my room. I prayed, I felt peace, and decided to return. I found them in the same place—Ivanka, Mirjana, Milka, and the two Ivans."

She added that Our Lady held the infant Jesus in her hands and uncovered and covered Him with her veil. The "two Ivans" she mentioned were Ivan Ivanković (20)—the oldest of the group, who was at Podbrdo only on that day—and Ivan Dragičević, who would become one of the six visionaries of Medjugorje.

"After that, she called us with her hands to come to her," Vicka told Marinko. "Nobody dared to come to her that night."

"Vicka, I believe you," Marinko told the girl. "But, when you told me that Ivan Dragičević saw Our Lady, if he told me like you just did, then I would believe him more than a hundred of you girls."

Marinko said he believed Ivan the most because Ivan was a very humble and shy young man. "For example, if I was working in the field and Ivan needed to pass by and greet with just 'Praised be Jesus,' his face would blush and the blood would rush to his cheeks. That's how introverted he was."
In the shyness and sincerity of the visionary Ivan, Marinko sought confirmation that something unusual had happened the previous day—something he would be able to believe.

. . .

That Wednesday, June 24, 1981, was the feast of St. John the Baptist. In Medjugorje, as in the rest of Herzegovina, holy days were non-working days. Consequently, both adults and children were free from their everyday duties and work in the fields and vineyards and with tobacco. That morning, Mirjana Dragičević woke up joyful because she didn't have to go to the field to pick tobacco. She had come to Medjugorje from Sarajevo to spend the summer holiday with her uncle and aunt. She loved those summer months immensely and would wait excitedly for the end of the school year so she could spend all summer in Medjugorje.

The day before, Mirjana and her friend Ivanka had agreed that they would spend the day together. Ivanka's house was right next to Mirjana's uncle's house, and when they met, they decided to walk outside the hamlet so they could talk in peace.

"Ivanka and I wanted to be alone, to tell her all my news, and she told me her own, because I had only just come from Sarajevo," Mirjana said. "We walked at the base of the hill, now called Apparition Hill."

The girls stopped in front of Vicka's house to ask her to join them. They were told that Vicka was napping, but that she would be told that they were looking for her.

Walking along the unpaved path in the shadow of Podbrdo, the two talked about the great storm that had recently hit the area. It had been so violent that lightning had struck the post office and disrupted all telephone and electrical lines, cutting off Medjugorje from the rest of the world. They also discussed school events, new friendships, the latest fashions, and other teen topics, but their conversation was overshadowed by the death of Ivanka's mother, Jagoda, whom had died less than two months earlier after a sudden illness. She was, as Mirjana testifies, a holy woman who embraced her suffering. Mirjana could hear the sadness in Ivanka's voice and see the grief that lingered in her eyes; she hoped that the fresh air would bring Ivanka some temporary joy, at the very least. Indeed, as she talked with Ivanka, Mirjana started noticing a smile on her face.

"At that time there were no houses there, everything was deserted, and when we got tired, we sat just at the foot of the hill," Mirjana remembered. "Ivanka was looking up at the hill and I sat with my back to it. At one point, Ivanka tells me, 'I think that is Our Lady on the hill.'"

It was between five and six o'clock in the evening. Ivanka continued looking up at the hill and repeated, "I think I see Our Lady."

. . .

"That's just what she said," Mirjana continued. "I didn't look because it was impossible for me. Namely, we grew up in Yugoslavia, under communism, especially in Sarajevo. Our parents taught us to pray. We prayed the rosary every night, we went to Mass, but they didn't tell us much about faith. It was more out of fear that we should not speak about it in school, or they could have problems. So, I had never heard of Lourdes, Fatima; I didn't even know that

Our Lady could come to Earth. [For us, all we knew was that] she was in Heaven, and we pray to her. So, when Ivanka told me that she thought Our Lady was on the hill, I did not look. I answered her with a little impudence. 'Yeah, she has nothing else to do but come to me and you.' And then I left her there and I wanted to go back to the village because, you have to understand, we grew up with the knowledge that the name of God must not be taken in vain in our speech. For example, if you just say, 'Oh my God,' you will immediately get hit over your head by grandma and be told, 'You are taking the name of the Lord in vain, shame on you...' So, when Ivanka told me about Our Lady, it bothered me a little, as if we had done something wrong."

However, as Mirjana made her way home and reached the first house, a strong feeling overwhelmed her heart and seemed to invite her to return. In fact, the feeling was so compelling that it stopped her and forced her to turn around and go back.

"And, when I returned, I saw Ivanka in the same place, and what touched me when I saw her was that she was the same as me," Mirjana continued. "Since I came from Sarajevo, I was always pale, so they used to tease me here that I was a city-child, whereas Ivanka had such ruddy cheeks. But now, she was as pale as me. Completely pale! She said to me, 'Look now, please.' I looked up at the hill and, amidst the rocks, I saw a woman in a long, gray dress holding a baby in her arms. I did not see the face of the woman or the face of the child. Everything about it was strange. Nobody went to the hill; there was no path like now made by the pilgrims' feet, and especially someone in a long dress—I don't know if anyone had a long dress then!—holding a small baby in her arms."

"At that moment, I felt all possible emotions at the same time, both fear and beauty and confusion, and not knowing whether I was alive or dead. It was so overwhelming that, to me, the only way out was just: Run! Run…! And I ran. I didn't understand it and just ran away. When I got home, my grandmother was home and I immediately told her that I thought I had seen Our Lady. She said to me, 'You take the rosary, go to your room, pray to God, and you let Our Lady be in Heaven—where she is.' I didn't have the strength to explain to her and tell her about what I saw. I just wanted to be alone and pray because that's how I had peace. Whatever caused alarm within me was calmed by prayer. So, I spent all night praying that God would help me understand what was happening to me."

While Mirjana and Ivanka were at Podbrdo, Vicka woke up and went to meet them.

"I went to school in Mostar that day, and when I came back from school, I rested a little," Vicka recalled. "My older sister Zdenka told me that Mirjana and Ivanka were looking for me…we would often meet to take a walk. When I got up, Zdenka told me, 'Vicka, Mirjana and Ivanka were looking for you and they told me where they were going.' And so I set out. This is the path straight from here, heading toward Cenacolo. As I was going there, Mirjana and Ivanka called to me, 'Hurry, hurry.'

"Coming closer to them, I heard them say, 'Faster, Vicka, faster!'" Vicka recalled. "I thought it wasn't a snake or any animal when they called me in that way. When I came closer, they said to me, 'Vicka, [it's] Our Lady!' I kicked my slippers off my feet and ran away. I moved away thinking that something wasn't right with them. How [could it be] Our Lady; what's [wrong] with them? I was waiting a bit over here when Ivan came. Our Ivan [Vicka's cousin] played soccer with Ivan the visionary. Ivan and Marija's sister Milka came. I told them that Mirjana and Ivanka saw Our Lady and that we should go to them. At that moment, I didn't see anything because I ran away as soon as they mentioned it to me."

Nevertheless, Vicka returned to Podbrdo, this time accompanied by Milka and the two Ivans. They found Mirjana and Ivanka in the same spot.

"I immediately fell on my knees and she was calling us to come," Vicka said. "That was the first night, but none of us had the courage to go. Then, she motioned with her hand to come, but we ran home from there. When we got home, we didn't want to tell anyone. We would remain silent, and if Our Lady comes tomorrow, then we would tell. If she didn't, then nothing. But, when we got home, our family could see that something was going on. When we told them, they told us it might be flying saucers; maybe someone with a lamp, maybe someone looking for sheep. We told only a few people and each of them had their own [theories] to add."

Meanwhile, Ivan Dragičević (who was mentioned by both Marinko and Vicka) decided to spend the feast day with friends, just like all of the other children in the village. After going to Mass with his parents at St. James church in the morning, he went to play soccer with friends.

"We played until 5 or 5:30 p.m.," Ivan remembered. "Leaving the meadow, we met some girls and some of my friends asked them where they were going and what they were doing. They said that they were going to take a walk and to go [look] for the sheep. I didn't ask anything because, at that time, I was very shy and I didn't even speak to girls."

Ivan and his friend then went home to change clothes, watch television and get something to eat.

"We ate quickly, and, from my parents' house, we went through the garden behind our house where there were several apple trees," he continued. "We picked some apples, put them in our T-shirts and came out on the road again. At one point, as we were walking, we heard a voice calling from afar: 'Ivan, Ivan! Come, come, Our Lady is on the hill!'"

According to Ivan, the path on Podbrdo was so overgrown with bushes and greenery at the time that only a sheep or cow could pass through it. Yet, despite not seeing anyone in the thicket, they went up the path following the voice that was calling them.

"We heard that voice getting closer and stronger," Ivan said. "Then, I saw Vicka running toward us and calling out in a trembling voice, 'Ivan, Ivan, Ivan! Come with me, Our Lady is on the hill, Our Lady is on the hill!' My friend and I stopped, looked at each other, and I asked him, 'What is she talking about, what [does she mean] Our Lady?' However, Vicka was so persistent and said, 'Come with me, what are you waiting for?' And, since she saw that we were standing still in the same place, Vicka ran to us barefoot, without anything on her feet."

Ivan, who knew Vicka well, said she had always had a special character and temperament—so much so that they called her "sheriff" at school. But, in that moment, Ivan marveled at Vicka's strange behavior because it was not the Vicka he knew.

"I told my friend that we should go with her to see what it was," Ivan recounted. "Looking at her, it's as if some kind of fear started entering us because we didn't know what was going on. As we came closer to that spot, from afar we saw Mirjana and Ivanka kneeling and facing the hill and looking at something. As we came closer to them, Vicka turned and said, 'Look up there.' I looked three times and I saw a beautiful figure of Our Lady, in light, of a normal size, with a clearly visible crown of stars. My gaze lasted no longer than five to ten seconds, maybe a little bit more. As soon as I saw that, I ran home. I was not interested anymore in anything else, whether my friend stayed or whether he fled. I just wanted to flee as soon as possible."

When he got home, Ivan said nothing to anyone—neither his parents nor his brothers; he just locked himself in his room.

"The night ahead of me was truly a night of fear, anticipation, questions," Ivan said. "Was it possible? How could it be? Was it really

Our Lady? I saw her, but still, I wasn't sure. Until I was 16 (and, at the time, I was 16), I'd never dreamed that Our Lady could appear. I didn't even have a particular devotion to Our Lady. I was a practicing believer, brought up and grew in the faith in those years, neither better nor worse than others. I never read or knew about Lourdes and Fatima or about any apparitions. The priests during catechism class, which I attended regularly, did not speak about it very much."

The night before him was a night of anticipation. What was going to happen?

"What I was most afraid of was that if Our Lady came to my room that evening, where would I run? As a child, I was very withdrawn, I never walked alone in the dark without my parents. My father always escorted me if I went to the village to watch television at night. My father would take me there and, when I finished, he would bring me back home. I was just waiting for the morning to come as soon as possible. I sat all night on the bed. I drew all the curtains shut. The night was as long as a year and it felt like morning would never come. Finally, morning came. My mother and father had already heard in the village that I had been with these girls. I can't describe to you my mother and father at that moment; they were so excited, fearful, nervous. So, they started telling me, 'Watch what you say. Don't play with it. It's not a game.' I told my father and my mother that I saw it, but that still I wasn't sure."

. . .

The same excitement seized Vicka, Ivanka, and Mirjana. Mirjana was so excited that she wondered whether she was alive or dead. She said her heart was in such turmoil that she could barely identify one emotion before another took over; she pinched herself to make sure she wasn't dreaming. She tried to remember exactly what she saw, but as she stood a hundred or more meters (110 yards) away, it was difficult to identify the face of the woman. Even so, she was sure she was wearing a bluish-grey dress and holding a newborn baby. Mirjana was sure that no mother would ever climb such a hill with her baby in her arms. Bursting into her uncle's house, Mirjana explained that she thought she had seen Our Lady. Her grandma Jela, who was alone inside, looked at her in shock.

"Let Our Lady be where she is, in Heaven," Mirjana remembered her grandmother telling her. "Take the rosary, go to your room and pray to God!"

Mirjana, too excited to explain to her that she had really seen something, did exactly what her grandma said. She ran into the bedroom and prayed. However, every time she closed her eyes, Mirjana could only picture that woman on the hill. She was sure it had been Our Lady—because of what she felt more so than what she saw. But, she wondered, shouldn't the Virgin Mary be in Heaven? She searched her memories for anything that might help her understand what she had just witnessed. Until that moment, Mirjana had never thought that anyone on Earth could see Our Lady. Specifically, she had never heard of other so-called apparitions. So, she assumed it was the first time that Our Lady had ever appeared to anyone. After all, in communist Yugoslavia, books with religious content were practically contraband, so their knowledge of miracles was limited to the measured homilies of the priests, who were always aware that secret government spies were lurking in the pews. The priests knew that anything that could be construed as an attack on the regime could put them in prison—or worse.

"I remember Vicka was looking for Ivanka and me, and when she saw what we were looking at, she kicked off her slippers to be faster and fled barefoot to the village," Mirjana testified. "And Ivan passed by because he was going to his house, and he fled when he saw it. Then, I said, who knows what it is, so I fled home, too. Jakov and Marija immediately said, 'How fortunate you are to see Our Lady, we would like to see Our Lady, too!' They believed immediately with the heart. And, the next day, they came, as did almost everyone from Podbrdo, to see what it was because, immediately, thank God, the news had spread throughout the village. The village was small, and news spread quickly. Then, Jakov and Marija also saw her that next day."

The children came running excitedly into the village. People were in their yards and in front of their houses on that warm summer evening. The children were met by one of their neighbors, Ivan Ivanković.

"The children came running to the house and said, 'We saw Our Lady!' I didn't understand what was going on, so I told them to sit down and drink some juice. My wife, Janja, made juice for them and gave them some cake. They sat for five or six minutes, as children often do, and then left. And that is how that evening ended."

Together with his cousin and neighbor, Marinko, Ivan Ivanković spent the most time with the visionaries in those first days.

FROM THE CONVERSATION OF FATHER JANKO BUBALO* WITH VISIONARY VICKA

FR. JANKO: "Since that is settled, tell me when and how the first apparitions came about. First of all, tell me when."

VICKA: "Father Janko, well, everyone at least knows this, but since you want to know—the first apparition occurred on the feast of St. John, June 24, 1981."

FR. JANKO: "Do you remember the approximate time?"

VICKA: "A bit after five in the afternoon."

FR. JANKO: "Now, tell me more about how it happened and how you happened to be there."

VICKA: "Well, that's a long story. Shall I tell it all or just the most important details?"

FR. JANKO: "Tell everything and the more the better, so that, once and for all—let me put it this way—that fateful moment might be as clear as possible."

VICKA: "Good. I'll speak, but you will have to help me with your questions, otherwise who knows where I'll wander."

FR. JANKO: "Alright, Vicka. I'll probably tire you with my questions, but let's proceed!"

VICKA: "Well, it was like this. As you know, that day was a feast day. However, I didn't go to Mass for I had to go to Mostar for summer school."

FR. JANKO: "What kind of summer school?"

VICKA: "Well, I failed mathematics, so I had to attend summer school."

FR. JANKO: "All right. So, then what?"

VICKA: "I arrived home somewhere around noon. It was terribly hot and crowded in the bus, you know how it is."

FR. JANKO: "And then?"

VICKA: "When I relaxed somewhat, I ate a bit and then fell asleep. But, just before that, Mirjana and Ivanka stopped by. That morning, we had agreed that we would go for a walk toward evening. We were always together."

FR. JANKO: "Good. And then?"

VICKA: "I fell soundly asleep. I slept long enough and then I was awakened by my sister Zdenka. She played games with me telling me I would be late for school, and the like."

FR. JANKO: "In other words, you became rather lazy?"

VICKA: "Well, I didn't become so lazy, but what can I say."

FR. JANKO: "And then?"

VICKA: "I got up, got dressed, and went to look for Mirjana and Ivanka."

FR. JANKO: "Where did you look for them?"

VICKA: "First off, I looked for them at Jakov's mother's house—she is Mirjana's aunt—so I thought they would definitely be there."

FR. JANKO: "And you found them there?"

VICKA: "No, no. They had been there, but then they went out for a walk. They told her [Jakov's mother] that they would go down the unpaved road toward the homes of the Čilići family and that when I come, I should follow them there."

FR. JANKO: "And that's the way it was?"

VICKA: "Yes, I went down that gravel road a bit and I saw the two of them and little Milka, the daughter of Filip. All three of them were staring at something and seemed to be kind of scared. They waved at me to come. I began to hurry toward them, but something seemed strange to me. What were they gazing at so intently?"

FR. JANKO: "Well, at what?"

VICKA: "As I approached them, they all shouted to me together, 'Vicka, look at Our Lady!' What's going on with them? What kind of Our Lady? I really thought they saw a snake and that they were trying to trick me. I kicked off the slippers from my feet and ran away barefoot. I ran like crazy."

FR. JANKO: "Where did you run?"

VICKA: "Well, down to the houses. Where else would I go?"

FR. JANKO: "And, thus, you didn't see anything that day?"

VICKA: "Well, hold on. I didn't finish yet."

FR. JANKO: "All right then, continue!"

VICKA: "I stopped down at the houses and began to cry. I just wanted to cry. How can they joke about Our Lady! And, I didn't know what to do nor where to go."

FR. JANKO: "Then, I suppose, you went home?"

VICKA: "No, no. While I was there, the two Ivans came by."

FR. JANKO: "Which two Ivans?"

VICKA: "Ivan, the son of Stanko, and Ivan, the son of the late Jozo. They were carrying some apples in a plastic bag."

FR. JANKO: "And, I suppose they offered you some apples?"

VICKA: "Yes, but I didn't care about apples. 'There's Our Lady!' kept popping into my head."

FR. JANKO: "And, what did ultimately 'pop' out?"

VICKA: "In tears, I begged Ivan (Stanko's son) to go with me to the three of them that claimed to see the Virgin. Ivan agreed, and we went toward them. I told him, 'We don't have to see Her, but let's go [anyway]..."

FR. JANKO: "And, Ivan, I suppose, agreed?"

VICKA: "Well, he did, of course!"

FR. JANKO: "And, when you arrived there?"

VICKA: "They began to point to show us where Our Lady was. And then, we, too, saw her. Ivan immediately ran away, jumping over the fences. He dropped the apples and everything."

FR. JANKO: "And you?"

VICKA: "I stayed and kept on watching."

FR. JANKO: "And, what, in fact, did you see?"

VICKA: "Well, I saw something like a beautiful young woman with a child in her arms. She continually covered and then uncovered the baby. And, she waved us forward to approach her."

FR. JANKO: "And you? Did any of you approach her?"

VICKA: "None of us. Who, out of fear, dared to even think about it?"

FR. JANKO: "And, why was she showing you the child?"

VICKA: "Who knows! Perhaps so that we could see him better."

FR. JANKO: "And, how long did you remain there?"

VICKA: "I don't know exactly. Perhaps five to six minutes. And then, I ran away again."

FR. JANKO: "Where to?"

VICKA: "Well, home, where else? I was extremely happy, but also afraid. I was afraid, and yet, I was also happy."

FR. JANKO: "And what about when you came home?"

VICKA: "I sat on the couch and started to cry. I just cried and cried."

FR. JANKO: "And, how did little Milka [Filip's daughter] find herself at the apparition?"

VICKA: "Well, that isn't important. I'd have to begin the story all over again."

FR. JANKO: "No, not the whole story. However, tell me if you know, just that because it is interesting, too."

VICKA: "All right, it was like this. When Ivanka and Mirjana went for a walk, Ivanka suddenly saw Our Lady and told Mirjana about it. Mirjana said to her, 'Get out of here, what kind of Our Lady, why would she appear to us?'"

FR. JANKO: "Mirjana didn't even see her then?"

VICKA: "No, no. Then they went home to look for me, but at the edge of the village they met little Milka and she asked them to go with her to let the sheep out of the pen."

FR. JANKO: "And, whose sheep were they?"

VICKA: "Milka's, for neither Mirjana nor Ivanka had any sheep at the time."

FR. JANKO: "And, then what?"

VICKA: "Milka let the sheep out and then she and the others began to head back toward the village."

FR. JANKO: "All right. They returned to the village and..."

VICKA: "Hold on! It isn't exactly like that."

FR. JANKO: "What is it now?"

VICKA: "Here is what it is: While they were heading back toward the village, Ivanka again saw Our Lady at the same spot. She told them. They looked, and they also saw her. It was Our Lady, and that's all there is to it. Shortly thereafter, I arrived, and the rest you already know."

FR. JANKO: "That's good. But, tell me, how did Ivan, the son of the late Jozo, come to be there?"

VICKA: "Well, he was there with Stanko's son Ivan. And, when we went up ahead, he also went with us."

FR. JANKO: "And, did he see anything?"

VICKA: "He saw her, too, but not quite as clearly as we did."

FR. JANKO: "Did anyone at that point hear Our Lady saying anything to you?"

VICKA: "No, no one heard anything. We only saw that she was waving to us to come forward. And she was showing us the child."

FR. JANKO: "All right. And, did Our Lady appear to be the same to everyone at that point?"

VICKA: "I don't know. She was quite far away at that point and..."

FR. JANKO: "You, as you said, returned home before Ivanka and Mirjana."

VICKA: "Shortly before. Our Lady left, and then they also went home."

FR. JANKO: "And, what happened when you arrived home? Did you tell any of this to others?"

VICKA: "Of course we did!"

FR. JANKO: "And they?"

VICKA: "There was everything. Some perhaps believed, some wondered, some explained it in this or in that way; that it was some kind of 'flying saucer' and the like. Well, all sorts of things were said."

FR. JANKO: "And then, everyone went to sleep?"

VICKA: "Well, what else were we to do! We had to pick tobacco at dawn and tend the animals and everything else. You know how it is."

FR. JANKO: "Good. And, also this, how did it occur to Ivanka to refer to the appearance of the beautiful young woman as Our Lady? Why didn't she think of something else?"

VICKA: "I don't know. Who else could she think of? A beautiful young mother with a child? A crown on her head? Our Lady as Our Lady is!"

FR. JANKO: "Good. Then, from now on, we will also freely call this beautiful appearance Our Lady."

* Janko Bubalo was born on January 31, 1913, in the small village of Turčinovići close to Široki Brijeg. In 1926, he entered the seminary of the Herzegovinian friars in Široki Brijeg and, in the summer of 1932, he wore a Franciscan habit and went to Humac near Ljubuški, taking the religious name Fr. Janko. After the novitiate, Fr. Janko returned to Široki Brijeg, where he completed several

high school classes. In 1935, he went to study in Mostar where, in 1938, he was ordained a priest of the Herzegovinian Franciscan Province. In 1941, he was appointed parish priest in Rasno and, in 1943, he went to serve in Vitina, where he remained until 1950. After World War II ended, Fr. Janko was arrested and imprisoned in a Ljubuški prison, where he was tortured in inhumane conditions. After five months in prison, he returned to Vitina and, in 1950, he went to Čerin, where he remained until 1981, when he went to Humac, where he died on February 21, 1997. Ten years before he died, Fr. Janko was admitted to the Croatian Writers' Association as the first priest to become a member of the Association. One year prior to his death, the President of the Republic of Croatia, Dr. Franjo Tudman, honored him with the *Order of Danica Hrvatska with the image of Marko Marulić* for a special contribution to culture.

THE SECOND DAY – JUNE 25

The six child visionaries

The excitement did not subside overnight, but rather overflowed into the next day, Thursday, June 25 (which would later be deemed the anniversary of the Medjugorje apparitions because, on that day, all six visionaries saw Our Lady and spoke with her for the first time). On the previous day, overcome by shock and excitement, the children did not speak with Our Lady. Additionally, on June 25, Marija's sister Milka and Ivan Dragičević's friend Ivan did not come to the apparition. Instead, Vicka, Ivan, Mirjana, and Ivanka were joined by Jakov and Marija. On that day, these six children became the visionaries of Medjugorje.

"On Thursday afternoon, Vicka's cousin ran to my mother and

asked, 'Josipa, they saw Our Lady again, do you have a rosary?'" Ivan Ivanković said. "Mom gave her a rosary and they headed for Apparition Hill just as I did. The children were already halfway up the hill. I ran after them, but I couldn't catch up with them."

Just as Ivan Ivanković did, many others also testified that the children were climbing the hill with incredible speed through the thorn bushes—where it was difficult to walk, let alone run; no one was able to catch up with them. They were already in prayer when others reached them.

Ivan Ivanković, then a vigorous young man, was the first to run after the children.

"When Our Lady called them, she was not where her statue is today, but about 30 meters (98 feet) lower on the hill where it is easier to see," he said. "I was up there, among the first of those who didn't see Our Lady that day. I had run up with them. They [the children] were kneeling and seemed to be talking, but I couldn't hear anything from them. That's why I was a little angry and I raised my voice. I used a swear word as locals do, and then they said, 'She left!' She left because of my anger and I was embarrassed by that."

But, not even fifteen seconds later, the children knelt again.

"Here she is! She is coming back again!" Ivan Ivanković recalled the children saying almost in unison.

"Ivan, when you said that word, the tears flowed down her face, we are sorry for that," visionary Marija reproached Ivan Ivanković, who made the sign of the cross in shame and asked them where Our Lady was.

"They told me that she was on a cloud," he said. "I raised my hand and felt the icy air—just like ice—I pulled back and I immediately believed. They talked with Our Lady again, but I did not hear anything."

In addition to the six children and Ivan Ivanković, Marinko's older son Juraj Ivanković, neighbor Mato Šego, and visionary Ivanka's brother also ran after the children.

"We came down from the hill and then the crowds, comments, and questions began," Ivan Ivanković remembered. "They [the children] were pale and looked lost. We were all in shock. I believed. I felt. But, I still had a worm of doubt wondering if that was possible. I had read only in books, in the catechism, in religious education classes, and I had seen a picture from Lourdes and Fatima, but it was still inconceivable to me that Our Lady could come to Earth."

. . .

Visionary Mirjana didn't know how she woke up the second morning because she didn't think she ever fell asleep the night before, given her state of mind.

"I helped my uncles that day, as on any other day," she said. "We picked tobacco and did other necessary work so that, during the day, I didn't have a chance to see any other visionaries."

As they were picking tobacco, her cousins reminded her about their plans to visit their aunt's house that evening. Mirjana nodded, but only wanted to think about the woman on the hill. Lost in the monotony of picking and stringing tobacco, she replayed in her mind the events from the previous afternoon, wondering if she had truly seen what she thought she saw. Then, as the time of the previous day's vision approached, a strange feeling began to consume her. Mirjana felt as though something within her was calling her back to the hill—a feeling that soon became too strong to ignore.

"At the time I had seen her the day before, I felt a call within myself and I said to my uncles that I had to go to the hill because I felt that something was calling me," Mirjana recounted. "They came along with me to see what was going on. My uncle always said that he felt responsible for me because I was entrusted to him by his sister, my mother, and he had to see what was going on. When we reached the base of the hill, it seemed like half of the village was already there, as someone came along with each of us. We saw Our Lady in the same place but, this time, she didn't have the infant in her arms. That day, June 25, 1981, was the first time we approached her, and this is how our daily apparitions began."

In fact, half the village had gathered at the base of Podbrdo, and Mirjana found Ivanka, Vicka, and Ivan in the crowd. Then, three flashes of white light drew their eyes to the hill and they were all amazed to see the same figure they had seen the day before but slightly further up the hillside. Marija and Jakov joined them and, together, they all ran up toward her. The onlookers below were baffled as they watched the children scale the steep slope at an impossible speed, seemingly coasting over boulders and thornbushes. Some people tried to run after them, but they could not keep pace. Notably, Mirjana was a city girl and not particularly athletic. Nevertheless, she said it felt effortless and as if she simply glided—or like something carried her—to the place where the woman was standing. Her uncle later told her that it takes at least twelve minutes to get up there and, yet, it seemed that the children did it in two; seeing that terrified him. The first time Mirjana gazed upon the woman up close, she realized that she was not of this world. Immediately—and involuntarily—they fell to their knees. Not sure what to say or do, they began to pray the Our Father, Hail Mary, and Glory Be.

To their astonishment, the woman prayed along with them—but she remained silent during the Hail Mary. A beautiful blueness encompassed the woman; her skin was imbued with an olive-hued radiance, and her eyes reminded Mirjana of the translucent blue of the Adriatic. A white veil concealed most of her long, black hair, except for a curl visible near her forehead and locks hanging down below the veil.

...

"It's indescribable," Mirjana said. "My words are insufficient to really describe the encounter. There was, at the same time, beauty and fear and admiration and confusion. It must be experienced in order to understand what I'm talking about because it is Heaven on Earth. I think that the people who are in Heaven feel that way. While meeting with her, you forget everything; you do not care about anything else, just that she may look at you and that you may look at her. You have no other desires like, for example, to touch her or anything else. I had the same desire the first time that I have today—just that she may look at me and that I may look at her. And this hasn't changed. After thirty-six years, it might be, as people say, that I got used to it. No, you cannot get used to it. It is always like the first time. I think that those who are in paradise—those who are with Our Lady all the time—feel that way."

Mirjana added that everything she saw seemed supernatural—from the unearthly, blue-gray glow of her long dress to the breathtaking intensity of her gaze. Her very presence brought with it a feeling of peace and maternal love, but Mirjana also felt intense fear because she did not understand what was happening.

Our Lady addressed them in perfect Croatian and said, "Djeco moja, ne bojte se!" (*My children, be not afraid!*) They said it was a resonant, melodic tone that no human could ever replicate or imitate; her voice was like music. The children were silent, and Ivanka was the only one who found the courage to pose a question, one that, as Mirjana says, had obviously been burning within her.

"How is my mother?" Ivanka asked.

Our Lady looked at Ivanka with tenderness and said, "*She is with me.*"

"Ivanka's mother had passed away a month before," Mirjana explained. "That was a shock for all of us because we all love our mothers. Her mother was truly a wonderful woman who suffered a lot. She had many illnesses, but she never complained. I never heard her say that it was difficult for her and that she could not go on anymore. She was, somehow, always a mother—she always thought of her children and not of herself. Ivanka asked where her mom was and Our Lady said, 'With me.'"

One of the others asked Our Lady if she would come again the next day, and she gently nodded in affirmation. Although, on the second day, unlike the day before, the children spoke with her, but little was said. It seemed as though the intent was for everyone to get comfortable with what would become a regular occurrence.

Mirjana had always been extremely shy as a child. When visitors came to her family home, she ran into another room and shut the door, and if her mother made her come out, she stood in the background and remained silent until the guests departed. That's how it was for her during the first apparition, as well; she was simply awestruck. Her only desire was to gaze at Our Lady's beauty and bask in the tremendous love she felt when Our Lady looked at her.

When the villagers finally reached them on the hillside, no one among them could see what the children saw. But, later, they reported that the children's facial expressions shocked them. And, although the children could hear the villagers' voices during the apparition, the villagers said that the children's lips moved without making any sounds—they could only hear the children speak when they prayed or, sometimes, when they answered questions. Later, when Mirjana heard others describe the apparition, she said it was unsettling, as if strangers had been watching her sleep. But, what the villagers saw convinced them that the children were truly experiencing something incredible; here were six children—only a few of whom had been friends before that day—kneeling on sharp rocks and briars; faces aglow; and eyes transfixed onto something unseen. Mirjana later learned that scientists categorized their experience as being in a state of ecstasy—but, she called it being in Heaven.

. . .

Vicka also decided to go for a walk again that afternoon, and Marija and Jakov told her to call them when she left for Podbrdo.

"Mirjana, Ivanka, and I went to the same spot," Vicka remembered. "But, this evening, Our Lady was right on Podbrdo—at the spot where Our Lady's statue is now. I ran into Marija's house to call Jakov and Marija. Together, we went to where Mirjana, Ivanka, and Ivan were. It was as if we were not walking at all. We were barefoot and there were so many rocks and thornbushes. But, it was as if something—not something, but Our Lady—took us by the hand and pulled us through the air, as if we were not walking on the rocks and thornbushes. She brought us right to the spot where Our Lady's statue is today. When we arrived, she told us not to be afraid. We all felt a little freer and we started asking something."

Vicka added that the children were most interested in whether Our Lady would leave a sign so that people would believe them and, to that, she said Our Lady simply smiled. Then, Vicka asked Mirjana what time it was. To Mirjana, it seemed like a strange request at that moment, as she was too mesmerized to even consider looking at her watch; she hoped the encounter would never end. "*Go in God's peace*," Our Lady told them. Then, quite suddenly, she began to ascend, fading into the blueness.

At the same time, Mirjana felt herself come back to this world—a transition accompanied by a significant amount of pain and sadness; she longed to be with Our Lady forever. Wiping her tears, she looked at the other visionaries. They, too, appeared to be struggling with the shift back to "reality." Ivanka was especially emotional—and for good reason. She now knew that her mother was with the Virgin Mary. Bystanders claimed that their vision lasted ten to fifteen minutes, but that seemed impossible to the children; it felt like so much longer to them.

Then, Mirjana looked at her watch to check the time, but what she saw perplexed her. The numbers and hands of her watch had completely turned backward; the 2 o'clock mark was in the place of the 10 o'clock mark and so on, and the hands were ticking backwards.

"I heard Vicka ask Mirjana what time it was," Ivan Ivanković said. "Mirjana looked at her watch and the clockwork of the watch was completely turned backward. I saw it. I took the watch in my hands and I looked at it. One of the policemen who was there took the watch and brought it to the watchmaker. The watchmaker said that he could restore the clockwork to the previous position, but that the watch would not work after that. That was the first tangible sign and I saw it with my own eyes. What happened with the watch later, I do not know. I have never asked Mirjana about it."

It all seemed so strange to the children. As they descended the hill, onlookers peppered them with questions, but they were still too stunned to give detailed answers. Together, Mirjana said, they had experienced something extraordinary—a glimpse of the divine, and a meeting with the Mother of God. And yet, for each of them, the encounter had been an intimate and personal one. In fact, Mirjana recounts how Father Slavko, a priest who would later serve in Medjugorje, once became frustrated because he could never get all six visionaries together in one place.

"If I were Our Lady," he said, "I never would have chosen the six of you. You're all so different, and that's a sign for me that it's true."

. . .

Indeed, the visionaries themselves agree that most of them never would have spent time together had it not been for the apparitions. According to Mirjana, when everything began, observers probably shared her first impressions of the others.

None of them were particularly pious compared to other children in the village, and they each had their own unique strengths and weaknesses. In spite of this, or perhaps *because* of it, Our Lady chose them and brought them together.

With a persistent smile, 17-year-old Vicka was a joyful and vivacious girl with curly brown hair, always first to take initiative in the group, per Mirjana. Furthermore, Vicka is her nickname; her real name, Vida, is the Croatian word for vision, Mirjana interpreted.

Likewise, Mirjana had never spent time with 16-year-old Ivan Dragičević prior to the apparitions. Tall with black hair, Ivan seemed shy and quiet; his name is the Croatian equivalent of John, a common name in the New Testament meaning "God is gracious," explained Mirjana.

Neither did she know 16-year-old Marija—a thin girl with short, brown hair whose name is the Slavic version of Mary. In the same way, Mirjana's name is also derived from the original Hebrew form of the name Mary—Miriam.

The youngest member of the group was Mirjana's 10-year-old cousin, Jakov Čolo, who lived alone with his mother, Jaka, and whom Mirjana had not associated with much. With his youthful innocence, Jakov—whose name is the Croatian version of James, the patron saint of the parish—always entertained the children and made them laugh, Mirjana shared.

And, of course, there was her dear friend, Ivanka, who, at 15 years old, was the youngest of the four girls. Ivanka had a penchant for being late and always seemed to be the last one to show up when all of the children met, Mirjana said.

They were all so different, but the extraordinary gift of seeing Our Lady bonded them together. Their interpretations of the experience were and would remain as varied as their personalities. But, through the years, they have always agreed on one thing: No words can describe the beauty of Our Lady and the feeling that comes with seeing her.

And so, on Thursday, June 25, 1981, Jakov Čolo and Marija Pavlović joined the other four on the second day of the apparitions and the six children became known as the Medjugorje visionaries.

"I was in the village at Marija's house and spoke with her," Jakov said. "Vicka came and said they were going again to the same spot where they had seen Our Lady yesterday. Marija and I said, 'If you see Our Lady again, call us.' Shortly thereafter, Vicka ran to us and said, 'Our Lady is on the hill, come with me.' That is when we went. We were at the base of the hill and we saw a female figure on the hill, which was calling us with her hands to come up. I did not know if I should go or not because I was afraid. I hesitated. Run home or go up the hill? But, the desire to go up the hill prevailed.

"What I remember most and what has been forever engraved in my heart—that crucial moment in my life—was when I knelt in front of Our Lady and looked into her eyes," he added. "At that moment, I felt Our Lady as my mother. Often, people ask me how beautiful Our Lady is, and I say that I have experienced Our Lady's beauty through her eyes—through the love that I saw in her eyes—and which, at the same time, I felt in my heart, even though I was just a child. That is when I felt like a child of a mother who is in front of me, who loves me. I felt protected, embraced by that mother. And that was the most beautiful moment because it was then when I fell in love with and accepted Our Lady as my mother."

Although Marija was not present on the first day of the apparitions, she felt as though she was part of the event from the very beginning because it happened in their "house."

"My sister Milka saw Our Lady while returning from Panja, right here where our house is currently located," Marija said.

She added that, from that night on, their parents did not sleep at all because who would have thought that Our Lady would appear?

"Is it Our Lady or not?" Marija recalled them wondering. "Are those Martians? What is this or what is that? It was very confusing."

On June 25, Marija's parents decided to bring her sister Milka with them to work in the field in another part of Medjugorje, in order to physically prevent her from going back to Podbrdo.

"Little Jakov came to my house," Marija recalled. "Vicka came to talk to my sister. She said that she felt the need in her heart to go there again. There, they found Mirjana, Ivanka, and Ivan, while the oldest Ivan—who was 18 years old—was afraid and never showed up again. And he has never had an apparition since. Likewise, my sister. Jakov happened to be in our house. When Vicka called us, we went with her. We certainly believed. We would not dare to joke with God. At that time, if I said something that was not true, my mother would peel the skin off me. She was like that, especially when it was about God and anything related to God. It was the age of communism. There was a fear of communism. We prayed in our home. More than once, my mother said, 'You are not an animal. Make the sign of the cross and ask God for a blessing.' I remember, when I was a child, my mother used to bless everything with holy water from the barn to the kitchen, the house, behind the house. It was normal to take a sprig of rosemary with holy water and, while praying the Creed, go around your entire property so that God and Our Lady would bless and protect your house and garden."

On that day, Marija said neither she nor Vicka nor Jakov were confident that Our Lady would appear again, although they were one hundred percent sure that it was Our Lady. On the second day, Our Lady appeared to them again.

"She had little Jesus in her arms and was calling us" Marija recalled. "She uncovered Jesus from the very beginning and called us to come closer to her. We were at the bottom of Apparition Hill, where we always were from the beginning, and we went up from the bottom. They said that we were going up the hill at high speed. I actually came with little Jakov more to be present than to see. There was no desire or thought within us to see Our Lady because we did not feel worthy. Our Lady appeared and called us with her hand, as she had done the first day, when all of them had fled. On the first day, Our Lady stayed for a long time—Milka went from above; Vicka, Mirjana, and Ivanka, from below, while Ivan and the other Ivan were there. I do not know how long it was, but it was a while. So, Our Lady did stay for a while. On June 25th, we were down below when Our Lady appeared and called us. That is when we decided to go up and get closer to her. Then, we ran as fast as if we were running on clouds, even though it was on stones, caves, trees, thornbushes."

Meanwhile, after hearing about the previous day's apparition from Vicka and Marija as he gave them a ride to Mostar, Marinko decided to go to Podbrdo that afternoon, as well, to see for himself what was happening.

"I came back from work and Ivan Dragičević told me the same things as Vicka had," Marinko said. "I misunderstood Vicka regarding the time it had happened; I thought it was at 6:50 p.m., but it was at 5:50 p.m. My brother-in-law had come from Germany and he was building his house and I was helping him, and around 6:45 p.m., I looked at my watch, finished with work, got in my car, and set out to go home. My brother-in-law called me, 'Where are you going? Why did you come at all? We can work another three hours.' I did not want to tell him why I was leaving. I was driving along the base of Križevac [Cross Mountain] when I reached the road at the base of Podbrdo. Everyone from my neighborhood—old and young and children—were standing in the street looking at the hill."

Marinko asked them what happened. They responded that the visionaries saw Our Lady and went up the hill. At that moment, Marinko, who was standing at the bottom of the hill while speaking with someone, saw Mirjana and his relative Ivanka descending.

"Ivanka came down," Marinko continued. "Her grandmother was standing near me. She reached for her grandmother, embraced her, clung to her, and started crying very hard."

"Ivanka, what's going on with you?" he asked. "Why are you crying, what is it? What has happened?"

"I asked Our Lady about my mother, and Our Lady told me, 'Go and listen to your grandmother. Your mother is with me in paradise,'" Ivanka told him.

"'Well, Ivanka, can there be any greater joy than this?'" Marinko remembered responding. "'Therefore, sing and rejoice. Your mother is in paradise with Our Lady! What more can you ask?' And she continued holding her grandmother and crying."

Marinko also wondered what to do now, after Our Lady appeared to the children on the second day. He thought that it would be best to tell the priests everything, so he headed toward the center of the village.

"I believe that God is with me and that Jesus leads me wherever I go," Marinko said. "I got in the car and went to the parish office. I found two nuns on the stairs of that old house."

"'Praised be Jesus and Mary, sisters, how are you? Is Father Jozo at home?'" he remembered asking.

"'No, he is not,'" they responded, according to Marinko. "'He went to Zagreb.'"

However, as they spoke, the chaplain, Father Zrinko Čuvalo, came out of the house and asked Marinko what he needed.

"Last night and tonight, six children have seen Our Lady," Marinko explained. "The mother of one of the girls died fifty days ago and she is crying a lot. Maybe it would be good for you to go to talk with her to see what's happening."

"Father Zrinko raised his hand up in the air and said, 'Marinko, if God chose for someone to see Our Lady, it is for them.' He then went into the house," Marinko recounted.

"I went to Vicka's house," Marinko continued. "There, Marija and Jakov jumped in front of me, 'This evening we saw Our Lady!' I didn't believe the children lied. Here, let me give you an example. If Milka saw her the first night and no longer sees her, why would she then not say that she still sees her."

Since that day, Marinko has been completely convinced that the children did not lie and that the apparitions are true.

FROM THE CONVERSATION OF FATHER JANKO BUBALO WITH VICKA

FR. JANKO: "Thursday has dawned, Vicka. Therefore, the second day of the apparitions is June 25th. Have you forgotten what happened the day before?"

VICKA: "Not at all. We dreamt about it and talked about it."

FR. JANKO: "Have you agreed on anything? Just to let it go or...?"

VICKA: "Well, it's strange. We could not simply let it go. The three of us..."

FR. JANKO: "Which three of you?"

VICKA: "Ivanka, Mirjana, and I agreed that we would go to the site again at about the same time of day. If it really is Our Lady, perhaps she will come again."

FR. JANKO: "And you went?"

VICKA: "We did—at about the same time. We went down the unpaved road and looked toward the place of the first apparition."

FR. JANKO: "And nothing?"

VICKA: "What do you mean nothing! Suddenly, a light shone and Our Lady appeared."

FR. JANKO: "With the child?"

VICKA: "No, no. There was no child this time."

FR. JANKO: "And, where exactly did Our Lady appear?"

VICKA: "The same place as the first time."

FR. JANKO: "Do you recall who saw her first?"

VICKA: "Ivanka again."

FR. JANKO: "Are you sure?"

VICKA: "Yes, I'm sure. Then, Mirjana and I also saw her."

FR. JANKO: "And, I suppose this time you approached her?"

VICKA: "Well, wait. As we went up, I told Marija and little Jakov that I would call them if we saw anything."

FR. JANKO: "And, it was that way?"

VICKA: "Yes, it was. When the three of us saw her, I told Ivanka and Mirjana to wait until I called them. I did call them, and they immediately ran after me."

FR. JANKO: "And then?"

VICKA: "When we all gathered, Our Lady called us to approach her by waving her hand, and we all ran toward her. Marija and Jakov didn't immediately see her, but they ran with us."

FR. JANKO: "Which way?"

VICKA: "Well, what way? There is no road there. We ran straight up. Straight through those thornbushes."

FR. JANKO: "And, it was possible?"

VICKA: "Well, we ran as though something was carrying us—as if there were no stones nor thornbushes, nothing! As though it were all of rubber, of sponge, of whatever. Well, it was beyond description. No one could keep up with us."

FR. JANKO: "And, did you see Our Lady while you were running?"

VICKA: "We did see her. How else would we know where to run? Only Marija and Jakov did not see her until they came all the way up."

FR. JANKO: "Then they saw her, too?"

VICKA: "They did. Vague at first and then more clearly."

FR. JANKO: "All right. Do you recall who arrived first?"

VICKA: "Ivanka and I arrived first, but we were mostly all together."

FR. JANKO: "Vicka, you say that you ran up so easily but, at one point, you told me that Mirjana and Ivanka fainted."

VICKA: "They did for a short while, but that was over in an instant."

FR. JANKO: "And, what did you do when you arrived up there?"

VICKA: "I don't even know how to properly tell you this. We were confused. We were frightened. It's not easy to stand before Our Lady. Nonetheless, we fell to our knees and began to pray."

FR. JANKO: "Do you remember what you prayed?"

VICKA: "Well, I don't remember. We probably prayed the Our Father and the Hail Mary and the Glory Be. We didn't know how to pray anything else!"

FR. JANKO: "On one occasion, you told me that little Jakov fell into a thornbush."

VICKA: "Yes, yes. In all the excitement, he fell into a thornbush. I thought to myself, 'Jakov, you're not going to get out of there alive.'"

FR. JANKO: "And, did he—we see that he did—pull himself out of there?"

VICKA: "Well, of course he did. And, he did it rather quickly. And, when he freed himself, he kept repeating, 'Well, I wouldn't regret dying now, for I saw Our Lady!' And, imagine, there was no sign he had fallen into thorns."

FR. JANKO: "How's that?"

VICKA: "How would I know? At the time, it didn't occur to me to think about it. But now, I know that Our Lady watched over him. Who else?"

FR. JANKO: "And, how did Our Lady look then?"

VICKA: "Do you mean how was she dressed and...?"

FR. JANKO: "No, not that. I'm thinking about her mood and her demeanor toward you."

VICKA: "She was beautiful, smiling, and joyful... Well, it cannot be described."

FR. JANKO: "Did she then—I'm thinking of the second day—say anything to you?"

VICKA: "Yes, she prayed with us and the like."

FR. JANKO: "And, did you ask her anything?"

VICKA: "I didn't. Ivanka did, however. She asked Our Lady about her mother, who had died suddenly in the hospital not long before, so...."

FR. JANKO: "Well, that is very interesting. What did she ask her?"

VICKA: "She asked her how her mother was."

FR. JANKO: "Did Our Lady answer her?"

VICKA: "Yes, yes. She told her that her mother was well, that she was with her, and that she should not worry about her."

FR. JANKO: "And, who do you mean by 'with her'?"

VICKA: "Well, with Our Lady. Who else?"

FR. JANKO: "Did all of you hear when Ivanka asked this?"

VICKA: "Of course we did. We all heard that."

FR. JANKO: "And, did you hear what Our Lady said to her?"

VICKA: "All of us heard, except Marija and little Jakov."

FR. JANKO: "And, why was that the case with Marija?"

VICKA: "Well, who knows? That's the way it was and that's it."

FR. JANKO: "Did Marija feel bad about that?"

VICKA: "I'm sure she did, but what can you do?"

FR. JANKO: "All right, Vicka. But, from this conversation, I don't see what happened to Stanko's son Ivan."

VICKA: "Ivan was with us and saw all that we saw."

FR. JANKO: "And, how did he happen to be there?"

VICKA: "The same way we did. He's a shy young man, so he looked to see what we were going to do and he followed our lead. And, when we ran up Podbrdo, he ran with us."

FR. JANKO: "All right, Vicka. And, it was, all in all, beautiful?"

VICKA: "Beautiful? It cannot be described. As if we were not on Earth, in spite of everything—the heat and thornbushes and the crowd of people. When she is with us, we forget everything."

FR. JANKO: "All right. Now, did anyone ask anything at that time?"

VICKA: "Well, I already told you that Ivanka asked about her mother. And, Mirjana asked for a sign to be given so that the people stop saying things about us."

FR. JANKO: "And Our Lady?"

VICKA: "Mirjana's watch completely turned backward."

FR. JANKO: "All right, I won't ask about that, for it isn't quite clear as to what happened. But, something else..."

VICKA: "Yes, we did. We asked her if she will come again."

FR. JANKO: "And she?"

VICKA: "She nodded her head indicating that she would."

FR. JANKO: "Vicka, you have stated (and it's recorded somewhere) that you, at the time, saw her in some kind of a thornbush."

VICKA: "Yes, I did say that. You know that I'm rather impulsive. I saw Our Lady through a thornbush, and it seemed to me that she was in a thornbush. But, she was in the midst of three thornbushes on a small patch of grass. But, why is anyone making a big point of that? The important thing is whether I saw her or not."

FR. JANKO: "Right. But, I heard you sprinkled her with holy water then."

VICKA: "No, no. That was the third day."

FR. JANKO: "Right. And, how long did you stay with Our Lady?"

VICKA: "Until she said, 'Goodbye, my angels,' and left."

FR. JANKO: "All right. Now, finally, tell me who all saw Our Lady that day?"

VICKA: "The six of us."

FR. JANKO: "Which six?"

VICKA: "Well, the six of us! Me, Mirjana, Ivanka, and then Ivan, Marija, and little Jakov."

FR. JANKO: "Which Ivan?"

VICKA: "Stanko's son Ivan. We already talked about that."

FR. JANKO: "Correct, Vicka. But, was anyone else with you at that time?"

VICKA: "There were at least fifteen of us. Even more. There was Mario, Ivan, Marinko… Who can remember who all was there?"

FR. JANKO: "Were there any adults present?"

VICKA: "Ivan Ivanković, Mate Šego, and a few others were there."

FR. JANKO: "And, what did they say about that later?"

VICKA: "They said that something was really happening there, especially when they saw how we went running up. Some also saw the flash of light when Our Lady appeared and the like..."

FR. JANKO: "And, were Milka and Ivan, the son of the late Jozo, there?"

VICKA: "No, they weren't."

FR. JANKO: "And, why not?"

VICKA: "How would I know? Milka's mother wouldn't allow her to go. Marija went, but Milka had to do some errand for her mother. And, as to the other Ivan...he's a bit older than us. What would he do with us children?"

FR. JANKO: "Right. And, when did you return home?"

VICKA: "It depends, it varied."

FR. JANKO: "Marinko told me that Ivanka wept bitterly upon her return."

VICKA: "Yes, she did. In fact, all of us did. But she, especially. How could she not weep?"

FR. JANKO: "And, why her, especially?"

VICKA: "Well, didn't I tell you that Our Lady spoke to her about her mother? You know how it is—a mother is a mother."

FR. JANKO: "Right, you said that Our Lady told her that her mother was with her and that all was well, so..."

VICKA: "All the same; who wouldn't love their mother?"

THE THIRD DAY – JUNE 26

"I am the blessed Virgin Mary"

"Those days were so shocking, they created such confusion in me," Marija Pavlović said about the first three days of apparitions in Medjugorje.

What's more, the confusion was even greater because Father Jozo Zovko, the pastor, wasn't in Medjugorje; he was in Kloštar Ivanić, where he was holding a spiritual retreat for Franciscan and Carmelite nuns. In addition, Fr. Jozo had no contact with Medjugorje because, the day before, there had been a storm and lightning that hit the post office, disrupting the telephone network. As a result, the visionaries, their parents, and the locals had no one to turn to for spiritual assistance.

. . .

Fr. Jozo Zovko had been the pastor in Medjugorje for a little more than half a year; he arrived eight months before the apparitions began. As such, he knew very few people in the parish and none of the children visionaries. Fr. Jozo began his priestly ministry as a chaplain in Čerin, where he spent nearly five years from 1970 to 1975 under the communist regime. In that village—six miles from Čitluk, which is near Medjugorje—he worked selflessly and labored with all his heart.

Fr. Jozo was a fan of Catechism Olympics (knowledge of faith competitions) and of all competitions for children. MAK (Mali Koncil, a Catholic periodical for children) organized competitions in Bible knowledge. Parishioners and the children from Čerin participated every year and they were always the best. In Čerin, they also opened a special catechetical center where the catechists, priests, and nuns provided catechesis. Fr. Jozo also went to lead retreats in Zagreb, Sarajevo, Subotica, Split, and Rijeka, and regularly held spiritual exercises for nuns and priests. He also became a member of the Catechetical Council of the Bishop's Conference of Yugoslavia and worked on religious education programs. Because catechisms were written for the whole of the former Yugoslavia, he often traveled to Split and Zagreb.

After Čerin, Fr. Jozo went to Austria to specialize, after which he was assigned as pastor in Posušje, where, with great enthusiasm, he continued working with children and parents. Once again, MAK organized the Catechism Olympics on the history of the Church and, with his high school students from Posušje, Fr. Jozo won first place. In the parish, he founded a prayer group, the Franciscan Third Order, the altar boy service, and the parish council. However, all of this work was too much of a burden for the communist government; they seemed to be unable to control him. They had official talks with him several times, but were unable to intimidate him or stop him in his work. Unshaken, Fr. Jozo built a catechetical center with five classrooms, a large hall, and housing for nuns. He was greatly anticipating beginning catechetical work at the new center, but his dream was not realized. The Communist Party authorities met and concluded that they would request his departure from Posušje. So, they directly asked his superior to transfer him from Posušje. Soon after, Fr. Jozo received a letter from the provincial elders that he had been transferred from the large parish of Posušje to the small parish of Medjugorje—a place with a large church surrounded by nothing but vineyards.

By now, it was the fall of 1980. Medjugorje—Fr. Jozo once recalled—had barely any pastoral or catechetical space relative to Posušje, so the catechism classes were held in the basement of the parish house. He said he was in love with religious education and loved to teach and educate children and young people—as well as their parents—in the faith. And, while he was in Posušje, Fr. Jozo had been particularly happy because none of the high school students nor their parents had enrolled in the communist party. In Medjugorje, he worked wholeheartedly with a prayer group of young people.

"When I arrived, I didn't know the children or their parents," Fr. Jozo explained. "I practically didn't know anyone. I led spiritual exercises, spiritual encounters, and retreats throughout Yugoslavia. We wrote books and catechisms for elementary and high schools, but I didn't have the time as a pastor to meet parishioners, and I was sorry about that. I had, in some ways, made it the priority of my heart to work with young people. I wanted to gather a group of young people and establish a prayer community. Thanks be to God, I succeeded with high school and university students. For the

May 1st holidays, I organized our participation in the prayer retreat in Split. Imagine what kind of a grace it was: A bus filled with youth at a prayer retreat! They were accompanied by chaplain Fr. Zrinko. It was a retreat led by the late Fr. Božidar Medvid and Fr. Josip Marcelić with a group of priests. Our youth participated in this retreat, and, after their return from Split, we continued our regular weekly meetings. The interest in our prayer meetings was enormous. Unfortunately, we didn't have the right space for them. We crowded together in the sacristy on the left. As God leads everything, how great is His providence! The apparitions began two months later and everything fell on the shoulders of these young people—praying, accompanying, and guarding the visionaries from the impudent crowd; praying at the cross; praying on the hill…And so it is to this day. Many of the young people specialized and became guides for pilgrims. We also started a course for guides of pilgrims. They have all persevered to the end in helping and serving the parish and pilgrims."

When the apparitions began, Fr. Jozo was in Zagreb, and before that he spent a week in Kloštar Ivanić where he led spiritual exercises for nuns who were preparing for final vows. When they asked him how he felt in a new parish, he told the nuns that he had accepted these spiritual exercises as a special vow and prayer for his new parish: For it to take root to awaken in the spirit of prayer, the spirit of love, the spirit of communion with the holy Church, and the spirit of hope; that he desired to see healthy and strong faith reign in it. Together, the nuns prayed for Fr. Jozo's intention and the spiritual exercises ended on June 24. That afternoon, Fr. Jozo had an appointment in Odra.

"I came to Odra, where late professor Ana Gabrijela Šabić, professor Josip Baričević, and I met regarding the final editorial for the Catechetical Manual 'The Way to Freedom,'" he explained. "We worked all day. During the break, Gabrijela asked me, 'Is there any other Medjugorje than the one you come from?'"

Fr. Jozo asked her why she asked.

"'Look, the lightning that struck…it hit the post office,'" he recalled her saying as she showed him the newspaper.

"I read it and said, 'Yes, this is my Medjugorje.' I could not reach Chaplain Zrinko by phone. Everything was burned, so the news of the apparition had to be spread by word of mouth, not by technology. There was no phone service, no running water, no electricity. The unprecedented severe weather turned seven electric poles into dust! They were destroyed by lightning—into dust!" Fr. Jozo said.

But, what happened during lunch in Odra—which preceded the apparitions—is a true mystery and a little-known secret about the announcement and happenings of the apparitions in Medjugorje.

"It was during lunch. They prepared a special meal for us," Fr. Jozo began. "We were not with the friars. Unannounced, an unknown priest entered and asked, 'Which one of you is the pastor from Medjugorje?'"

Fr. Jozo said he was the pastor and the unknown priest told him that he had a letter for him.

"He handed me a letter, which I later read on the airplane," Fr. Jozo continued. "The friar described his own vision in Canada. He carefully described his dream and adventure—his experience. Apparition of Our Lady in Medjugorje! That's something fantastic! He writes that in the dream he saw Our Lady appearing. She stopped at a church and said, 'Here, this is Medjugorje.' That night, after this dream, he did not close his eyes again. He wrote down his vision. He didn't know where Medjugorje was. He described a church with two towers not knowing where it was. Finally, he learned from other friars that it was in Herzegovina. He was happy. And, when the brothers in the monastery told him that I was from Herzegovina, that is, from Medjugorje, he said, 'Excellent!'

"He looked at me with tears in his eyes because he had experienced it deeply," Fr. Jozo went on. "And I did not know what he had experienced and what he had written in the letter. I asked who he was, so they told me that he was a Friar of the Third Order living in Canada. The letter was addressed to me and I read it only when I was on the airplane."

The memory of this event is described and confirmed by Father Jerko Penava, also a Franciscan of the Third Order, as well as Father Teodor Badurina. According to Fr. Jerko, Fr. Teodor—who was serving in Canada—first asked him whether he knew where Medjugorje was because Fr. Jerko was a native of Herzegovina. He told him that he knew it was about 50 kilometers (31 miles) from his village, but that he didn't know exactly where it was, but that it was "somewhere near Ljubuški."

"Fr. Teodor told me that Our Lady would appear there, that he had such a vision—a dream," Fr. Jerko said. "I even think that he told me when this would happen."

Fr. Jerko added that he had told one of his fellow friars in Odra, as well, because he didn't know Fr. Teodor well enough. The friar told him that it was nonsense and that he didn't believe in such delusions.

"I only knew that Fr. Teodor was a quiet, withdrawn, and God-fearing friar," Fr. Jerko said. "And you see what later happened."

Meanwhile, Fr. Jozo planned to return to Medjugorje on June 26, but his flight was delayed, so he had to spend the night in Posušje.

"The flight was an hour and a half late," Fr. Jozo explained. "Fr. Zrinko didn't meet me in Posušje. He went back home due to the situation in the parish—the situation that Fr. Zrinko did not discuss with Fr. Viktor, the parish priest, at all…The next morning, I decided to go with Fr. Viktor to visit my mom, who was in the hospital in Mostar. My eighty-year-old mother had a hip surgery. At the entrance door of the hospital, I met a parishioner, Draga

Ivanković, Marinko's wife, from Bijakovići. When she saw me, she cried out at the top of her voice, 'Where are you, my friar!? Our Lady has appeared and you are not there!' I looked at her and I thought she was crazy—she was all wrapped in white."

Draga's husband, Marinko Ivanković, confirmed her words.

"My wife worked in the Čitluk Soko factory where they manufactured refrigerators," Marinko explained. "The manager told them to come to work on that Saturday because they had to clean the whole factory. She graduated from high school, having studied economics, and she worked in an office. She had been working about an hour or two when she took a heavy piece of metal from near the radiator to clean it. When she tried to put it back, it fell and injured her leg and arm. So, they had to take her to the hospital in Mostar. When she was getting out of the car in front of the hospital, someone called her, 'Dragica, Dragica, what happened?' When she turned, she saw Fr. Jozo."

"'Run, Jozo, to the parish. Fr. Zrinko doesn't believe it. Our Lady has appeared!'" Draga told Fr. Jozo, according to Marinko.

"Together with [Fr.] Kosir, he went to visit his mother at the hospital in Mostar," Marinko continued. "He asked Kosir whether he heard something happened in the parish of Medjugorje. 'No, I haven't heard anything. Let her go, she seems to have hit her head, not her arm and leg,' he replied jokingly. Fr. Jozo celebrated an early morning Mass on the following day and, after it, he asked my wife, Draga, to forgive him because later he met with Fr. Zrinko who told him everything."

In Medjugorje, everyone was excited. Fr. Jozo arrived at exactly noon on Saturday, June 27. All the parishioners gathered around the parish office. Fr. Zrinko was out.

"When we arrived in Medjugorje, there was much to hear," remembered Fr. Jozo. "The nuns were in front of the parish office and many people were on the hill. They all asked, 'Well, where are you? The people are gathering. Six children say that Our Lady appears to them.' I was silent. I had that letter in my head. I put it on the table. Later, it was taken by the members of UDBA [communist secret police] who imprisoned me."

The letter mentioned by Fr. Jozo disappeared after the police raid on August 17, 1981, during which Fr. Jozo was arrested. That is when most of the parish archives and chronicles, as well as the records of the apparitions, all of his personal belongings, and the recordings of the first conversations with the visionaries also disappeared.

"Zrinko heard the people talking, but he did not care," Fr. Jozo continued. "For Zrinko, this was an UDBA hoax. Imagine that he didn't even mention this to Fr. Viktor in their conversation! When I came to Medjugorje, I saw the nuns were worried. I asked them if they knew the children, but they didn't know all of them. Did they know their parents? Sister Vladimira said, 'I teach Jakov."

"Well, what is he like, is he healthy?" Fr. Jozo asked the nun.

"A lively boy, he is good," she replied, according to Fr. Jozo. "He has a mother. He is without his father."

When Fr. Zrinko returned, Fr. Jozo asked what was going on in the parish.

"He said, 'Well, let it go. It is certainly UDBA at work," Fr. Jozo recalled. "They constantly followed me—everywhere. The noon bells rang, we prayed the Angelus, and I thought about how I could reach these children. We had just finished the Angelus prayer when a van entered the yard. The children—the visionaries—jumped out of it like birds from the nest and ran to me, saying, 'Behold, the pastor has come to us!' they delightedly shouted. I greeted each of them and the driver, Jure, with a smile. I decided to listen patiently and watch each child individually. I vigilantly focused on my posture during the conversation in order to not confuse them; not to encourage a false or inaccurate answer. I invited them into the office along with Fr. Viktor and Fr. Zrinko. My wish was that they would also see and hear their experiences."

"'You stay here in the office, talk with each other and have something to eat, and I will talk with everyone separately in my room,'" Fr. Jozo remembered, "I had a tape recorder, which I turned on after explaining I would record our conversation."

"First, I called Mirjana because she came from Sarajevo," he continued. "An intelligent girl, very open and honest. She answered all questions without any difficulty. From our conversations, I found out what had happened in those three days I had been out of the parish. I felt a bitter prejudice against the communists, thinking they manipulated children to make fun of the faith, the Church. I thought about how they only needed a little time to prepare such scenarios and pranks. Then, I thought, maybe they gave drugs to the children. I wanted to uncover all of it in conversations with them. And they, simple as children, spoke only of Our Lady, about Her beauty, about the neighbors and the encounters with them.

"The children were initially somewhat blocked and reserved, but soon they relaxed and began sharing their experiences," he said. "Only Ivan remained reserved. I first called Mirjana for a conversation. She came from Sarajevo and I suspected she might have brought drugs or some sort of intoxicant from Sarajevo. Had someone perhaps manipulated her? I knew her father and uncle. Her uncle was a priest—a friar—who had left our community and became part of the diocese of Šibenik. He was a very good priest. So I optimistically relied on the fact that Mirjana was from a priestly family and that she should not cheat. I was afraid of drugs. We had to know these issues and their effects. I saw from the conversation that they knew nothing about it. That they had not been given something; they had not been manipulated."

Fr. Jozo recalled a previous event that had initially led him to believe that the communists were trying to trick the villagers.

"Something rarely mentioned had happened here in Herzegovina, in the parish of Raško Polje after World War II," he began. "The communists manipulated people. In the woods outside the village, they connected a car battery to an electric bulb using a cable. At night, from the village, they watched it in amazement as if it was some kind of miraculous sign from Heaven. They knew that there was never a light there, but they suggested to the people that it was perhaps Our Lady—some kind of a sign from Heaven. The people believed and began to pray. Then they disconnected the battery and, mockingly, announced that Our Lady was no more. They used it as evidence later at their conferences: 'This is how the friars manipulate you. There is no God, it is a friar's fabrication.'... They can do just about anything. They use everything to achieve their goals."

"I preached on the feast of St. Elijah at the cemetery in Rastovača. After the Mass and the sermon, UDBA called more than four hundred people and asked every one of them separately what I had preached about. And I preached about the Church in Poland, about the recent event in Nova Huta where Archbishop Karol Wojtyla consecrated the new church. The Poles from Chicago sent a tabernacle in the form of a spacecraft. Poland has 50 parishes in and around Chicago. Wojtyla delivered a sermon, from which I learned how the church was built in that working-class, steel-producing settlement. They wanted a church, but the government said that there would not be a church, but a house of culture. The people defended the area with their bodies. Some of them were even killed, but they managed to have a church there. And Wojtyla, from Krakow, commended this powerful and courageous attitude of his people. I said that Nova Huta was like our Zenica, the steel-producing center, and how they bravely got what they wanted—the church. This newly built church was consecrated by the Archbishop of Krakow. He would later become pope. I went to Rijeka to lead a summer catechetical school for priests and nuns who were catechists. Posušje talked only about the sermon and UDBA. Fr. Veselko Sesar, my chaplain, called me and said that all the workers from the factory, without exception, were called in for the hearing because of my sermon. He asked me what I had said. I told him to just stay calm because there was nothing special. After returning to the parish, I was also called to the hearing and questioned for seven to eight hours. And then, again and again. In the end, they transferred me to Medjugorje. In February, I already knew the UDBA sought my transfer from Posušje. It would indeed happen in the fall of that year."

At the time, Medjugorje was an ordinary, rural parish that was moderately wealthy. Many priests and nuns came from there. In part, it was richer than other parishes; there were some so-called passive parishes where there were no vineyards and where the railroad was far away. However, the railroad was close to Medjugorje in Šurmanci.

"Some families were rich, in our Herzegovinian terms, because in this part [of the region] where they could plant tobacco and produce wine and sell it, people could make a good living from it," Fr. Jozo continued. "So they were able to live decently. But those who were poor, they were simply poor. Whoever had a small field was poor. It was an ordinary parish, but a parish in which the Communist Party did not stand well. The parish did not have a Communist Party branch. I remember meeting a group of young intellectuals while I was in the neighboring parish of Čerin. The group of students—on Savka's [a Communist leader from Zagreb] invitation in 1971—were called to join the Communist Party to make it more popular. I dissuaded them from doing so by explaining how the Communist Party always remains atheistic. Whatever else they promise is a scam, a lie. They did not join the party. Ten years later, in 1981, these students were the great guardians and activists of the Queen of Peace.

"The parishioners of Medjugorje built a new church. It was rare that a parish had a church; that was a sign of economic power. It was rare that someone had a school in the village, as the Franciscan nuns had in Medjugorje. Along with the public school, there was a private school from the era of old Yugoslavia. The school was burned by enemies before I came to the parish. This was all a sign that they [people from Medjugorje] could do more than others—like the cross that was erected on Križevac. Once it became a municipal headquarter, the neighboring Čitluk was able to do more as buildings and apartments were built; new jobs were created; a department store and tobacco factory—which was previously in Ljubuški—were opened. It was only a small step forward."

Fr. Jozo feared the communists' frauds and provocations, even though they didn't have a strong hold in Medjugorje.

"I had lots of problems," he went on. "First, the fear of a fraud. Second, when someone discredits your faith…I loved and venerated Our Lady, as well as Jesus, of course. For example, I wanted people to come to May Marian devotions, but they said they didn't have time because that is when they worked in the tobacco fields and vineyards. I came to terms with it but, in Posušje, I managed to organize the May devotions."

With all of these thoughts in his head, Fr. Jozo began to question the children one by one. As soon as they introduced themselves, it was Mirjana Dragičević who captured Fr. Jozo's attention. She was the first one to enter and she looked cheerful. Fr. Jozo asked her why she was in Medjugorje since she lived in Sarajevo. She explained to him that her parents were from Medjugorje and that she came here for summer break. He asked her if she went to church, if she prayed, and if she had heard of Lourdes, Fatima. She told him that she had never heard of apparitions. He then asked her if she attended the catechism classes, if she prayed to God, how they prayed in her family, and so on; he was interested in what kind of a family she came from, and Mirjana answered all of the questions calmly and normally. Throughout the conversation, Fr. Jozo learned that Mirjana's family led a Christian life. He was impressed with her because she was intelligent and lively and didn't give the impression of a person who invented or talked about something she had not experienced.

After speaking for about an hour, Mirjana remained adamant about the experience of the apparitions. He was surprised that she had never heard of Lourdes or Fatima, so he gave her a book about the apparitions in Fatima. When she went home with the book, Fr. Jozo later regretted it.

"Why did I give her the book!" he said.

Unfortunately, Mirjana compared the apparitions from Fatima with their apparitions and later made a statement about how many more encounters they would have with Our Lady, based on what she had read in the book.

"I asked her, 'Mirjana, have you heard that Our Lady had appeared in Lourdes and Fatima? Do you attend Mass, catechism classes...?' I turned around because I knew exactly where each book was and I took a book by professor Božo Vuce from Makarska. I asked her if she had read it, because there is a book about it, and she said, 'Please, give me the book!' And, when I gave her the book about Fatima, she said, 'We still have so many days!'—she thought it had to be the same for them, because it was about Our Lady's apparitions. She also argued with those who challenged them, pointing to the book, until I told her, 'Bring the book back to me.'... That is why Mirjana made statements regarding how many days Our Lady would appear to them; Fr. Božo's book created a big problem for us. You can't prove it to anyone because it all happened spontaneously."

Mirjana has confirmed everything associated with the controversial book.

"I think Fr. Jozo asked only me about this," she said. "A night or two before that, Marinko told me about Lourdes. That Our Lady had already been to Lourdes; that she appeared there 17 times. I said, 'Really? She didn't come from Heaven only to Medjugorje?' And, when Fr. Jozo asked me how many more times Our Lady would appear, I will never forget how shocked I was that a friar asked me something like this. I thought, 'My dear God, didn't he read about Lourdes? I hadn't heard of it, but is it possible that he hadn't heard of it?' Then, I said to him, 'Well, 17 times.' I thought if she appeared 17 times in Lourdes, she would appear 17 times in Medjugorje, as well. I didn't know then about Fatima, Guadalupe, and other apparition sites. I thought, as many times as she appeared at one site, that it would be the same at the other site as well."

She described Fr. Jozo's reserved and strict attitude toward the children.

"When Fr. Jozo came back from Zagreb, Marinko went to tell him that six children were seeing Our Lady, and he replied a bit arrogantly, 'Those who see, let them see, and those who do not see, let them come to the church and pray to God and that's it.' And, only a few days later, when Our Lady took him in her arms, he invited us and started calling us 'his angels'— hugging us, kissing us—and he was completely changed."

Coming from Sarajevo, Mirjana said she was always "under the spotlight."

"They thought, as I came from Sarajevo, that I had prepared something, some drugs or something similar," she said. "I had no idea what a drug was. I grew up with my dad and mom. I never went into the city without my dad. I was attached to my family and it was in Medjugorje—not in Sarajevo—where I had freedom. They thought that I brought drugs but, for me, the freedom was here! In Sarajevo, I didn't go out anywhere without my parents or anything else. Those accusations were very difficult for me but, over the years, I got used to them."

"I was afraid," Fr. Jozo admitted. "I had to go slowly, little by little. You know why else? Because, at first, the police didn't interfere at all. There were no policemen at all! They watched only through spies. I decided in my heart, in order to not fall under the influence, I wouldn't climb the hill. Everyone, even friars who came, said, 'Let's go! Let's go!' Fr. Tomislav said that he would organize the prayers up there, and I said no! Instead, I said that we would organize prayer in the prayer area [in church], because it was risky to do it up there and the government would stop everything by declaring it a crime. It was known that they could declare it a people's gathering or something similar. That was so sensitive. Having a rite—as they called it—outside the church, without previous registration, meant to risk up to three, five, or more months in prison for nothing."

When Fr. Jozo learned that Ivanka—the daughter of the late Jagoda, a good, young woman whom he had just buried in May—was among the child visionaries, he immediately began the conversation with a question about Ivanka's mother, asking if she had asked Our Lady anything about her mom. Ivanka replied that she had asked Our Lady to show her her mother, and that since she didn't, Our Lady did promise that she would. Fr. Jozo asked when, and Ivanka began to explain everything to him. In his heart, Fr. Jozo said that he rationalized that Ivanka had such a great and human desire to see her mother—whom she loved and whom she couldn't forget—that now, in her imagination, in her projections, it seemed as if she had seen her; as if she had had a vison. He explained to her that it might be her imagination; in her soul, it could be her mom, but she called her Our Lady. And that, with her suggestion, she influenced the other children, so now everyone sees Our Lady. In this way, Fr. Jozo, from the beginning, convinced himself not to believe the child visionaries, because, to him, their words were so unconvincing.

After the conversation with the withdrawn and vulnerable Ivanka, Vicka—who was joyful and overflowing with words about her experience—came in. Fr. Jozo questioned her about the same things as he did the others—about her family and prayer. But, she quickly finished answering these questions and changed the subject to Podbrdo, testifying about what she had seen and what she had said there. He also asked her about Ivanka's mother's funeral, but she responded quickly and again changed the subject back to when they were on the hill in front of Our Lady. He simply couldn't find anything particularly problematic to confirm his views. Yet, at the same time, Vicka didn't convince or disarm him, so Fr. Jozo still suspected that the children were manipulated or that somebody had given them something. He wanted to continue to examine everything very carefully.

After Vicka, it was Ivan's turn. Fr. Jozo barely spoke with him because the withdrawn and quiet Ivan replied only with "yes" or "no." In fact, Fr. Jozo mentioned that this boy couldn't express himself in words or give any testimony, so he even wondered if Ivan spoke at all; he didn't say anything! Fr. Jozo talked and talked, trying to encourage Ivan to talk, but he didn't succeed. At the end of the conversation with Ivan, Fr. Jozo wondered if it was possible that someone could have manipulated the children in such a way that they could hardly say a word!

During the conversation with the youngest, Jakov, the boy's eyes were burning with fire. He described everything to Fr. Jozo, who listened to it with his heart and was open to Jakov disarming and convincing him. But, Jakov didn't succeed, either.

Fr. Jozo's intention had actually been to record these conversations and to listen to them at night, but he found it demanding and difficult.

Meanwhile, Fr. Jozo described Marija as a fearful, but open person. After the conversation, he sent the children home because it was late afternoon and getting dark.

Fr. Jozo did not feel the need to go to Apparition Hill on that day or on the following days; he wanted to distance himself so that nothing would influence him, and so that he could judge for himself. He feared that the people were influenced by some kind of false enthusiasm, and he wanted to be realistic and cautious. He knew that this was his responsibility because people openly asked him what, as a pastor, he thought about all of this.

. . .

Although the return of Fr. Jozo to the parish brought back peace, excitement among the people continued to grow. Meanwhile, news about the apparitions spread widely, and people from all over started coming to Medjugorje. According to Marinko, there were about a thousand parishioners on the road where the visionaries had seen Our Lady on the first and second evenings.

One evening after work, Marinko went to Vicka's house, where he found five of the six visionaries (Ivan was absent). He asked if they were going to see Our Lady tonight, and they said they would.

"Please, if Our Lady comes, ask her why she came here and what it is that she asks from us," he said to the children.

"When we got there, Ivan Dragičević joined us at Podbrdo," Marinko said. "I looked at my watch and it was 5:50 p.m. The visionaries said, 'See the light, see the light, see the light.' They said that they saw the light three times and that Our Lady was on the hill! I asked them, 'Where on the hill is Our Lady?' There were around twenty people about fifty meters (55 yards) down from where Our Lady's statue stands today. I asked them if Our Lady appeared where those people were standing. Vicka took my hand, 'Come on, Marinko. There, see where Our Lady is!'"

Earlier, when they had left Vicka's house, Vicka's grandmother gave her a glass of holy water and instructed her, "Make the sign of the cross with the holy water and pray the Creed and the seven sets of Our Father, Hail Mary, and Glory Be. Say, my child, 'If you are Satan, flee from us. If you are Our Lady, stay with us.'"

"It rained the night before," Marinko continued. "I gave Mirjana my hand a dozen times—because she was a city child from Sarajevo—so I could help her step over the stones because it was still slippery. Ivan was able to run up because he played soccer every day. As we approached him, I looked at him, and he seemed to have lost something. I turned and noticed that the visionaries no longer stood beside me—they knelt between two stones where there was green grass. I asked them if Our Lady was there, and they said she was."

"'Where is Our Lady standing, on which stone? On this one? On that one?'" Marinko recalled asking the children.

"'No, Our Lady is standing on a bright cloud; she is not touching the ground,'" they replied.

Then, Marinko gave Vicka the glass with holy water. Vicka took it and threw the holy water saying, "If you are Our Lady, stay with us. If you are not, leave us!"

"Then, I asked if Our Lady was there and she told me, 'She is looking at all of you and smiling,'" Marinko said.

Marinko inquired to the children if they asked Our Lady why she had come to Medjugorje and what she asked from them. When they said that they didn't, he told them to ask.

"There were about forty of us present there," Marinko said. "While the first event was convincing for me, this time, when I told them to ask her—all six of them—I heard all six of them speaking as one. At the same moment in one voice, they said, 'Our Lady said, "I came here to this parish because in this parish there are still many faithful who believe and who pray a lot. I came to convert and reconcile the people.' After that, a man from another parish told them to ask Our Lady to give us a small sign so that everyone could see that she was there. All visionaries said in one voice, 'Our Lady said, blessed are those who have not seen and yet believe.'"

Afterward, Marinko reported that the children were exhausted and tired, so the adults gave them a hand down the same path that is used even now to come down from Podbrdo. As they descended, they prayed the joyful mysteries of the rosary.

Additionally, because this third day was swelteringly hot, the air felt suffocating as the crowd pushed in on the children. Yet, no amount of discomfort could prevent them from being there. Witnesses later told them that their apparition lasted thirty minutes. During this time, the visionaries said that Our Lady greeted them with the words "Praised be Jesus"—which they all recognized as part of the traditional Croatian greeting *Hvaljen Isus i Marija* or *Praised be Jesus and Mary*. Only later did they understand why Our Lady said only the first part; as a most humble servant of God, she would never praise herself.

"Marija went down the hill with my cousin Ivan," Marinko added. "She went off his side and was with Our Lady for two minutes—just her, no one else. That is when Our Lady told her that she wanted peace between man and God and among people."

The event was witnessed by Ivan Ivanković. In those first days, he was with Marija every time while they were still allowed to go to Podbrdo—until the police prohibited it.

Ivan Ivanković remembers, "On the third day, a few of us went up the hill. A great crowd of people gathered on the hill, but the visionaries were not there. At almost 6:00 p.m. they were not there yet. That is when someone called us from down the hill saying that they had run to another spot where she appeared on the third day. I went up the hill - I knew every stone - I ran up there and they came to a cliff almost at the same time as me. As they knelt down, people gathered together, scrambling through the thorn bushes. The children spoke, but their voices were not heard. As I was on the closest rock to them, practically behind Our Lady, I descended to a lower rock to get closer, when they all screamed: 'Ivan, you stepped on her dress!' I froze and stood petrified, and now they all looked at me. I couldn't go back because the rock, that I had been standing on, was behind me. I stood there for four to five minutes, and after that they said: 'She left!' And in that moment—between me and the visionaries and people—a white dove appeared and flew into the air. People were weeping, screaming, and becoming emotional" – remembers Ivan Ivanković, who was right next to the visionaries.

"Everybody went with somebody," he said. "We were returning from that spot and, at the place where today stands the plaque with the second joyful mystery of the rosary, Marija—all pale and barely moving—let go of my hand my hand. The people were following us. It was crowded. We were the first. All of them rushed to ask her something. She just ran from me to the left to a dry pomegranate tree where it happened. She knelt and there she saw Our Lady with a bloody cross. She was kneeling there for two or three minutes. The crowd from above stopped. She was pale, lost, and she said that Our Lady appeared to her with a bloody cross."

Marija confirmed the additional apparition as well.

"When the apparition ended, we went home," she said. "It was closer for me to go down the old path on the hill, not from this side where the blue cross is now. Goats and sheep went that way and we went that way to gather firewood. It was a wider path, as it is a little wider even today, and I went home that way. At one point, Our Lady appeared! And she gave the first message. This is absolutely the first message that Our Lady gave, 'Peace, peace, peace. Peace within man, peace among men, peace between man and God, and peace in the world.' Behind Our Lady, there was a dark cross without Jesus, and she began to cry. Her tears streamed down her cheeks and she went to the cloud on which she stood.

Then I started crying and my school friends were shocked with my openness, my strength, because I was shouting, 'Convert! Reconcile!' Our Lady later said that she came here with the name Queen of Peace, that peace is needed and that I should pray for peace."

On that day, Our Lady told the children who she was—the Blessed Virgin Mary, the Queen of Peace.

"By the third day, there was already a lot of people," Vicka said. "People asked about this, asked about that. Ask her for this, ask her for that. Everyone thought they could get an answer. At the beginning, Our Lady just said, 'I am the Blessed Virgin Mary. I have come here because there are many believers.' At first, she prayed with us; she did not immediately begin to give messages. But I remember well that she said, 'I came here, I chose this parish because there are many good believers here.'"

According to Mirjana, one of the children asked Our Lady why she had chosen to appear in Medjugorje and not somewhere else.

"'I have come because there are many true believers here,'" Mirjana recalled that Our Lady replied. "'I have come to convert and reconcile the whole world.'"

"Why are you appearing to us?" Mirjana remembered asking. "We are no better than others."

Mirjana said that Our Lady replied, "'Because I need you the way you are.'"

Ivan Dragičević also confirmed that, on the third day, there were many people on Podbrdo who protected them from communist authorities and the police.

"We brought with us the holy water that Vicka's grandmother had given us, and we went spontaneously with the people," he recollected. "We didn't go together so that the police would not recognize us. One group went with me; the other group went with

Vicka. And when we were about twenty meters (22 yards) from the place where the statue of Our Lady is now (before there were shrubs), she was already waiting for us holding little Jesus in her arms, smiling, and waving her hand, 'Dear children, come closer.' I will never forget that day for the rest of my life. I was standing still; I could not move—neither forward nor backward. I thought of running away again, but something was stronger than me. At one point—not with my power; as if I was floating over those stones, the bushes—we came closer to her on our knees. When we came closer to her, I cannot describe that moment. I trembled. I kept looking up and down. It was more than excitement, and then Our Lady began to say the first words, 'Dear children, I am with you. I am your mother. Do not be afraid of anything. I will protect you. I will lead you. I will help you. Do not be afraid.'

"One of the girls, who was the calmest among us at that moment, asked her who she was and what her name was. She replied, 'I am the Queen of Peace. I am coming, dear children, because my Son sends me to help you.' These were the first words that Our Lady conveyed through us to the world. Then, I was sure, and that is when we started talking with her for the first time. I recognized her and I was sure."

Ivan added that every hour brought new developments.

"The police tortured our parents—even during the night," he said. "We were exposed to them 24 hours a day. For many nights, I slept in the field in a bedsheet. People from the village used to come to tell us that the police and secret service were coming. My mother would give me the bedsheet and I would go sleep in the vineyard."

Other parents were also troubled, but they all stood firm with their children; they believed them and supported them. Mirjana's parents came to Medjugorje immediately. They were troubled when they saw her during an apparition for the first time, especially because of the extreme emotions on her face and the tears flowing down her cheeks. Yet, knowing her as well as they did—and fully aware that her shyness would have made it impossible for her to be the center of attention in such a large crowd—they never expressed any doubts. When they returned to Sarajevo, they asked her to come back with them; they were worried about her safety as every day seemed increasingly chaotic with bigger crowds and more police. Mirjana, however, was not ready to go back. In truth, she wanted to stay forever. She assumed that Our Lady could only appear in Medjugorje, and nothing was more important to Mirjana than seeing her.

The encounters with Our Lady in those few days changed the children greatly. But, they also encouraged them and literally steeled them overnight, as visionary Marija explained.

"My schoolmates told me, 'Marija, when we saw you, instead of Marija who was shut down like a hedgehog, we found a girl who was ready to die for what she was saying,'" she recalled. "I always say that when God's Spirit comes down on us, He begins to transform us and everything changes. I remember those first days when I scrutinized what I was going to wear every morning because I thought that it would definitely be the last day of my life. Thinking about what communism did to us, how we lived from the very beginning…they forbade us to do things; they took us to the psychiatric ward in Mostar in an ambulance; they came to our homes. How did we survive that, I do not know. Today, I always say, at that time, only God and Our Lady helped us endure everything and remain normal."

FROM THE CONVERSATION OF FR. JANKO BUBALO WITH VICKA

FR. JANKO: "And, that is how the third morning and day of the third apparition dawned. The excitement, as you once told me, was all the greater. For, as you say, you really met with Our Lady for a second time. I suppose it was a bit easier this time?"

VICKA: "Well, yes, certainly. Nonetheless, it was still a torment, for no one really knew what was happening, nor what would come of it."

FR. JANKO: "Perhaps you began to waver as to whether you would go or not?"

VICKA: "Not at all. No way. We could hardly wait until it was six o'clock in the evening. We did our daily chores as fast as we could so that we might go up even sooner."

FR. JANKO: "And, that is how you went, then?"

VICKA: "Yes, of course. What else? We were a bit afraid, but Our Lady was drawing us to her. From the moment we left, we only looked for where we would see her."

FR. JANKO: "Who all went on that day?"

VICKA: "Well, the six of us, and many people."

FR. JANKO: "Which six of you?"

VICKA: "The six of us visionaries and the people."

FR. JANKO: "And then what—you arrived up there and Our Lady wasn't there?"

VICKA: "Well, hold on! Why are you jumping ahead! First, we took the path beyond the houses to see if Our Lady would appear."

FR. JANKO: "And, nothing?"

VICKA: "What nothing! Soon the light flashed three times."

FR. JANKO: "What was the purpose of the light? That was one of the longest days of the year. The sun was high, very high."

VICKA: "The sun was high, but Our Lady shone in order to show us where she was."

FR. JANKO: "Who all saw the light?"

VICKA: "Many of us saw it. I don't know how many. The important thing is that we, the visionaries, saw it."

FR. JANKO: "Did you see only a light, or..."

VICKA: "The light and Our Lady. What good is the light only?"

FR. JANKO: "And, where was Our Lady? I suppose the same place as the first two days?"

VICKA: "Nowhere near that place. She was in a completely different spot."

FR. JANKO: "Lower or higher?"

VICKA: "Much, much higher!"

FR. JANKO: "And, why is that?"

VICKA: "Why? Why don't you ask Our Lady?"

FR. JANKO: "Marinko related to me (that is, when he was there with you for the first time) that it occurred under a cave and there was an old wooden cross—perhaps on an old grave."

VICKA: "I know nothing of that. I was never there before nor after."

FR. JANKO: "All right. What did you do when, as you say, you saw her?"

VICKA: "We ran forward as though on wings. The place is all thorn-bushes and stones; it's awfully steep. But, we flew like birds. We just flew. Both us and the people."

FR. JANKO: "Then, there were people with you?"

VICKA: "Well, of course! I already told you that!"

FR. JANKO: "How many of them were there?"

VICKA: "Who counted? They said there were more than a thousand. I think even more. Well, of course, there were even more."

FR. JANKO: "And, at the sign of light, you all ran up?"

VICKA: "First us, then all the people after us."

FR. JANKO: "Do you recall who was first to reach Our Lady?"

VICKA: "I think it was Ivan."

FR. JANKO: "Which Ivan?"

VICKA: "Well, this Ivan—Our Lady's."

FR. JANKO: "Well, I'm glad that he, as a man, was the first to arrive!"

VICKA: "Right. Just rejoice!"

FR. JANKO: "Vicka, that was a bit of a joke. But, what did you do when you reached the site?"

VICKA: "We got a little confused because, once again, Ivanka and Mirjana didn't feel well. We occupied ourselves with them a bit, but that quickly passed."

FR. JANKO: "And, what was Our Lady doing at the time?"

VICKA: "She disappeared. We began to pray and she reappeared."

FR. JANKO: "And, what did she look like?"

VICKA: "The same as yesterday, only she was happier. She was beautiful. Smiling."

FR. JANKO: "Then, as you already said, you sprinkled her with holy water?"

VICKA: "Yes, yes we did."

FR. JANKO: "Good. Now, that is very interesting to me; why did you sprinkle her?"

VICKA: "Well, you don't know how it was. No one was yet certain about what was taking place. Some said this, some said that. Until then, I had never heard that Satan could also appear."

FR. JANKO: "Then, I suppose, someone remembered that Satan is afraid of holy water."

VICKA: "Well, yes. How many times did I hear from my grandmother,

'He is fearful like the devil is of holy water!' Some of the older women told us to sprinkle her."

FR. JANKO: "And, where did you get 'holy water' at this time of year?"

VICKA: "Come on, why are you now pretending to be an Englishman? As though you don't know that in every Christian home here we have blessed salt and also holy water."

FR. JANKO: "All right, Vicka. But, tell me, who made that holy water?"

VICKA: "I know as though I'm seeing it happen. My mother made it."

FR. JANKO: "And, how did she make it?"

VICKA: "As though you don't already know! She combined the blessed salt with water, mixed it, and that's it. While she did that, we all prayed the Apostles' Creed."

FR. JANKO: And, do you know who carried the water?"

VICKA: "I know. Our Marinko; who else?"

FR. JANKO: "And, who sprinkled Our Lady?"

VICKA: "In fact, I was the one who sprinkled her."

FR. JANKO: "You threw the water toward her and that was it?"

VICKA: "I sprinkled her and said in full voice, 'If you are Our Lady, remain with us. If you are not, you better go away.'"

FR. JANKO: "And, how did she respond?"

VICKA: "She smiled. It seemed to me that she was pleased."

FR. JANKO: "And, she said nothing?"

VICKA: "No, nothing."

FR. JANKO: "What do you think—did any of the water fall on her?"

VICKA: "Well, of course! I came quite close to her and I didn't spare the water."

FR. JANKO: "That is truly very interesting. By that, I would say, the custom of blessing the house still prevails among you, as it did in my own childhood?"

VICKA: "Well, of course! As if we are no longer Christians!?"

FR. JANKO: "That is nice and it really pleases me. But, what did you do with Our Lady on that third day?"

VICKA: "We prayed, sang... And, we also asked Our Lady something."

FR. JANKO: "And, what did you ask Our Lady?"

VICKA: "I know that Ivanka asked about her mother again."

FR. JANKO: "What did she ask her?"

VICKA: "She asked if her mother had a message for her."

FR. JANKO: "And Our Lady?"

VICKA: "Our Lady said that her mother told her to obey her grandmother since she is old, and the like."

FR. JANKO: "Did the rest of you hear Ivanka ask that?"

VICKA: "Yes, all of us did."

FR. JANKO: "And, Our Lady's answer?"

VICKA: "Only we, the visionaries, heard it."

FR. JANKO: "It is not clear to me, but ok. Did anyone else ask anything?"

VICKA: "Mirjana asked her who she was and what her name was."

FR. JANKO: "And Our Lady said nothing?"

VICKA: "What do you mean nothing? She said loud and clear, 'I am the Blessed Virgin Mary.'"

FR. JANKO: "Did she also say the word, 'blessed'?"

VICKA: "Yes, she did. Why do you ask that?"

FR. JANKO: "Oh, nothing. But, now it was easier for you?"

VICKA: "Well, of course! But, again, it wasn't easy for us. A hundred questions ran through our minds."

FR. JANKO: "For example, what?"

VICKA: "Well, why did the Virgin come here? What does she want with us? What will come of this? Everything!"

FR. JANKO: "And, in the end?"

VICKA: "I've told you enough about it already. When Our Lady said farewell to us, I mean, when she said goodbye and left, we slowly returned to our homes. Well, where else were we to go?"

FR. JANKO: "And, at home?"

VICKA: "The people gathered at our houses again. Everyone wanted to know everything. What happened, how it was. Thus, into the night. But, I haven't told you something that happened to Marija, and I'm sure it will interest you."

FR. JANKO: "Of course. Tell me!"

VICKA: "Well, she is rather swift-footed. She went a bit ahead of us—alone. And, suddenly, as though she was thrown, not knowing how, she went off to the side."

FR. JANKO: "To the left or to the right?"

VICKA: "To the left."

FR. JANKO: "And then?"

VICKA: "There, Our Lady appeared alone to Marija with a big cross. Marija said that Our Lady was very sad, and that she spoke something to her through tears. Marija was very frightened. She was unable to stand on her feet."

FR. JANKO: "And?"

VICKA: "At that point, we arrived. We saw her and helped her until she got her wits about her. And, slowly, we managed to get home."

FR. JANKO: "All right, Vicka. Marija told me this twice extensively. That is quite interesting and very important. But, I will come back to this at a later time, so let's end this for now."

THE FOURTH DAY – JUNE 27

Medical examination

On the fourth day, June 27, the six visionaries met at Marija's house to rest and talk before the apparition. Vicka and Mirjana laid in the cool shade underneath a large, covered table and the others sat on a couch. Then, a policeman suddenly barged in.

"'Where are the ones who claim to see Our Lady?'" Mirjana recalled him saying to the surprised children. He then told them to get in the car.

As the visionaries left the house, Marija's family pleaded with them.

"Don't let them give you any pills or injections!" they said.

The policeman drove them to the police station in the neighboring town of Čitluk.

"The local authorities, it seemed, were getting pressure from the Yugoslav government to 'put out the fire,'" Mirjana recounted. "But, this was a flame that no one could extinguish. The officers interrogated us and accused us of lying. When we continued to insist that we were telling the truth, they yelled and cursed at us. It was the first time I had ever heard such vulgar language. Naturally, we were frightened, but our persistence began to confuse and soften them. Some of them may have even believed us, but they never could have shown it. In Medjugorje and Čitluk, many of the policemen secretly baptized their children and even got married in churches under the cover of night. On the job, however, they had to follow orders. After the interrogation, they took us to a clinic to be examined. We all sat nervously in the waiting room. The doctor called Ivan in first, followed by Vicka. Through the thin walls, I could hear her refusing to let him examine her. By the time he summoned Ivanka, it was fifteen minutes to 6 p.m.; I worried that we'd be late for the apparition, so I went in with her."

Mirjana said the doctor glared at her and asked who called her.

"We're in a hurry," Mirjana said she told him. "We need to go back."

"No. You all need to stay," the doctor replied.

He lit a cigarette and offered Mirjana one, but she declined. Then, he asked her what her name was and where she was from. She replied that she was from Sarajevo.

"Ah, Sarajevo," he said and asked her to hold out her hands. He wanted to check to see if her hands trembled, but they were steady.

"We *really* need to go back," Mirjana said to him and, in that moment, the phone rang.

There was a sense of urgency in the doctor's voice after he took the call. He came to them and said that now they would be examined by a psychiatrist in Mostar.

"No," Mirjana replied.

"No?" he questioned.

Mirjana continued, "Maybe you think we're all crazy, but what more do you want from us? Goodbye. We have to leave."

Then, Mirjana said she opened the door and the children left. At a local inn, they asked for someone to drive them to Bijakovići.

"A local man offered to take us, so we piled into his car," she continued. "With the time of the apparition fast approaching, we were distraught to find police blocking the road leading into Medjugorje. Hundreds of parked cars lined the roadside; people who came for the apparition had parked and walked. The police were ticketing the cars and writing down the registration numbers. We hopped out of the car and ran to the hill. As soon as we arrived, three flashes lit the hillside."

Father Svetozar Kraljević—a Herzegovinian Franciscan and leader of Mother's Village in Medjugorje—confirmed that Dr. Ante Vujević, a general practitioner, first interviewed Ivan for more than an hour. Vicka was supposed to be next but, as the apparition time approached, the children wanted to go to Apparition Hill to see Our Lady. Vicka remained in the doctor's office for a very short time and, at 5:45 p.m., five of them—without Ivan—left the doctor's office. They managed to find a ride and headed to the hill, while Ivan was taken home by his relatives.

"When I arrived home, they were all already on the hill," Ivan remembered. "Then, Our Lady appeared to me in my parents' house. It was a brief encounter. I was in shock."

The visonaries and their parents were completely confused by everything that was happening. Their lives changed overnight; the quiet, ordinary days turned into something that no one could ever imagine. Plus, the excitement was so strong that they were unable to sleep at night, according to witnesses.

"It was a shock to everyone," Marija said. "Communism was strong and great. Fr. Jozo thought that the communists wanted to trick him, and the communists thought that Fr. Jozo was working against them since he had just arrived. We didn't depend on anyone in all of this. Some thought one thing, others another thing, but God acted just as He does today. They wanted to invoke Medjugorje and the messages of Medjugorje in many situations that have nothing to do with Medjugorje. Our Lady is free as a butterfly here, like the air! And, Our Lady speaks and says, 'Answer in freedom.' The police started coming to our homes—looking for us, watching us, and taking us away. We were taken by an ambulance from the local clinic to Mostar. A friend—a lawyer—said that we were underage and that we must not go anywhere without adults. Vicka's mom was afraid. Vicka's dad, who worked in Germany, said that if he came, his passport would be taken away, so they would all starve to death because he was the only one working."

The telephone lines in Medjugorje were still down at the time.

"I had three brothers in Germany then," Marija continued. "In those days, one of them dreamed that there was confusion in our house. What else could it be, he thought, but death. He phoned, but no one answered. He got on the bus and it was there that he heard Our Lady appeared in Medjugorje, in Bijakovići, in our hamlet under the hill. In Mostar, he heard that it was about his sister! When he arrived home, the first thing he thought to do was to see if I was normal because he knew me well. When he saw me, he started crying and hugged me. He saw that I was normal, that I had not gone crazy."

On Saturday, more people came to Medjugorje than on all three previous days combined, and the police was everywhere. Police officers who were not in uniform were monitoring and recording, hoping to hear Our Lady's voice. They asked where she was and what she was doing, according to Ivan Ivanković, who was spending most of his time with the visionaries.

However, the one who suffered the most was the pastor, Fr. Jozo Zovko. He returned to the parish from Zagreb the day before and he was shocked with what he found there, and first thing he decided to do was to talk to the visionaries whom he did not really know. It was important for him to meet with them in order to hear their experience, and to make sure that he would not miss anything, he recorded all the conversations. Those recordings however—as well as many other materials that would be useful to reconstruct those early days—were seized by the police on August 17, 1981, after his arrest.

Mirjana spoke about her first meeting with Fr. Jozo.

„Fr. Jozo's dark brown eyes matched the color of his hair, and his face might have looked friendly if he was not trying so hard to be stern," she wrote in her book. "Without even the hint of a smile, he asked me to sit and describe the previous evening's apparition."

"We went to the hill," Mirjana reported saying to him, „and then we saw the sky light up three times. I looked at the hill and said, 'There she is!' This time, she was even farther up than she had been before."

Fr. Jozo asked what they did.

"We ran up as if it were nothing," she explained to him. „When we reached Our Lady, we immediately knelt down in front of her. A lot of people came up the hill. As we were kneeling, some people stepped on our legs and some put children in front of us. I fainted because of all that and from all the emotions."

"You fainted?" Fr. Jozo asked.

"Yes, Ivanka and I fainted, probably because of the humid air and all," Mirjana reported replying to the pastor. "Everybody wanted us to ask Our Lady something. I asked her, 'How is my grandfather?' I loved him very much. She said, 'Grandfather is fine.'"

Mirjana recounted that Fr. Jozo then asked her to describe what Our Lady did during the apparition.

"No words could truly describe what it was like to be with her, but I tried," Mirjana said. "She often looked around at the people. We asked her to leave us a sign so that the people would believe us, so they don't laugh at us. But she did not answer. She simply said, 'I will come tomorrow.'"

"Is she beautiful?" Fr. Jozo asked, according to Mirjana.

"Oh, incredibly!" she replied at the time. "She has black hair—a little bit pulled back—and blue eyes."

Fr. Jozo asked if Mirjana had ever seen a girl like her, and Mirjana replied, "Never."

"How tall is she? Is she smaller than you?" she recalled the pastor asking next.

„Like me, but she's slimmer. She's *really* beautiful." Mirjana told him. She said she wanted to describe what made her so beautiful, but couldn't pinpoint anything specific.

„When people speak of physical beauty, they often highlight someone's eyes, hair, or other distinguishing feature. But, Our Lady's beauty was different. Every feature was beautiful, and everything was harmonized. A white veil framed her oval face. The color of her skin was similar to the sun-glazed complexion of most Mediterranean people and, paired with her black hair, she resembled a person from the Middle East. Her diminutive nose was perfectly aligned with her almond-shaped eyes, and the slight rosiness on her cheeks was similar to the color of her lips, which were small, full, and tender-looking. But her appearance was also a feeling, one best described by the word 'maternal.' Her expression conveyed the qualities of motherhood—care, compassion, patience, tenderness. Her eyes held such love that I felt like she embraced me every time she looked at me."

"And how was she holding her hands?" Fr. Jozo continued, according to Mirjana.

"She opened her arms in different ways," Mirjana explained. "They did not remain in one place."

Fr. Jozo then asked if she was afraid at all to look.

"Not at all," Mirjana recalled responding. "I was really happy. I wouldn't mind if she took one of us with her, so the people can see that it's really her."

The priest then looked at her skeptically.

"*Takes* one of you? Would you like it if she took you?" he asked.

Mirjana answered him that she would.

"Seriously. You wouldn't regret it?" she recounts Fr. Jozo pressing.

"I wouldn't," Mirjana replied. She added that the immense feeling of love she felt during the apparitions was like nothing she had ever experienced on Earth, and that her only desire whenever she saw Our Lady was to stay with her forever.

Mirjana then said she shared that it hurt her that they were saying she had brought drugs from Sarajevo.

"Who says that?" Fr. Jozo asked, concern filling his face.

"The policemen," Mirjana replied at the time. "Two of them called me over and asked me to show them my watch. I showed them and told them how it happened, and then I left. But, I overheard them saying 'That one from Sarajevo, maybe she brought some drugs from the city,' and so on. Other people said the same, too."

"What do they mean by drugs?" Fr. Jozo asked her.

"As if we were drug addicts, that we took drugs and that's why we see Our Lady," she responded.

Fr. Jozo then asked what Mirjana thought about that.

"I would like to tell them straight in the eyes: Let a doctor examine me to see if I'm on drugs," she answered him.

In the coming years, Mirjana would be examined by more doctors than most people ever see in their entire lifetimes. But, instead of finding what they all suspected—drugs, epilepsy, mental illness, or deception—it was her normality that left them all baffled.

. . .

Speaking with Mirjana was almost like talking with an adult—an equal. But, that day, before the apparition, Fr. Jozo called for a conversation with the youngest visionary—ten-year-old Jakov, who surprised him with his simple, sincere, and direct answers. Fr. Viktor Kosir also participated in the conversation, which Fr. Jozo recorded. He began by addressing Jakov like a baby.

"Jakov, go ahead. Let's talk about how you talked with Our Lady. Come on," the priest said.

Jakov told him that, when they first came, Our Lady did not tell them anything. More precisely, only when they were leaving did she say, "Go in the peace of God."

"When we arrived the second time, we asked, 'Our Lady, Our Lady, why have we all gathered here? '" Jakov began. "She said, 'So that we may all be at peace.' And, she told us, 'There are many good believers here. '"

Fr. Jozo then asked him to describe Our Lady.

Jakov said that her eyes were blue and that she had a white scarf on her head and a gray dress. He added that her legs could not be seen because of the long dress. Fr. Jozo seemed surprised by his description, and then Jakov exclaimed, "How beautiful she is!"

When Jakov shared how the children prayed seven Our Fathers

and Hail Marys, Fr. Jozo prompted him to describe what happened during the apparition in a more systematic and detailed way.

"Before we left [people told us], 'Tell Our Lady to leave us something, some kind of a sign!' And we just said, 'Our Lady, leave some sign,' when she said, 'I will come again tomorrow,'" Jakov said, almost in one breath.

"At what time did she say she would come?" Fr. Jozo asked.

"At six, like yesterday, at six," the boy said. "But, today, she will come to another place, where we were on the day before yesterday. That's closer over there. It was far away yesterday."

Fr. Jozo asked him what they would ask Our Lady today during the apparition.

"I will ask her again, 'Our Lady, why have we all gathered here? Why are you coming to us?'" Jakov answered.

The priest then inquired about what it looked like in the moments before Our Lady's arrival, and Jakov told him that there were three flashes of light before they saw her.

"It flashed three times and then, suddenly, Our Lady appeared up there," he said. "We immediately ran up there. I said, 'There is Our Lady up there,' and we all ran up. And, while she spoke with us, she told us, 'Stand up.' We stood up, and she said, 'Do not kneel anymore.'"

Jakov spoke excitedly and added that Our Lady "moved her head like this" while she was talking to them and said that she would come again tomorrow.

Fr. Jozo asked whether Our Lady told them anything else and how long the apparition lasted.

"She did not tell us anything else," Jakov replied. "Half an hour. So, less than half an hour."

The priest then asked him if he would know how to get to the place of the apparition again. Jakov responded that he would, but that they only know the exact place at the moment Our Lady appears to them and then they go toward her.

Fr. Jozo was also interested in what Our Lady stood on.

"She stands like this in the air," Jakov described. He explained how she was not far away and that she had the same clothes on as she did in the previous days. And, although he said he personally hadn't said anything to her yet, he thought that he might say something during that evening's apparition, because he was "a little scared" at first.

"So, were you afraid of her?" Fr. Jozo asked.

"Who?" Jakov replied.

"You!"

"I wasn't there. The first time, I wasn't there, so I wasn't [afraid]."

Jakov explained to the priest that, on the first day—Wednesday—he was not present at the apparition. He confirmed to Fr. Jozo that all of the visionaries hear Our Lady in the same way when she is speaking to them.

And, when Fr. Jozo insisted that Jakov saw something that the others did not see—for example, when Our Lady was leaving—he answered, "Who? I don't know! I see her spreading up all like this and suddenly disappearing. When she talks to us, it is like singing."

"What do you mean, like singing?" Fr. Jozo asked.

"She can speak nicely. Well, that is what I am telling you! She speaks beautifully," Jakov explained.

Fr. Jozo then requested further details, which he would later compare to the conversations he had with other visionaries. Specifically, he asked Jakov whether the other visionaries also saw Our Lady in that moment when he said, "Here, I see Our Lady."

"Well, I don't know; I saw her," the boy replied. "And then, when 'There is Our Lady,' that is when all of them looked and saw her and we all immediately ran up there and how we ran and that's it. But, when I came down from up there…"

"What do you mean when you came down?" the priest asked.

"When we couldn't—we couldn't as if we ran up there."

"It was more difficult for you?" Fr. Jozo asked.

"It was harder for us," Jakov said. "But, still, as we were climbing uphill, but when you are descending, it is even easier. But, it wasn't for me."

Everyone who watched the children after the exclamation "There she is!" could not believe how fast they climbed uphill every time, and all the way through brambles and thornbushes. No one could keep up with them, and many reported that it seemed as though the children simply flew toward what they saw. Moreover, the children themselves testified that they felt as if an invisible force was carrying them upward with ease. They did not feel tired at all in that moment—unlike the descent, which was more difficult for them, as little Jakov testified to Fr. Jozo.

Fr. Jozo was most interested in the children's description of Our Lady's appearance—that is, if it resembled an image that the children had seen somewhere. So he asked Jakov if he loved Our Lady and if he had a picture of her in a prayer book or in a catechism book.

"I don't have a prayer book," the boy responded. "I have the catechism of Our Lady here. And I would also like to have a prayer book to…"

"I will give you a prayer book," Fr. Jozo told him. "And tell me: Will you be scared tonight?"

"I won't, I won't," Jakov replied. "Why would I be afraid? Only the first time I was a little scared. And now, I'm not."

Fr. Jozo then revisited the subjects of the children's conversation with Our Lady from the previous day. In particular, the priest said he wanted to detect any kind of detail that would help him discern whether the children were telling the truth or if they had made up everything. So, once again, he asked Jakov what he had heard.

"I heard her telling us all to be at peace, that all reconcile," Jakov repeated. "And I heard when she told us, 'Because we're all here, because in this country'—our Yugoslavia—'there are many believers.'"

"And that is why she came, right?" Fr. Jozo persisted.

"That is why she came," Jakov confirmed. "We asked her why she had come, and she said, 'Because there are many believers in this country.' I said, 'Leave us some kind of a sign.' She said, 'I will come again tomorrow.'"

"Where shall she come?" Fr. Jozo asked.

"She will come where we were for the first time—the day before yesterday," Jakov said.

Fr. Viktor Kosir—who, with Fr. Jozo, participated in the interview—engaged in the conversation and told Jakov that Our Lady did not say that she would come to the first place of the apparitions.

"Yes, she did," Jakov replied confidently.

"How did she say?" Fr. Viktor asked. Fr. Jozo joined in asking Jakov if he would know how to get there now, or if he was being led by some kind of sign like the night before.

"Well, I wouldn't know that," Jakov said. "But, we see her, Our Lady, and then, when we see her, we only go when we see her."

The friars were very interested in whether the children had seen Our Lady's picture somewhere. Or, perhaps, they thought, the children had watched a movie about her that later roused their imagination so that they, too, wanted Our Lady to appear to them. And, while Jakov did confirm that he had watched Our Lady in a film, he then uttered a sentence that, for years, would shock everyone who heard it come from the mouth of a ten-year-old boy. That's because, after the apparition, even Jakov was ready to die:

"And now I say, I said: If I die now, I would not be sorry after I saw Our Lady."

"You didn't hope that Our Lady could appear to you? You didn't even think of that?" Fr. Viktor persisted.

"I didn't even know that," Jakov said.

"That she could appear?" Fr. Viktor clarified.

"Yes," Jakov replied. Then, Fr. Viktor turned the conversation towards confession, counting with certainty on the possibility that this was where he might discover a possible lie and fraud.

"Tell me, when did you last confess?" Fr. Viktor asked little Jakov.

"When you confessed us," the boy said.

"Aha! Then, you received Holy Communion, did you?" Fr. Viktor asked.

"I did, I received Holy Communion," Jakov admitted. "If I have a grave sin, I confess and..."

Fr. Viktor interrupted Jakov to ask if he received Holy Communion often.

"Yes."

"More often, on Sunday and thus?" Fr. Viktor persisted.

"Yes."

"You do it right," the priest replied, and ended his part of the conversation.

Then, Fr. Jozo asked Jakov directly, "And, tell me this, Jakov. This, what will you say to her tonight? Has anyone told you what to say?"

"No one has. It is like this in my head, in my thoughts," Jakov responded casually in his boyish style.

"What do you have in mind now? What will you say to her?" Fr. Jozo asked.

"To say to her, 'Our Lady, why have you come here?'" Jakov began. "And I will say to her, 'Why have you come here to us, and what is it that you want to tell us?' So, I will say to her. That's what I have in mind. What could anyone tell me? I don't know."

With this, Jakov disclosed identical details of the conversation with Our Lady, which would later be confirmed in all of the statements of the visionaries, who—in those first days—testified that they prayed with Our Lady and talked with her primarily about why and with what intention she came to Medjugorje. They also asked about deceased relatives, and later conveyed the questions and requests of people who attended the apparitions.

Fr. Viktor then rejoined the conversation by asking Jakov if he was tired of kneeling, to which he replied that he was not. Then, Fr. Jozo and Fr. Viktor alternately questioned Jakov again about Our Lady's voice and whether he was afraid, as well as about the place where Our Lady would appear to them on that day—hoping to catch him in an inaccuracy or inconsistency. The friars also wanted to know whether Jakov prayed at home with his mother on a regular basis. Jakov confirmed that he was praying, and when asked what he said to his mother when he returned from his first apparition, he replied:

"I said, 'Mom, mom, I saw Our Lady.' She said, 'Come on, my son, what?' I said, 'Seriously, mom, I saw Our Lady.' She said, 'Maybe you did; how would I know?' She said, 'Okay, I'll see.' She will come again tomorrow when she is looking there, when Our Lady is up there, up there, like this. Up there in the sky, like this."

"Mom saw it, too?" Fr. Jozo questioned.

"Yes!" Jakov replied.

"And, who else of the adults saw it, Mom...?"

"It was then when we first saw her, everyone came there," Jakov said before Fr. Viktor interrupted him.

"Hold on, brother, take it easy," the priest said.

Little Jakov confused them with who had really seen Our Lady during the first evenings. There were many people from Bijakovići who went to Podbrdo when they heard the news of the apparition, and many saw a flash of light on the hill. Jakov said that he was sure that even the friars could see Our Lady.

"I could see her?" Fr. Jozo asked.

Fr. Viktor was interested in what made Jakov conclude that Fr. Jozo could see her, and added, "I guess because he celebrates Mass."

"Well, that's what I'm saying. Well, Jozo could see her, too," Jakov said.

Fr. Jozo laughed from his heart because of the childlike simplicity with which Jakov believed that everyone could see Our Lady, especially priests because they were at the altar.

Then, they asked him if Fr. Zrinko Čuvalo, the chaplain of Medjugorje, could see Our Lady too. Jakov replied that he could, just like all of the other friars could also see Our Lady.

"So, you're glad that you saw it?" Fr. Viktor asked.

"How could I not be glad?" the boy replied.

"Will you now, let's say, be better than before?" the priest continued.

"Well, I will. I guess I'll be better now. How can I not be better?!" Jakov said.

Fr. Jozo asked the boy if he would go tonight, as well, to which Jakov replied affirmatively. The priest then told him to ask Our Lady if the friars should also come to the apparition. And, when they asked the boy if he would still go to the hill even if, for example, his mother forbade him, Jakov replied:

"Who will prevent me when I want to go? I'm pulled by the desire to go up there. I can't be stopped. I want. I would say, 'Mom, I'll go even if you kill me. Even if you kill me, I'll go anyway!'"

"I know, but when God says that you should obey your mom, what will you say then?" Fr. Jozo probed.

"I will go up there to God, I will go up there to Our Lady, and that's it," Jakov said. The youngest visionary wasn't willing to give up even an inch.

. . .

In those first days of apparitions, one of the central figures was certainly the chaplain of Medjugorje, Fr. Zrinko Čuvalo. He was the first priest to receive information about the apparitions when Marinko Ivanković excitedly told him, although he did not seem to be too upset about it. Those who knew the Franciscan—who was ordained a priest in 1963—attributed it to his nature. The only preserved conversation from that period was published by Fr. Svetozar Kraljević, to whom Fr. Zrinko said that "he received the first news exclusively as news, and not as something to be believed or not to be believed."

"I simply took it as news, the news which, if you like, didn't even surprise me as much as it normally should," Fr. Zrinko said. "In fact, at that moment, I reacted pretty coldly, neither contemptuously nor enthusiastically, but simply, 'What can be—why should it not be.' I have always believed that something like that could happen, but for it to happen here was something unexpected and strange, but not impossible. So, I simply acted accordingly. While Marinko was talking, I kept silent and, at the end, I made only this simple remark: 'Thank God, go about your business, we shall see, we shall hear.' Then, I went to bed. But, during the night and the next morning, the news began to disturb me. The next morning, I was not calm. I was worried. How could I have reacted to such news in such a way? How could I have so superficially passed over it? How could I have missed it?"

Fr. Zrinko added that his "intimate turmoil can be better understood in the context" of "what Dragica Ivanković, Marinko's wife, told me two days later, when she attacked me because I was not coming to the place where the apparitions were occurring. 'Where on earth are you?! Are you human? Are you a priest? Who are you? As if it didn't affect you at all?'

"As I have said, it tormented me that night and the next day because I didn't know the background of the events—whether it was truth or just a fraud; an ordinary story or children's machinations; result of illnesses, etc. I thought of nothing else but of that news and the way I took it. I mean, I took it so coldly. I did not come out against it. No, I didn't, nor did I accept it as something true. You see, as for those children—the visionaries—I could say the same even today. Not only today, but all this time, I have been struggling with myself and I have not been clear what is happening with me—why, up to this day, those children have never interested me at all and I don't pay attention to them, even though all of this is actually impossible without them because everything happens through them. They are a transmitter, a bridge, and there is no crossing from one riverbank to the other except by that bridge. But, you see, that bridge does not interest me at all and that is what surprises me. It puzzles me."

Fr. Zrinko was honest in saying that he could best portray his attitude toward those events with the example of the signs that happened during the first days in Medjugorje—from the sun "dancing" to the spinning of the cross on Cross Mountain, for example.

"I didn't see the sign with the sun, and I didn't see any special signs at all except that strange whiteness around the cross on the second day of Father Jozo's trial," he said. "That happened in the early morning hours. I also saw the fire that many talked about. When I came out of the office and saw what people were looking at, my first reaction was that it was an ordinary bonfire, as our people call the fire which they light on the eve of the great holy days. I was angry with those who had done it and scolded them in my mind. I still attached no value and no importance to it later, even when I heard that there was no sign of the fire and that there was absolutely nothing burned. If it was a miraculous flame, which it very likely was, even I, myself, in some way, agree to it. Then, after all, it is a sign of some type—a visible sign. It doesn't have to be a miracle, but it is a sign, after all. And, you see, that kind of sign was of no importance to me."

"It doesn't matter to you?" Fr. Svetozar asked him with confusion.

"Yes, it doesn't matter to me," Fr. Zrinko explained. "It is of no importance. For me, it has hardly any value in relation to the events in Medjugorje. You see, for instance, that fire or that whiteness around the cross have hardly touched my faith this year. If I needed to measure, I don't know how small that measure would be."

He added that he was touched by something after the disappointment he had experienced on the hill when he, for the first and only time, attended the apparition on Saturday, June 27. That is when, he said, he was disappointed because of what he had expected to see and what he actually saw during the apparition.

"I didn't experience anything, and that's why I was disappointed," the Medjugorje chaplain admitted. "I gave Fr. Jozo a recording of the conversation I had with the children immediately after the apparition, when I asked each child a short question. After we had listened to it together and when I told him my impressions, he regretted that we hadn't gone there earlier; that we hadn't told people to stop going to the hill; that we hadn't forbidden it; and that we hadn't dispersed the crowd. The disappointment was caused by what I had seen on the faces of those people who had been coming. For example, when I was going up the hill, I heard one blaspheme God and Our Lady because he couldn't catch up with the children who were running up the hill. I later learned that he was a police officer in civilian clothes. Another one blasphemed God and Our Lady for not having appeared to him, and I said to him, 'I, myself, wouldn't appear to you either, let alone Our Lady!' That attitude of the people was repulsive. They pass by the church in a hurry. We stand in front of the church. Nobody says to us, 'Praised be Jesus and Mary! Father, how are you?' or 'Is the church open?' Instead, they came back from the hill with their cameras and seemed void of any spiritual experience."

However, something "woke me for the first time from that resulting darkness," he said, which was increasingly taking hold of him and Fr. Jozo Zovko.

"What was the light that first shone in that darkness?" he began. "It was not the events on the hill, nor was it that whiteness around the cross, but an encounter with a woman. One morning, when I went to church for morning prayer and Mass, I saw a woman waiting in front of the church. She immediately grabbed my hand and asked to confess. I told her to wait a little and I went to open the church, when she said again, 'I'd like to confess.' I answered, "But for God's sake, woman, don't you see—I'm going to open the church. Can't you wait until after the morning prayer?' Namely, we used to say the morning prayer first and then come out ten minutes or so before Mass to hear confessions, if there were any. She said again, 'I'd like to do it now. I'm in distress.' 'All right, if you insist,' I said. She came and knelt, trembling and shaking all over. 'What is the matter? What is the big problem?' I wondered. And then I heard her confession. Afterward, I called her to the office where we talked and she gave a written statement. Therefore, I am allowed to talk about it now."

Fr. Zrinko explained that she was a barren woman. She had done everything she could to have a child; she made promises to God, she fasted, and she went on pilgrimages. Yet, she remained childless, although she was still relatively young and had been married for about fifteen years.

"When she heard of the apparitions in Medjugorje, she cursed Our Lady, 'Our Lady! Nonsense! If she existed at all, she would hear me! How many shrines have I visited barefoot; how many times have I fasted?' However the next Sunday, she went to Mass, and when she came to the church, she had difficulty entering—as if something had petrified her. Once in the church, she was seized by anguish and the other women had to lead her outside. Her husband took her home, where she was again seized by anguish. She said that when she saw Our Lady's statue in the church, she simply froze. When she got home, she asked to go to confession in the middle of the night. Her husband did not let her go at that hour to bother the friars. And it was this woman's breakdown that enlightened me in my darkness. It was a sign that God must have a hand in this, regardless of my doubts and of what I was saying. For this was already a sign—a sign of true faith, which to me was much clearer and more tangible than the faith on the hill. You see, this ordinary event, we would say, seemingly trifle, enlightened me more than that hill—more than the fire on Crnica or that whiteness around the cross. This is what I wanted to say to portray my walk in faith."

For Fr. Zrinko, the only genuine sign was when "people adopted a spirit of penance, a spirit of conversion." He said that a person could do penance and convert in other places, as well. And that is also what the government officials from Čitluk kept telling him—that everybody has a church, everybody has their priest, friar, sacraments, Mass, rosary, Fridays…

"Everybody can do it in their church," he continued. "This is what we, if you like, said from the beginning: 'Go home and say your prayers, for your parish church stands empty and you come here to tread on thorns on the hill!' Yet, after all, we must admit that this is where the Spirit prevailed; that He had somehow come here. It was not forced. Well, it followed a priest's call, but we know that every priest on almost every Sunday calls for penance, for conversion. But, here, the response was different."

The massive and genuine response of the people in Medjugorje—where, as he said, the people simply "stuck with that Spirit"—was a sign for Fr. Zrinko; a sign that he couldn't fail to see.

"Just as the situations I listed were difficult for me, it was also difficult for me that people didn't see the obvious signs of conversion and that they so easily dismissed it," he said. "That they saw nothing there, but that they clung to some statements from the children or some less important signs, let's say signs of healing. I came to the point that I would simply force people to come to Medjugorje and experience what I had experienced. As for the image that people have of us, that's the image they had to get; those who accepted this as our sincere position—both mine and Fr. Jozo's—for example, how we set ourselves up at the beginning, had to get such a picture of us. We knew where we were and what the future had in store for us because, on the first day, I warned the children to tell the truth with these words, 'One day, we shall all come together—including you, my little one—to be judged. Don't think now that they are going to put you in prison and try you, but you shall appear before the Church court. This is not a frivolous thing.'"

Fr. Zrinko added that the friars were aware of their responsibilities from the very beginning, "regardless of whether it was truth or lie; the time will come when we would be the most responsible."

"We were aware of it from the beginning and, therefore, we behaved accordingly on the first Sunday when we addressed the congregation at Masses and every time after," he explained. "At times, perhaps, we would say what we maybe didn't mean or want to. We were all in fear. We had to be in fear precisely because of the future, of what was to come after the initial events, whether it was good or bad. I think every man would find himself in fear, in anxiety, at that moment. Mind you, aside from this anxiety, it pained us to see that people of our kind and rank—I mean clergy and sisters—were not truly with us. We wondered why they should run ahead of us; why they should go up the hill in habits and not in secular clothes; why they should stand out and be recognizable. I spoke to everyone who walked up there and some did change to civilian dress. This was not because of my disbelief, but simply because we were in fear. Whether it was true or false, the priests would be immediately accused, whether they are 'for' or 'against' it. We used to say that it was better for us priests to be on the sidelines."

Fr. Zrinko added that, nonetheless, they were still open to the events.

"We didn't know what it was, but we kept the door open to let it in—whatever it was," he said. "We neither obstructed nor stopped it, although it was on the tip of Fr. Jozo's tongue to say to everyone as he once had said to me, 'Go and disperse it!' But, we did not disperse the crowd; we didn't tell them not to go to the hill, but we grieved: Why go up there? Is there anywhere else to go but there? But, we were not closed to the events or to the children; Fr. Jozo was especially soft. I am strict in my nature. You can see from this conversation; I am the same with the children, as well. I have always been that way."

Fr. Zrinko shared with Fr. Svetozar that children were always afraid of him—not only the visionaries, but all of the other children, as well. He said they were afraid of him because he looked strict, although he was not strict toward them.

The priest added that the friars were open "as much as possible." But, in that openness, they were also very cautious—maybe too cautious—mostly because of the fear and anxiety in which they found themselves. However, that anxiety was not due to the crowds or the various issues and time constraints. Rather, it was due to "something vague; you see what's going on, but you don't know what it is or what position you will take, how you will defend yourself, how you will accept it. That is anxiety: You see something coming; you don't know what it is, but when it comes, you don't know whether it will crush you."

FROM THE CONVERSATION OF FR. JANKO BUBALO WITH VICKA

FR. JANKO: "Well, we somehow managed to get as far as the fourth day. Perhaps that day was a bit more favorable?"

VICKA: "Yes, sure! Even more unfavorable."

FR. JANKO: "How's that?"

VICKA: "Well, we were called in to the SUP [Secretariat of the Interior] in Čitluk."

FR. JANKO: "All right. Well, that isn't all that awful! And, why did they call you in?"

VICKA: "I don't know, either. Let's not talk about it now."

FR. JANKO: "I suppose they questioned you about something. They then returned you to your homes and everything was ok."

VICKA: "They did, but when we escaped by ourselves."

FR. JANKO: "What's this?"

VICKA: "They, from SUP, took us to some doctors for an examination, as though we were sick, or drug addicts, or... who knows what they thought."

FR. JANKO: "So, were you, in fact, examined?"

VICKA: "My dear Father! We were and we weren't. I think that they knew we were healthier than they, but they still went through the motions of examining us."

FR. JANKO: "Who examined you?"

VICKA: "Some doctor. I've never seen him before."

FR. JANKO: "I'm surprised that a lady doctor didn't examine you girls. That is, if there were any present."

VICKA: "They spoke to one of them, but she, as an intelligent woman, didn't want to examine us."

FR. JANKO: "All right, then. Tell me, then, how did your examination seem to you?"

VICKA: "Well, first—which was the worst—they took Ivan in. That was somewhere about four o'clock in the afternoon. He—poor guy, being as good and timid as he is—allowed the doctor to question him for more than an hour."

FR. JANKO: "And, what did he say to him?"

VICKA: "What do I know? The doctor droned on and on, while Ivan remained quiet. Then, I entered."

FR. JANKO: "You were called in, I presume?"

VICKA: "Lord, no. I let myself in and said, 'Is it over?' They called Mirjana, but I went, instead."

FR. JANKO: "And, the doctor?"

VICKA: "He told me it wasn't my turn yet, but to sit down anyway. I told him, 'I'm young and healthy, thank God, and I can stand!'"

FR. JANKO: "And, that's how [the] examination began?"

VICKA: "What examination? I told him, 'When it's time for an examination, I'll come in myself. Now, is it over?'"

FR. JANKO: "And he?"

VICKA: "He was laughing. Then, he said to me: 'Come on, stretch out your hands.' I stretched out my hands and told him, 'Here are two hands and on them, ten fingers. If you don't believe me, count them!' And, immediately after that, I left of my own accord."

FR. JANKO: "And then?"

VICKA: "It was almost six o'clock by then. And, where are we? Where is Our Lady? We took a taxi home. I said, 'Get in, and we're off.' And, that's the way it was. Only Ivan remained behind with one of his relatives."

FR. JANKO: "In all likelihood, you were late for Podbrdo?"

VICKA: "No, no. We just drank some water at home and went straight up there."

FR. JANKO: "You didn't, I guess, hesitate?"

VICKA: "Not at all. Well, we wouldn't even if guns were awaiting us up there. But, something else hindered us a bit."

FR. JANKO: "Perhaps tiredness, or..."

VICKA: "No. Rather, we didn't know where or how."

FR. JANKO: "Why was that?"

VICKA: "Because we were not sure where Our Lady would appear. You know how the third day unfolded. That's why Marija and Jakov remained down by the road and watched to see where she would appear, while we went up ahead. We agreed that whoever saw her first should let the others know."

FR. JANKO: "And, as far as I know, Marija and Jakov were the first to spot the flash of light and run up like the wind. Those who were with her (there were also two friars) ran forward with her. They weren't even halfway up before Marija was already at the site of the apparition. And, the rest of you, how did you know where to go?"

VICKA: "Well, we also saw the light and ran toward it... Only it was quite a bit closer to us."

FR. JANKO: "And where, exactly, did Our Lady appear that day?"

VICKA: "She wasn't at the place of the second or third apparition."

FR. JANKO: "Where, then?"

VICKA: "She was a bit to the left, and a bit higher."

FR. JANKO: "And, you felt fortunate you were able to meet with her despite all the obstacles?"

VICKA: "Well, of course! But, there was a mass of people. Everyone wanted to get as close as possible to Our Lady and to us. They all but trampled us. Our neighbors looked after us, but the crowd surged and what could be done?"

FR. JANKO: "And, what did Our Lady do?"

VICKA: "Easy for her! She gazed over the people... She smiled... She gazed over Križevac and over the fields."

FR. JANKO: "Over which fields?"

VICKA: "Well, over our own meadows. We call them fields."

FR. JANKO: "Someone said that they were also stepping on Our Lady?"

VICKA: "Not on Our Lady! Well, who could step on her? But, they were stepping on her dress, or, rather, on her veil."

FR. JANKO: "And, what did she do? Was she angry?"

VICKA: "My Lord! Father! Our Lady doesn't get angry. She is not like us. It's easy for her. The people crowd around us. They know that Our Lady is where we are, so they press forward and then step on her veil."

FR. JANKO: "And, what does she do?"

VICKA: "She disappears for a moment, and then again…"

FR. JANKO: "Right. But, for what does she need such long a veil?"

VICKA: "How should I know! It's not for me to ask."

FR. JANKO: "Not for me, either. But, somehow, I asked it nonetheless."

VICKA: "Oh no, you don't! That's not so. You intended something."

FR. JANKO: "What can I say? I wanted to make a bit of a joke about how Our Lady seems to like long dresses, too. Somehow, it must be the woman in her."

VICKA: "Well, what else is she but a woman, but you intended something else."

FR. JANKO: "Really, nothing else, except that she is a Woman, but written with a capital letter."

VICKA: "All right, then, you managed to get out of that one somehow, but…"

FR. JANKO: "So, Vicka, you told me, and I read it somewhere, too, that Our Lady appeared to all of you more than once that day."

VICKA: "She did. Three times."

FR. JANKO: "Why was that?"

VICKA: "I don't know why. You would have to ask her that."

FR. JANKO: "Good, then. And, did Our Lady say anything to you that day?"

VICKA: "Yes, she did, in general. In response to what we asked her."

FR. JANKO: "And, what did you ask her?"

VICKA: "We asked her all kinds of things that time."

FR. JANKO: "Tell me some of them."

VICKA: "First off, little Jakov asked her something about the friars."

FR. JANKO: "And, what did he ask her?"

VICKA: "He asked, 'My Lady, what do you wish of our friars?'"

FR. JANKO: "Surely, one of the friars asked him to ask that?"

VICKA: "Most likely he did."

FR. JANKO: "Did Our Lady answer him?"

VICKA: "Yes, of course she did."

FR. JANKO: "And, what did she say to him?"

VICKA: "She told him that the friars should guard the faith and believe firmly."

FR. JANKO: "And, did anyone else ask her anything?"

VICKA: "Yes. Jakov and Mirjana asked Our Lady to leave some sign because people are saying all kinds of things about us—that we are liars, that we are drug addicts. Everything."

FR. JANKO: "And, Our Lady?

VICKA: "She said, 'My angels, there has always been injustice. Have no fear.' And the like."

FR. JANKO: "Did the rest of you hear what Mirjana and Jakov asked?"

VICKA: "Well, of course we heard! We hear them and Our Lady."

FR. JANKO: "And, the people around you?"

VICKA: "They do not hear Our Lady. But, we tell them afterward."

FR. JANKO: "All right, then. And, how long did the apparition last?"

VICKA: "Who worried about that? It was quite long."

FR. JANKO: "I suppose until it wearied Our Lady?"

VICKA: "It didn't weary us. Well, when you look at her, you feel no anxiety."

FR. JANKO: "Nonetheless, she departed?"

VICKA: "Yes, but she didn't say goodbye upon departing."

FR. JANKO: "Well, what is that? That isn't that important."

VICKA: "Right. It isn't. But, for us, it is."

FR. JANKO: "Then, you went home?"

VICKA: "Yes, where else?"

FR. JANKO: "Did you at least ask her if she would come again?"

VICKA: "We did. She nodded her head indicating yes."

FR. JANKO: "But, she said nothing?"

VICKA: "No, only that."

FR. JANKO: "All right, Vicka. As far as I can remember, Ivan was not present at the apparition that day?"

VICKA: "He was not."

FR. JANKO: "And, why not?"

VICKA: "Well, I already told you that he remained in Čitluk with one of his relatives, and when he came home and told his parents what occurred, they told him not to go to Podbrdo for he was tired and he was already late."

FR. JANKO: "Therefore, he didn't meet with Our Lady that day?"

VICKA: "Well, of course he did. He went out a little beyond his house. He knelt and he prayed. And, Our Lady appeared to him there."

FR. JANKO: "Did she say anything to him? Perhaps she rebuked him for not being there?"

VICKA: "No, no. None of you knows how kind Our Lady is and how she understands us. She told him to be at peace and to have courage. She bade him farewell and departed. What can the boy do? He's not to blame."

FR. JANKO: "Good. And, the rest of you went home about that time?"

VICKA: "Yes, about that time. However, on our way, Our Lady again appeared and she sent us on our way."

FR. JANKO: "And, what did she say to you?"

VICKA: "She said, 'Farewell my angels. Go in the peace of God!' Then, she disappeared and we went slowly homeward... The heat was terrible. The people were shouting, running downhill since there is no pathway, and the like."

FR. JANKO: "And, you finally arrived home?"

VICKA: "Well, where else?"

FR. JANKO: "And, how did you feel?"

VICKA: "Good. Excellent!"

THE FIFTH DAY – JUNE 28

"May they all believe as if they see me"

It was Sunday, June 28, 1981—the fifth day since the apparitions began. Around noon, Medjugorje was already filled with people who came for the apparition. The visionaries were at Mass and, afterwards, they split up to go home.

"As the news of miraculous events spread in all directions, a huge crowd of people came to the site of the apparitions from neighboring villages and parishes," reported Dr. Father Ljudevit Rupčić, one of the best chroniclers of the Medjugorje phenomenon. "Some estimate that there were about fifteen thousand people that day. The visionaries stood in one place and would kneel as soon as Our Lady appeared. The rest of the people sought to get as close as possible to the visionaries, thinking—which is natural—that in such a way, they get closer to Our Lady. But, despite such a large crowd, everything went smoothly. However, one of the visionaries recounted that someone had cursed something—probably God, as they were likely in some distress—and Our Lady, in some way, saddened. Everything else ended nicely. When Our Lady disappeared, the visionaries and the people descended like a river flowing to the base of the hill. They were looking for some refreshments. The locals could sell hundreds and hundreds of liters of it, but it never occurred to anyone to do something like that. No homeowner had charged anyone for anything."

It is interesting to note that the parishioners at that time, as well as in the coming months, shared everything they had, including water, wine, and brandy. They even provided free accommodations to pilgrims who came from afar—even giving them their own beds—because there were no hotels or guest houses in Medjugorje or the surrounding area. However, the people of Medjugorje themselves lacked water; they collected rainwater in concrete tanks, which quickly began to empty. So, they had to order a tanker truck to fill their water tanks with drinking water. But, when the communist authorities found out, they forbade tanker trucks from coming to Medjugorje. Nevertheless, the ingenious Herzegovinians had an idea: They would light a fire somewhere on the hill and call the firefighters to extinguish it. Then, when they brought a water tank, they would pour water into their water tanks so that the pilgrims had something to drink.

In the meantime, as more and more people started coming to Medjugorje every day, it became a challenge to protect the visionaries during the apparitions. So, after Sunday Mass, Marinko Ivanković and his friends went to the hill to fence off space for the visionaries.

Using stakes and rope, they blocked off an area that was approximately where the visionaries had experienced apparitions several times previously.

"There were a lot of people," Marinko recalled. "I went up the hill with the visionaries and I shouted, 'Clear a path for the visionaries to go up!'"

Also with the visionaries on that day was amateur radio operator Grgo Kozina, who recorded interesting conversations and people in the surrounding villages. He decided to record the apparition on his tape recorder.

"I got a tape recorder a long time ago, and I recorded all kinds of things in the village: speeches, weddings, Masses...It's a hobby for me," Grgo said. "As I am an electronics technician, this was natural to me. I was on good terms with Fr. Zrinko. They thought that Mirjana was playing some sort of game. He dressed in a civilian suit and put on his glasses—no one would say he was a friar—when he went up the hill. The children lined up and I stood on the sidelines and recorded them when Our Lady came. They prayed to God. Initially, they thought that since Mirjana was from Sarajevo, she was playing some kind of a game. The friars thought she was playing a game when [the children] would say, 'There she is.' Later, they realized that she was not, but everything was considered. They said, 'Our Lady in the thorns.'"

Grgo explained that their hesitation stemmed from the fact that Josip Broz Tito had died a year earlier and the communist authorities thought that it was all organized by those who had emigrated—that Fr. Jozo had come here and that he was coaxed. Then, people said that it was hypnosis or some kind of a telepathy, among other explanations. But, in the end, it turned out to be none of these.

Grgo was near the children on Podbrdo that day at the very spot of the apparition. His voice is heard on the tape recording: "It is 6:20

p.m…It is already 6:30 p.m…Some wind is blowing. Brambles are swinging. The six of them stand up; they were kneeling...They are praying Hail Mary...They knelt again. Has she come? Here, Our Lady has come at 6:30 p.m. And she is asking everyone to kneel..."

"Silence!" he shouted to the assembled people, who quickly fell silent.

"My Lady, what do you wish from us? My Lady, what do you wish from us?" the visionary Vicka asks aloud in the recording.

"Where is she? There? Here? Is she telling you anything?" a male voice asks Vicka.

"Faith and respect for me," Vicka says.

The male voice repeats, "She said, 'faith and respect for me.'"

"My Lady, what do you wish from our priests?" Vicka can be heard asking three times on the recording. She conveyed that Our Lady invited them to firmly believe.

The children are peppered with questions from people who have come in droves to Podbrdo from all directions. Many of them have been waiting under the scorching sun since noon for the evening apparition and are wondering why she appears here.

"My Lady, why don't you appear in the church so that everyone sees you?" Vicka asks twice in a row before sharing Our Lady's reply: "Blessed are those who have not seen and have believed."

The response is immediately conveyed to the people.

"My Lady, will you come again? She will. She will come here again to the same place," Grgo dictates in the recording. "My Lady, what do you wish from the people that have gathered here? Our Lady looks at the people. There she is, here. She disappears; she disappears...slowly. She's gone! She left! We will pray again because she has not said anything to us. The children speak and pray again the

Our Father, the Hail Mary, the Glory Be. It is 19 minutes before seven o'clock."

The prayer is heard: "Our Father, who art in Heaven, hallowed be thy name...Hail Mary, full of grace, the Lord is with thee...Glory be to the Father and to the Son and to the Holy Spirit..."

"Here she is! Here she is!" the children's voices can be heard in the recording before they begin to sing to Our Lady, "Mary, how beautiful you are."

"Has she come? Yes, she has. It's 6:40 p.m. and she came again to the same spot," Grgo dictates.

"She is telling us that we are her dear angels," the children say. "She tells us so. My angels, my dear angels! My Lady, what do you wish from the people? My Lady, what do you wish from the people?"

The children repeat their question with their gaze directed toward the sky. Vicka says that she will ask that question aloud and she does so.

"She said, she answered, let these people here—who do not see [her]—believe the same way the six of us who see her believe," say the children.

In the first days, they asked primarily the same questions. Among those, the most common was when she would leave them a sign because they were afraid that people would think they were lying and that they were joking about her.

"My Lady, are you going to leave us a sign here, on Earth, to convince these people that we are not liars; that we were not lying and that we didn't toy with you?" Vicka asks aloud.

A murmur from the people is heard around the children. At one point, the children say that she left.

"Is she going to come again?" someone asks.

"She will tomorrow," the children respond.

Next, they begin singing the hymn of Our Lady of Lourdes, "Immaculate Mary!" Jakov also begins the song, "Mary, oh Mary, oh how beautiful you are," which everyone recognizes. Jakov seems to be in charge of the singing because, after that, he starts the song, "Glory, glory, hallelujah." Then, someone (most likely Fr. Zrinko) asks Jakov if Vicka or Ivanka have whispered something to him. Jakov says they have not.

"Did you see anything tonight?" he asks the visionary Marija. "Why didn't you say, 'There she is,' like you did last night?"

Marija claims to have said it and, when asked if Vicka whispered something to her, she replies that she did not. Ivan was also asked the same questions, but his answers were not heard due to the noise of other people around them.

Grgo continues to report on the scene, including that the road was "full of cars, which were parked on both sides of the road" from the "shop to the Čilić houses."

"It's 7 p.m. and the people are going toward the road," he continues. "People are going downhill on all sides. Since there is no pathway, everyone takes the most convenient way for themselves. From up here on the hill, you can see everything—car after car, all the way to the new school."

As he was nearest to the children, Grgo was best able to hear and record what they were saying, so he conveyed the content to others.

"They were lined up, side by side, and I was on the other side," he recalled. "Suddenly, little Jakov said, 'Our Lady is coming down.' The tape recorder was in my hand and I repeated what Jakov said. One of the nuns, who was by my side, told me that the friars resented my saying that Our Lady was coming down. I only repeated what the little boy had said. He was far away and I had the tape recorder with me to record his voice."

Grgo also remembers when the children warned him for stepping on Our Lady's dress.

"I was already recording when the children said that Our Lady was over the brambles now," he recounted. "They knelt and, as Vicka was on the other side, I wanted to get closer to her because she was the one who commented the most. I was on the left and I wanted to pass in front of them when they said to me, 'You are stepping on Our Lady's dress!' As there was a thornbush, I stepped back and just hopped to the other side. Ivanka told me how I stepped on the dress. I asked them later how it was possible that I didn't see anything, and they told me that I stepped on her veil."

Otherwise, the fifth day seemed to be mostly devoted to filming. Fr. Jozo spoke to the visionaries in his parish office after Mass and, as usual, recorded that conversation. The first in line was Jakov.

"Tell me, you were up there last night, as well?" Fr. Jozo asks.

Jakov replies that he was.

"And what did you see last night?" Fr. Jozo continues.

"I saw Our Lady," Jakov shares excitedly. "And, when we set out, she was there, and we went there. And I asked, 'Our Lady, give some sign to convince the people. She said, 'I will come again tomorrow. You are my angels, my angels.' And then, she rose up and a cross appeared up there, gray as her dress."

Fr. Jozo interrupts him to ask when Our Lady will appear to them today.

"At the same time. People are up there now, marking where Our Lady will be..." Jakov responds.

Fr. Jozo replies that he doesn't care what people do and not to tell him about it, but rather that he cares about the apparition itself.

"Tell me this, Jakov, did anyone else see her last night?"

"We all saw her, as we have all seen her previously," Jakov says. "Me and Marija were first to see her up there."

Fr. Jozo then asks who went with whom from home to Podbrdo, in order to get more detailed insight into the previous night's events. Jakov replies that all five of them did not go together from their houses, but that he and Marija were already up there. They were the first to see Our Lady, and then the other visionaries ran after them and met them.

"Did they run after you or did they go the other way?" Fr. Jozo clarifies.

"They went after us," Jakov explains.

"Did you go the same way up to the apparition?" Fr. Jozo asks.

Jakov replies that they did and also confirms that there were people at the apparition last night.

Notably, the conversation between Fr. Jozo and little Jakov, as it can be heard on the recording, is swift with short and precise questions from Fr. Jozo and Jakov's shorter and faster answers. There is no hesitation or calculation in the answers; Jakov replied directly and precisely. But, this did not quite suit Fr. Jozo. It would have been easier for him if the answers were longer and more extensive because, in this way, he could more easily detect the inconsistencies in the children's story. But, there were no such inconsistencies.

Fr. Jozo then asks the boy what Our Lady is saying and what she is telling people.

"She says, 'Let the friars believe,'" Jakov said.

"And what else?" Fr. Jozo presses.

"'People who believe in me, but do not see me—let them believe as if they see me,'" Jakov relays.

"And what else did she say?" Fr. Jozo continues.

"When we returned, she said, 'You are my angels, angels,'" Jakov shares. "And that she is the Blessed Virgin Mary."

"Aha, who asked her that?" Fr. Jozo asks.

"Vicka," Jakov replies.

Fr. Jozo wants to know what, exactly, Vicka asked Our Lady, so Jakov quotes what Vicka said, "What is your name?" and that Our Lady replied, "I am the Blessed Virgin Mary."

"And she will be there today as well, will she?" Fr. Jozo asks.

"Yes, she will," Jakov replies.

Fr. Jozo wants to know if Our Lady said anything else, but Jakov says that she didn't.

"Did she say anything else to the people?" Fr. Jozo persists.

"Yes, 'Let them believe as if I were here, as if I were with them in the same way, as if they see me,'" Jakov says.

Fr. Jozo wondered if she had blessed them and if she did something different from what Jakov was dryly saying to him.

"She returned three times," Jakov says.

"Where?" Fr. Jozo asks in amazement.

"Like this," Jakov describes. "She would come down and leave. Then, she would come back and leave again, and then come back."

"Well, what did she look like when she was returning and leaving?" Fr. Jozo asks.

Jakov was obviously using his hand to try to explain to him that "Our Lady looks like this."

"How was she dressed yesterday?" Fr. Jozo asks.

Jakov replies that she is dressed the same every day.

"Please, what is she like? Tell me." Fr. Jozo asks, almost pleading in a soft voice.

"She has, like, this white shawl and grey dress," Jakov explains. "Her legs are not visible; her dress covers her legs."

"Please," Fr. Jozo spoke as if somewhat surprised.

Jakov tells him that, after Our Lady left, "a star appeared in the sky."

"But, really. How big was the star?" Fr. Jozo asks, still surprised.

Jakov says that it looked small. Fr. Jozo wants to know if he also saw angels.

"I didn't," Jakov replies quietly and contritely.

"How come? Our Lady and angels are always together," Fr. Jozo says.

Jakov smiles and says that he did not see angels.

"Was there a swallow yesterday?" Fr. Jozo probes.

"No, just the star. And a cross appeared, too," Jakov remembers.

"What was the cross like? Was it wooden or...?" Fr. Jozo asks.

Jakov shares that it was made of wood.

"How could you not take it when it was made of wood?" the priest wonders.

"Well, it was up there," Jakov says.

Fr. Jozo asks him where up there, and Jakov replies, "Up there, in the sky."

"Seriously? How big was it?" Fr. Jozo asks, a bit surprised.

Jakov must have showed with his hands that, "It was big. This big."

Fr. Jozo asks if she had appeared at the same place where she promised to come the day before yesterday.

"No, no, no," Jakov suddenly replies.

"But, do you remember the day before when she told you where she would be? That she would come to the previous place?" Fr. Jozo says.

"Yes, but she didn't come," Jakov states, as if it were the most normal thing.

"She didn't?! Well, then how will she…Why didn't you ask her, 'Our Lady, you said down below?'" Fr. Jozo wonders aloud.

"I don't know," Jakov replies.

"Well, how do you not know?" Fr. Jozo persists.

"She was closer there than where she was now," Jakov explains. "It was on the other side, and now it is on this side."

Fr. Jozo asks if Our Lady was pleased that so many people had gathered this time, and if she told them anything.

"No, she didn't," the boy responds. "We asked her before, 'Our Lady, why are you coming to us?' She said, because there are many believers here."

"That was the day before yesterday?" Fr. Jozo clarifies.

Jakov responds that it was.

"And yesterday?" the priest continues.

"She did not tell us anything yesterday," Jakov says. "Just let them believe as if they see her here."

Fr. Jozo inquires what Jakov would ask Our Lady during that day's apparition.

"I will ask again," Jakov confirms quickly. "Yesterday, I asked, 'Our Lady, why are you coming here?' She said that there were many believers. She had answered that way before. [To the question] if she would leave some sign that the people may believe, she said that she would come again tomorrow."

Fr. Jozo asks whether Our Lady had said how many days she would come and whether Jakov would ask her this.

"I will," Jakov responds boldly. "I'll ask her today. Now, I'm not afraid of anything."

"Seriously?" Fr. Jozo asked, laughing.

"The first night I was scared," Jakov admitted.

"Did you pray yesterday when you saw her?" Fr. Jozo asks.

"Yes, we did. The Hail Mary."

The priest also wants to know if they had sung anything; Jakov shares that they did.

"We sang Marijo [Mary] and Zdravo Marijo [Ave Maria]."

"Do you think anyone else—besides you—sees Our Lady?" Fr. Jozo suddenly changes the focus of the conversation—which he often did when examining visionaries—as he wanted to deliberately confuse them.

"They saw her, too," Jakov responds, referring to the five other visionaries.

But, Fr. Jozo was obviously interested in whether anybody else except the six of them had seen Our Lady, or why others could not see her.

"Well, I don't know that," Jakov answers modestly.

"You don't know?" Fr. Jozo asks. "What do you think? Who among you sees her the best [most clearly]?"

"I think that it is Marina. Shall I tell her to come?" Jakov replies and then invites Marija, whom the children, among themselves, also called by the nickname Marina.

"Go ahead, let her come in," Fr. Jozo says.

Marija entered the room in the parish house and, for the first time, met Fr. Jozo, who said he had not spoken to her thus far. He asked which grade she was in school.

"In the first grade [freshman], in Mostar," Marija says.

"Have you finished the first grade?" he asks.

"No, I haven't," she responds. "I have a make-up exam in August."

Together with Vicka, Marija traveled to Mostar for summer school classes.

Fr. Jozo wanted to know who Marija lived with; she replied that, at home, she had a father, a mother and a younger sister Milka—who was at the apparition on the first day, but not allowed by her parents to go the next day—as well as three brothers who lived and worked in Germany.

"What Mass did you attend today?" Fr. Jozo asks.

"At the daily Mass [at 11 a.m.]," Marija replies.

Then, Fr. Jozo wants to know "whether and how many times" in the last year she had missed Mass or catechism classes. Marija replied that it was "almost never," but that she did stay at home sometimes. Fr. Jozo asked her "if she prayed for anything" when she stayed at home, but Marija's answer is not heard.

"What do you particularly like to pray about? Do you have a prayer book?" Fr. Jozo asks, slowly introducing her into the conversation, but also questioning her about her spiritual life in order to get an impression of how "serious a believer she was."

"I do have. I do read, I kind of read something," Marija replies.

Fr. Jozo suddenly moves straight to the point and asks her if she was the first one to see the light.

"I wasn't. I didn't see it the first time at all," Marija recalls, thinking of the first day of the apparitions, when she wasn't there.

"Were you there?" Fr. Jozo asks.

"I wasn't," she responds.

"Who spoke to you about it?" he asks.

Marija then describes her experience from the second day when she saw Our Lady.

"We are almost always together. I kind of listened to them, but I didn't believe them. Even before, I wanted to see what she looks like; what she was like. They were at my home and they said they were going to see if she would appear to them again. I asked them to have one of them come for me, and Vicka said that she would. Later, I had already forgotten about it, when she ran in and said, 'Let's go!' I said, 'Where are we going?' I put on my shoes, but I left one shoe at home, and the other one after 20 meters [21 yards]. I came and I saw. Everybody said, 'There she is; here she is.' I saw her up on the hill and said, 'Let's go up there!' They said we should wait to see if she will still be there, so I set out alone and they came later after me. I went up there and she wasn't there. I didn't see her. I wonder now what it was. I stood on that spot and they came up to me. They knelt down and made the sign of the cross. I also made the sign of the cross and then I saw her. I knelt down, and when I knelt down, I said how nice and beautiful she was."

Fr. Jozo asks Marija how beautiful Our Lady was and if she could describe her a little better.

"I didn't see her very well, as if there was fog around her," Marija remembers. "First, I saw the shape of her face, and I saw the redness there. It was the first thing I remembered. Then, gradually, I saw her body, too."

"How was she dressed?" he asks.

"The white veil and the dress—how would I say it—gray, but it is not gray, it is not even cream," she responds. "I don't know what color it is. We were there and when we came down to the village..."

Marija is interrupted by Fr. Jozo, who asks if Our Lady said anything at the time.

"The first time, I didn't hear her at all," Marija replies.

"When did you first hear her? Did you hear her last night?" he asks.

Marija responds with a simple, "No."

"You have never heard her?"

"I have heard her..." she clarifies. "The first time when I went, on Thursday, that is when I didn't hear her at all."

"On Friday?"

"On Friday, I heard her"

"What did she say on Friday?" Fr. Jozo presses for a more detailed answer.

"She answered all the questions we asked her," Marija explains. "This girl asked how her mom was. She said, 'She is good.'"

Marija referred to the question that Ivanka had asked about her recently deceased mother.

"You saw that she was talking?" Fr. Jozo inquires with interest.

"I did hear," she replies. "But, the first question was kind of unclear to me. Same as her figure when I first saw her. The next day, Mirjana asked her if she would come again, and she nodded and said that she would."

"Our Lady didn't say anything; she just nodded?" Fr. Jozo asks her, obviously wanting to find out more about Our Lady's posture and the way in which she communicated with the children.

"She just nodded that she would come," Marija responds. "We spoke among ourselves, and she looked toward here, toward the valley, and toward the cross. We watched her turning her head."

Fr. Jozo then asks Marija if she had been present at the apparition on the previous night, to which she replies that she was.

"Well, where and from where did you first see her?" Fr. Jozo asks, looking for precise information.

Marija explained to him that she was "down there"—that is, at the base of the hill—with Fr. Zrinko. They were supposed to wait there for the visionary Ivan, who had remained in the infirmary in Čitluk. His cousin would be bringing him home; the other visionaries had returned home without him. Ivan and Marija had previously agreed that they would go to the hill with Jakov that day.

"Jakov went with me, and Ivan stayed in Čitluk," Marija explains.

"Describe to me what happened yesterday," Fr. Jozo goes on. "What did you notice in your soul? What started to emerge?"

Fr. Jozo was interested in what was going on with Marija internally.

"The first time I was on the road, on the unpaved road, when they walked there, I didn't see her," Maria recalls. "The second time, they were down the hill and I was up the hill. The third time, they said that I would stay. Little Jakov came, I took his hand, and a light appeared. I asked Jakov if he saw it. He said that he did. For the second and third time, it was the same and she appeared."

Marija's response had been somewhat incoherent; she was talking more about what was going on among them than about what Fr. Jozo had wanted to know about her inner feelings.

"It happened last night?" he asks.

"Yes. And her figure appeared," Marija says. "And then, I saw her and I started running up. Then, she was in front of me. A local man said that he ran after me and that he couldn't keep up with me. Little Jakov stayed back; I have no idea. When I got up there, her figure disappeared. They were down there in the previous place. I was maybe twenty meters [21 yards] farther. I was watching; no trace of Our Lady's figure. I stood there and I froze; I didn't know where to go now. And she appeared to them down there, on the previous spot. Maybe I was supposed to go down there, as well, but I was pulled up the hill. When she came, they began to pray."

Marija's response was somewhat confusing regarding the previous day's meeting with Our Lady.

"Was she with you or with them?" Fr. Jozo asks.

"She was with me until I came and she disappeared," Marija explains.

"Did you see her after that at all?"

"On that spot?"

"Yes."

"Then, she appeared to them and she also disappeared," Marija explains. "They came to me and we prayed the Our Father, Hail Mary, and Glory Be. We sang the song 'Marijo, Marijo' [Mary, Mary], and then she appeared."

Marija then described to him what it looked like.

"She appeared just a little?" Fr. Jozo clarifies.

"She appeared and there she was."

"Was she the same the first and second time?"

"I didn't see her the first time, when she had a child [with her], as they said," Marija responds, referring to the first day of the apparitions, when she had not been among the visionaries.

"And when you prayed..." Fr. Jozo continues.

"When we all prayed, the people began to pray with us," Marija explains. "Then, she appeared. She had a veil, and her dress was down to where she was standing. It hung on the ground and they stepped on it."

Marija explained how the people crowded around them had stepped on Our Lady's dress.

"Why didn't you tell them not to step on it?" Fr. Jozo asks.

"Everyone was rushing to the place and watching where she was," Marija responds. "A few of them stood there, and we just watched her disappear up into the clouds. Later, we prayed again and stopped when we finished the prayers. Then, we sang, and she appeared for the second time. We asked those questions that you had asked. I didn't ask any questions. Somehow, I didn't have the strength."

The girl explained to him what happened on Podbrdo the day before, and Fr. Jozo added, "Or you didn't need it."

Marija explained to him that Our Lady had returned again, and how one of her neighbors had suggested that the adults make a circle around the children, holding hands to prevent people from approaching them too closely. But, the neighbor stepped on the veil, as did a nine-year-old boy.

"Then, she appeared in the same place a third time," Marija says. "They made a circle and we asked her questions."

"Do you recall what you asked her?"

"Jakov asked what you had told him, for the friars," Marija responds.

Fr. Jozo said that he didn't tell Jakov to ask that.

"He asked about the friars and she answered, 'Let them firmly believe and keep their faith,'" Marija continues. "Then, Mirjana told her that people call us drug addicts and say that we have epilepsy, and she replied that there were always exceptions and injustices among the people, but that we shouldn't pay attention to it."

"What do you mean, 'exceptions'?"

"That there were always dishonest people."

Fr. Jozo asks if she had heard Our Lady saying that.

"Yes. We all had heard," Marija confirms.

"How nice is her voice? Have you ever heard such a voice as hers?" Fr. Jozo asks. Evidently, he had heard, prior to this conversation, that Our Lady spoke in a particularly gentle voice, as if she were singing.

"Never, never. She has a voice like—as if she sings, something like that," Marija says, confirming the information about Our Lady's way of speaking.

"Is that voice loud?" Fr. Jozo asks, in order to get as much information as possible.

"It's not particularly loud; it's gentle. Medium," Marija shares. "And then, the third time, she said nothing to us except, 'Go in the peace of God.' Every time, she told us that. And then, she disappeared again. We thought she might appear again, but she didn't. And we all went home. And we came to the place where I, alone, had seen her the day before yesterday, when Vicka and I saw—and those who were behind us also saw—Our Lady and the cross. The same one I had seen."

Marija told him about the apparition that had occurred after they had begun to descend from Podbrdo.

"How big was it?" Fr. Jozo asks.

"I think up to two meters [6.5 feet]. Big," the girl explains. "But, there was no crucifixion on it."

Marija explained the appearance of the cross that the other visionaries would also tell Fr. Jozo about. Then, Fr. Jozo asked Marija if Our Lady had said anything afterward.

"Afterward, she said, 'My angels, my dear angels,'" Marija replies. "And she said to us, 'Go in the peace of God.'"

Fr. Jozo wanted to know how Marija had felt after that apparition—whether she felt joy in her heart.

"I cannot describe it in any way. Great joy! Great, great," Marija said enthusiastically.

"And when did your joy cease?" Fr. Jozo asked, a bit skeptically.

"Before, some things used to hurt me," Marija describes. "But now, I'm indifferent. Before, if someone told me to do something, I'd say I couldn't, and now, I somehow can."

Fr. Jozo laughed.

"Even if they tell me I need to bring something with a wheelbarrow from the field—nothing is difficult for me anymore," Marija continues.

Fr. Jozo wondered if Marija had prayed for something special after the apparition the night before, and whether she thanked God for everything, especially for Our Lady.

"I prayed Our Lady's rosary last night," Marija discloses. "We were up late. I planned to pray even more last night, but I couldn't. We were at Marinko's and we wrote a diary, in order to write everything down. We left about 10:30 p.m. or 11 p.m.; I don't know. I was sleepy, but I prayed the prayer my dad taught me and the Creed with seven Our Father, Hail Mary, and Glory Be prayers. Then, I prayed many Our Father prayers until I fell asleep."

"Did she say anything suggesting that she would appear today?" the priest asks, to which Marija replies that she did.

"What?" he asks.

"We asked her if she would come today and she nodded," Marija responds.

Fr. Jozo wondered what it meant when she "nodded."

"She had done that before," Marija explained. "Little Jakov asked her—when she appeared with that cross—to leave a sign, and she said, 'Go in the peace of God.' Jakov was the one who asked the last question if she would leave us a sign, and she shook her head like this, as if she won't, whatsoever. And she disappeared. That was the end."

Then, their conversation ended. Fr. Jozo thanked Marija and said "Let the one from Sarajevo, Mirjana, come in."

. . .

Mirjana remembers that day and the conversation with Fr. Jozo well, and she describes it in her book, "My Heart Will Triumph." On that day, when they complained that people were accusing them of using drugs or having some medical condition that caused their visions, Our Lady told the visionaries that there had always been injustice in this world. Mirjana also remembers that, on that day, Our Lady told them that she was the Blessed Virgin Mary and she gave a message for the priests—*"Let them believe strongly"*—and for the people who wanted to see her—*"Blessed are those who believe without seeing,"* that is, *"Let them believe as if they see me."*

But, in addition to Our Lady's messages that were very clear, Fr. Jozo's sermon from Sunday Mass also imprinted itself on Mirjana's memory.

"Earlier that day, the six of us had gone to Sunday Mass at St. James Church," Mirjana wrote in her book. "It was overflowing with people, many of whom had come from distant parts of Herzegovina. It was clear that many of them had come out of curiosity, not devotion, as they mostly talked about signs and miracles. Few of them prayed or made the sign of the cross during Mass. Even more distressing, Fr. Jozo's sermon seemed to be aimed at the six of us."

In his sermon, Fr. Jozo said, "It's true that God can reveal Himself and has done so before. And, indeed, Our Lady has appeared on

Earth before. But, why do we need such wonders when we have the Eucharist, the Bible, and the Church? Jesus is here! My friends, we are only human beings, and human beings can be manipulated so easily. We live in challenging times and we have to always be prudent. More than anything, we must constantly pray to the Lord."

After hearing his sermon, Mirjana admitted that she dreaded having to meet with Fr. Jozo that evening.

. . .

Since she had received the book about the apparitions in Lourdes, France, Mirjana admitted that she was fascinated to learn that someone else had also seen Our Lady. In 1858, a peasant girl named Bernadette saw her while she was out gathering firewood along a riverbank. She suddenly heard a gust of wind and looked up to see a beautiful woman in a grotto.

"When I read that Our Lady had appeared to Bernadette 18 times, I assumed it would be similar in Medjugorje—as if something kept telling me that she'd appear for just a few more days—and I related this to the other visionaries," Mirjana wrote in her book. "At some point, we began believing it was true. With the communists terrorizing us and the apparitions rousing our emotions, we'd barely eaten or slept, and it was easy to get confused. But, deep down, I desperately wanted the apparitions to continue. How would I go back to living a normal life after experiencing Heaven?"

Mirjana explained that those days were marked by contrasts—joy and fear, solitude and suffering, the love of Heaven and the animosity of the police.

"I had been an ordinary, teenage girl, living in peace with my family, when everything suddenly changed," she said.

Meanwhile, as she got to know the other visionaries and observed their different personalities, she began to think that Our Lady wanted them just the way they were—with all of their quirks and flaws included.

"Later, when I learned more about Lourdes, Fatima, and other apparitions of the past, I saw how Our Lady usually visited young people and I wondered why," Mirjana wrote. "Was it because we were not yet burdened by plans and obligations? Were the hearts of children purer than those of adults? If I had been older, perhaps I would have comprehended everything faster, but her messages don't require lengthy commentary or theological interpretation. She speaks to all of us, and she does so with simple words."

. . .

Fr. Jozo had prepared a set of questions for Mirjana, just as he did for other visionaries. First, he asked if she had a Bible at home. Mirjana replied that they did not have one, but that they sometimes read the Bible at her godmother's house in Sarajevo. However, she shared that, at home, they had a book entitled "Bible – Is it the Word of God?," although she did not know who the author was; just that it was bought by her mother and that it had a shiny green cover.

"The closest thing we had at home was an illustrated children's book of Bible stories," Mirjana remembered.

"Do you feel the need to learn something now? For instance, to pray to Our Lady?" Fr. Jozo asked.

"I'd love to do that," she replied. "I asked people to write down some prayers for me because I wanted to learn them by heart."

Mirjana testified that the experience of seeing Our Lady had inspired her to embrace the faith with all her heart. So, Fr. Jozo suggested Mirjana to communicate with Our Lady, who had also taught the visionaries in Fatima to pray.

"Try to ask Our Lady to teach you some prayers—how we should pray, what prayers we should pray...," he said.

"So that she tells us what we should pray?" Mirjana asked, a bit surprised.

Fr. Jozo directed her to ask Our Lady which prayer was pleasing and valuable to her; or which one was the best and most pleasing to her, so that everyone could pray those prayers.

"Will you ask her?"

"I will ask her what she would like us to pray and which prayer is pleasing to her," Mirjana promised. "Because the people—together with us—accept everything we pray and sing."

"What do you think about starting to pray Our Lady's Rosary today?" Fr. Jozo asked.

"I could," Mirjana replied. "She doesn't ask from us any additional prayer; she just smiles and looks at us. Then, we start singing, and then she is somehow even more pleased."

Mirjana described Our Lady's meetings with the visionaries, and Fr. Jozo wondered if she saw Our Lady in the same way that she looked at him during their conversation.

"Just as I am looking at you now," Mirjana confirmed.

"Really! Is she closer or farther from you than you are from me now?" Fr. Jozo inquired.

"It's like this," she began and demonstrated to him. "We are kneeling in front of her."

"Oh, my God! And how tall is she? Is she like you?" he continued.

"Well, like me," Mirjana responded.

"Do you see her hair?"

"Not completely," she said. "Just a little. She has black, curly hair. Her hair is long, and it is hanging down here a little bit [below the veil]."

Then, Mirjana described Our Lady's appearance. Fr. Jozo wanted to know about the cross with which Our Lady had appeared to the children on their return from Podbrdo.

"She was holding the cross with her hand?" he asked.

"No, it was down there when we were coming down. The cross stood next to her," Mirjana explained.

"So, how did it not fall?" Fr. Jozo pressed.

"I don't know," Mirjana admitted. "She was not holding it."

"And Jesus was not on the cross?"

"Jesus was not on the cross," Mirjana confirmed.

Fr. Jozo found this interesting and wanted to know what Mirjana would ask Our Lady that evening.

"I'll ask her exactly this, if she prefers that we sing or pray," she said.

The priest wondered what else Mirjana would ask her.

"I'll ask her for a prayer that she would prefer," the girl said. "I don't know; they told us to ask something else, too. How many days will she appear to us, if she could tell us."

Then, Fr. Jozo suggested that it would also be good to ask her why she had been appearing. Mirjana explained to him that they had already asked that, and Fr. Jozo asked what she had said.

"Because we are all faithful and that we [may] be together. And she turns around and looks at the people," Mirjana said.

On several occasions, Fr. Jozo asked the children if they thought he might also be able to see Our Lady.

"I'd love to see her," he said, as if confiding in her.

"I don't know; I think that she will not appear to priests and nuns," Mirjana said of her theory. "I have that feeling. I don't know if she would like to appear to you."

Just then, Jakov entered the room, and Fr. Jozo invited him to come in. Ivanka also came, and Fr. Jozo immediately began a conversation with her.

"You were there every night?" Fr. Jozo asked Ivanka.

Ivanka confirmed that she was. And, because she had found out that her mother was with Our Lady in paradise, Fr. Jozo asked Ivanka if she now felt sorry for her mom—or if she was glad that she was now with Our Lady.

"I'm glad, but I wish she was with us," Ivanka replied honestly.

"What did Our Lady tell you?" Fr. Jozo.

"On the second night, I asked her how my mom was," the girl replied. "She said she was fine. And then, on the third night, I asked if my mom had said anything. She said we should be obedient to Grandma and help her."

"When Our Lady speaks, how does she speak?" Fr. Jozo asked Ivanka, repeating the same question that he had previously asked other visionaries.

"As if she sings, beautiful voice," she replied.

"Is she tall, like you?" he asked Ivanka, just as he had the others.

Ivanka replied that she was, and Fr. Jozo wanted to know if Our Lady was older than her.

"Yes," Ivanka said.

"How did her cheeks look last night?" Fr. Jozo asked, knowing that the other children had described Our Lady's rosy cheeks.

"Beautiful, kind of rosy," Ivanka confirmed.

"Did you see her like you see me now?" he asked.

"The same," she replied.

"Really?"

"Really," Ivanka replied.

Fr. Jozo asked if she was afraid, and the girl said she was not.

"How did you see her last night?" the priest continued. "Did you know that she would be there where you saw her?"

"First, we went up there," Ivanka began.

"Who?"

"Vicka, Mirjana, and me. Marinko led us," she continued. "They said, 'There is Marija up there, she saw Our Lady.' She said that, when she was there, she just saw her and then she disappeared. When we arrived, she appeared again."

Fr. Jozo commented that it happened on the first day.

"No, it was last night," Ivanka corrected him.

"Last night? And, when you got up the hill, you saw her?" he asked.

Ivanka replied affirmatively. Next, Fr. Jozo wanted to know what she did when she saw Our Lady, as well as "what she felt inside."

"Well, I was glad," Ivanka shared.

"I know that you were glad, but did you feel a need to put your hands together in prayer?" Fr. Jozo asked.

Ivanka replied that they knelt down when Our Lady came.

"I know, but do you feel a need to kneel down?" Fr. Jozo persisted with his questions in order to understand the child's mind.

"I do feel it," she said. "So, we say a prayer and she tells us to stand up."

"What do you mean to stand up?"

"So, when we finish the prayer," Ivanka explained, "we talk with her about something, and then slowly, like this, with her hand, she invites us to kind of stand up."

"Really? And then, what else does she tell you?" Fr. Jozo asked, a bit surprised.

"We ask her, she responds," Ivanka replied.

"What did she say last night?" Fr. Jozo went on.

Ivanka told him that they had asked her to leave a sign for the people, and Our Lady answered that they should believe as if they see her.

"Did anybody say this to the people?" Fr. Jozo asked.

Ivanka responded that someone did, and that they asked Our Lady for her name.

"And what did she say?"

"I just asked her and she said, 'The Blessed Virgin Mary,'" Ivanka replied.

"You asked her?" Fr. Jozo asked in astonishment.

"Yes, Marinko said [to ask her] that, and then he spoke to the people," she said to Fr. Jozo, who wanted to know if she said anything else to Our Lady that night.

"Mirjana told her that the people say that we are drug addicts and epileptics, and she said, 'My children, there has always been injustice, so there is now, as well,'" Ivanka said.

"Did she say anything to you at the end? She didn't?" Fr. Jozo continued, although he already heard it in the previous conversations.

"That was the third time she appeared," Ivanka said. "First time, we saw her and prayed, but they stepped on her [veil]."

Fr. Jozo was curious to know if the children had seen her when people stepped on her veil and, if so, why they didn't tell people not to do so.

"We did see, and we told them," Ivanka recalled. "And she disappeared again. But there was the light again. We prayed and she came back. Then, when we went down to our homes, I saw what Marija saw—the great cross—and we started singing, 'Marijo [Mary], how beautiful you are.' And she told us, 'Angels, my dear angels,' and 'Go in the peace of God.' And, up there, she hadn't told us to go in God's peace."

Fr. Jozo wanted to know more about the cross and whether Jesus was on it.

"No. As her dress, it is so," Ivanka told him.

"She was carrying it in her hand?" he asked.

"No. It was behind her. It stood above her," she clarified.

"It was not next to her?" Fr. Jozo asked, wanting to know the exact position of the cross.

"It was up behind her, like this," Ivanka replied.

"Interesting," the priest responded. "What do you think, could I see Our Lady?"

"Maybe you could, I don't know," the girl admitted. "Some women say they saw her, too."

This was a new piece of information because it was known that only the children had seen her so far.

"Where are those women from?" Fr. Jozo asked.

"I don't know," Ivanka said. "Marija says that a woman from Ljubuški also saw her. And we saw the light last night around 9 p.m."

"Where?"

"Vicka, Marija, and Vicka's mother saw the light, which appeared and then disappeared," Mirjana interjected.

"On the hill?" the priest asked.

"No, but up there in the sky," Ivanka said.

Fr. Jozo asked if she had told anyone about it.

"Yes, I had," she said.

"And Marinko believes you?" Fr. Jozo asked.

"I think everyone believes us. I think so," she replied.

Fr. Jozo wondered if it bothered her when someone didn't believe, or how she explained it to them so they believed her.

"I tell them to believe if they want to, and if they don't, they don't have to," she replied simply. "I'll believe in it. When they come and convince us that this is an accidental thing, it can't be accidental."

"They don't believe and it is coincidental for them," Fr. Jozo added. Then, he asked if she would say something to Our Lady tonight.

"I don't know what I would tell her," Ivanka responded honestly. "We will ask her to leave some kind of a sign that they may believe."

"Are you perhaps going to ask her about the people, or about you, or about yourself, about God?" Fr. Jozo inquired, before giving her instructions on how to expand the range of questions. "Ask her what her son's name is. Ask her who sent Him and who He is. Who did she give birth to, and why, and who is He. And where did He come from. Ask something like that and let her explain to us. Do you have some kind of plan? Will you pray to God there? Do you have a need to pray more than before? Did you pray anything in particular last night?"

"Well, yes, we did. I always...My grandma would not allow me to fall asleep," Ivanka said, explaining that they pray and had prayed in their home even before Our Lady appeared.

"I know, but do you now have more joy and love in your heart than before?" the priest pressed on.

"I do."

"For example, if someone were to say, 'We will kill you if you say that you saw Our Lady,' what would you do?" Fr. Jozo asked hypothetically, to convince himself of the seriousness of what the children were witnessing.

"I would say, 'Kill me!'" Ivanka replied genuinely.

"Would you really be ready?" he asked.

"I would," she replied determinedly.

"Would you be sorry to be killed?" Fr. Jozo continued.

"I wouldn't," Ivanka answered decisively; Fr. Jozo wanted to know why.

"Because I saw her."

"Then, would you joyfully go to her?" he inquired.

"I would," Ivanka replied without a doubt, and their conversation ended.

...

Next up was Vicka, with whom Fr. Jozo had not yet spoken. So, he asked what year of high school she was in and what her grades were in school, and Vicka replied that she had finished the first grade in Mostar, but that she would take a make-up exam in math because of a failing grade.

Then, Fr. Jozo began the conversation with the usual question of whether she had seen Our Lady the night before.

"I did."

"Is she taller than you?" the priest asked, to which Vicka replied that she was.

"Seriously? What is she like?" he continued.

Vicka explained that when they looked at her, Our Lady was floating in the air in front of them. She added that her eyes were blue;

she was wearing a gray dress and a white veil; and "there is nothing down there"—most likely referring to the fact that they did not see her legs and feet, as they had previously mentioned.

"Is she beautiful?"

"Yes, she is," Vicka replied. "I wouldn't give her more than 20 years."

"How do you know that she will appear?" Fr. Jozo questioned. "How can you see her while others do not see her?"

"I can see her," the girl explained. "When we are to see her, a light suddenly appears to us and it is a sign that she will come. Then, we look again. The light appears at most three times. And, when it appears for the third time, that is when we go up. People walk and it is crowded, but we know where we are going because we feel it within ourselves."

Fr. Jozo expressed interest in how she felt.

"I am really glad, for something within me…something within me makes me feel as if I am talking with her, although I am not talking," Vicka described. "When I think that I'm going to talk to her, it feels as if I get the answer from within myself. Well, what shall I say to her when we go up to her there?"

"When did you go up there last night?" the priest continued.

"First, when we went up there, we prayed the Our Father, Hail Mary, and Glory Be seven times," Vicka began. "Suddenly, she appeared, and the people trampled on—and demolished—everything. When we were halfway through the prayers, she left, and we prayed again to see if she would come back. We prayed and prayed, and she came back again, and we asked her what she wanted from the many people who had gathered. If she couldn't tell them, tell us, and we would tell them. She said that all those who were there and didn't see her should believe as if they did see her."

"That is how she talked?"

"She did talk like that."

"You heard her talking?"

"I did hear her."

"And was she opening her mouth?" Fr. Jozo continued to ask questions that would allow him to gather as much detail as possible to complete the picture of what was happening in Medjugorje—already in the fifth day—which he still couldn't fully accept.

"She was, and she did it slowly; it's not like we see it now," Vicka explained. "She did it all slowly, as if she were singing. Mom told Fr. Zrinko that we should ask about you, about what would she say to the priests. And she said that they should firmly believe and not to give up their faith for anything. Everyone from the crowd said something, 'Ask, ask.' It's easy to ask. In all the commotion, we got pushed and hit with fists. Then, they said, 'Come on, ask her what her name is. Let's see what she'll tell us.' And we asked. Mirjana was the one who asked, 'What is your name?' She said, 'The Blessed Virgin Mary.' We listened to everything up there, but little Ivan was not with us. He stayed home. Since they drove us to the doctor's office, his uncle brought him back later. We came by another car—we did not want to be driven by that ambulance. We went up there. His Mom and Dad didn't allow him to go up there. They thought it was a lie and why would he fool around with it. They didn't let him leave the house at all. But, when he came home, Our Lady said, 'Where is that boy?'"

Vicka gave the most comprehensive answers of all the visionaries.

"Did she say his name?" Fr. Jozo asked about Ivan.

"No. She just asked where that boy was," Vicka replied. "Ivan told us later that, at the moment when she was saying this, he had cramps in his stomach and legs; he couldn't get up at all. Then, suddenly, he jumped up and said to his mother and father, 'I am leaving, I am going to see her!' He left the house and they followed him. He went on the road and said, 'You can't do anything about it; I see her again.' And, whenever she came to us, she also came to him. He was down here, and we were up there."

Next, Fr. Jozo wanted to know how far Ivan was from the rest of them.

"He was maybe two kilometers [1.2 miles] away, approximately," Vicka said.

"He saw her at the same time you did?" the priest continued. "When she came to you, did she also come to him?"

"She did, the same," Vicka confirmed. "When she came the first time and the second time, as well. And we said that if she came the third time, then she would surely tell us something, such as to go in the peace of God. Mirjana told her, 'My Lady, people say that we are drug addicts, that we have epilepsy, and that we are sick.' And she said, 'Let the people talk. There has always been injustice in the world and there always will be. Don't listen to them.' And so we told Marinko. Because whatever she said to us, we said to Marinko, and he spoke out loud so that everyone could hear what she had said. So that no one would ask us later, when we hear something, we tell him and he conveys it to the people. When she came for the third time, she was already letting go of her veil and slowly leaving, we could see her ascending."

"You could grab her by the veil?" Fr. Jozo asked, interested in that detail, as well.

"We grab her dress and the like, but our hands seem to slide off immediately and separate from her dress," the girl explained. "It's kind of slippery. I can't grab hold as when I grab hold of my pants; I can't do it."

Fr. Jozo wondered if her veil fell all the way to the ground.

"Yes. I saw the veil from behind. It was all over on the side," Vicka responded.

"Could it be trampled when people pushed around?" Fr. Jozo asked. He wanted to confirm with Vicka what he had heard in the previous conversations about the trampling of the veil.

"Yes, on the dress," Vicka said. "As they were trampling, she disappeared. When Marinko came, he kept moving people away from himself and told the people not to trample on her [veil], to move back. Because even if they did not see, they would at least hear what was being said here. When it happened the third time..."

"Could you hear what Marinko said?" Fr. Jozo interrupted.

"We didn't hear anything," she said. "We just saw him moving them. And he later told us what he had said when we got home—when people were departing and the like. For example, if we were now seeing Our Lady and someone told us something, we wouldn't hear any of that. We would just see her—and for as long as she stays; nothing until she leaves. And, when she leaves, then it's a little different. We could see someone. Some of them we see, but some of them we don't see. Even when it happened the third time, she told us, 'Go in the peace of God.'"

The priest admitted again that he was tormented by why Our Lady appeared "in the brambles up there," and not in the church. He also asked whether Vicka would ask her that night why she didn't appear in church, even pleading with her to do so.

"I will ask her," Vicka promised.

"It would be easier for people to come to church," Fr. Jozo justified.

"Yes, it would, but she appears up there," Vicka replied. "There is a bramble—there are two brambles—and on the one side there is another bramble, and in the middle, there is something like a little lawn. She appears in that light-colored grass and we see when she comes – as if she illuminates something. And, when she leaves, there is always some light left behind, and a lot of people see that light. It's not just us who see it, but everyone feels [sees] that light. As to why everyone cannot see her, I really don't know. And when we went up there and she told us to go in the peace of God, we went down lower, the four of us went together."

"She didn't tell you, 'Go in the peace of God,' yesterday when you were up there?" Fr. Jozo clarified.

"When we left? Yes, she did," Vicka confirmed. "This was a sign that she would not come again. If she told us the first time to go in the peace of God, we would have gone immediately because we would have nothing more to wait for."

Fr. Jozo wondered if Jakov had asked anything.

"As we were coming down, the four or five of us looked and suddenly fell to our knees," Vicka testified. "Our Lady appeared to us again, but it was not quite the same as before; like in the shadow, a figure appeared to us and she was holding a big cross. There was nothing on the cross. It was gray, the same as the dress."

"She was holding it?" Fr. Jozo asked. He was most likely interested in this because he wanted to catch the children in a lie if someone reported different information than what he had already heard.

"She was holding it," Vicka said, demonstrating with her hands. "She extended her arms like this. Reverend—how would I say it—the cross was like above her, and her hands were like this."

"It was not next to her?" he asked.

"No, not at all," she replied. "The cross was up there, and her hands were like this, and as if she was telling us to come to her. We all approached her. 'My Lady, leave us a sign for the people here to be convinced,' Jakov said, and she shook her head like this and left. Something like, 'I'll come tomorrow, too.' Then, when we went down in the crowd, the people kept on asking. We were tired of it; everyone was saying the same things. Everyone wanted to know, but it was tiring to tell it all over again."

Next, Fr. Jozo asked Vicka if she would continue to tell the people what happened to her during the apparition and about what she had said to Our Lady.

"I will, I'll tell everything," she said.

Then, Fr. Jozo wanted to know how Vicka felt when someone said that they didn't believe that she saw Our Lady.

"It's as if someone insults me," she said, sounding hurt. "It's as if someone now tells me that I'm on drugs, but all I know is that I'm not. Why would anyone tell me that I'm on drugs?"

"Wait, it doesn't matter about drugs," Fr. Jozo said. "This is what I'm interested in. If someone said, 'I will kill you if you continue to say that Our Lady appeared,' what would you do?"

Vicka didn't stand down from what she saw.

"I would still look at her, and let them—whoever that is—kill me," she replied. "As for the people, if they don't believe in it, I do believe."

"Not the people, but if someone, such as the police, threatens to put you in jail and tell you that you must not speak any more?" Fr. Jozo clarified.

"I would still talk," she replied. "Let me go to jail; I don't care. That means nothing to me. I'd go to jail; I wouldn't be scared. We all would do that."

"What would you all do?" the priest asked.

"All six of us would be in jail," Vicka said, convinced of her words. "We would still go."

"You can't go if you are in jail," Fr. Jozo pointed out, thinking that they couldn't be together at an apparition if they were in jail.

"No, I mean, if they told us that we would go to jail—that we should not go anymore—and if we weren't in jail, I would go again," she clarified. "For example, like the doctor, he thinks we're so crazy. And he told me—when I went in and he was sitting like this at the table—to say some nonsense. I said, 'Do you know who is talking nonsense? If you're a fool, talk. I'm not.' This is how I said everything to his face. He told me to hold on, to take it a little more seriously, not like that. I told him why I wouldn't do so. We came at 4:20 p.m. and we were still up there at 5:45 p.m. and they wouldn't let anyone go. And there were still five of us to be examined. If he were a real doctor, he would have examined 105 [people] during that time. If it was, I don't know what kind of a disease, it would be diagnosed in the hour we spent there. We went there at 4:20 p.m. and they let us go at 6 p.m. And he asked everything."

. . .

After the conversation with Fr. Jozo, the children went home and prepared for a new meeting with Our Lady on the hill. Their neighbor Ivan Ivanković, who was with them all the time, remembers that day by the unusual event that occurred during the apparition and meeting with the curious people—most likely tourists, as he calls them—who came with a Polaroid camera to "film" Our Lady during the apparition.

"I was standing next to them and a woman was telling a man that she could not take a photo of anything at the place where the visionaries said Our Lady was," Ivan Ivanković testified. "The camera simply wouldn't shoot. But, when she turned it to the other side, it worked. She turned to one side, to the second side, and to the third side, and it worked. But, there on the spot where Our Lady was, it did not work. Then, all of a sudden—click! It did take a photo! She pulled out a photo on which [it looked] as if there was a cave. I turned it around 180 degrees and then it showed a silhouette of Our Lady, who seemed to have her arms spread. I experienced and I saw this."

Meanwhile, that fifth day began to cause great anxiety in all the hearts of the then-communist authorities. Dispatches from all directions—Mostar, Sarajevo, Belgrade, and Moscow—began to arrive at the municipal committee of the Communist Party, and top-level officials asked municipal party colleagues how such a thing could not be stopped. The National Security Service was also interested in the whole case, and the local police sensed that they would be assigned special tasks. The police commander, in particular, was angry because he had to work all weekend. In addition, the medical examination did not go as expected, as it was confirmed that all of the children were completely normal. However, the greatest pressure on local authorities and police came from the "well-meaning" supporters of the order, who demanded the use of tear gas to disperse believers. Fortunately, the police did not do it.

Around the same time, political officials and the chief of state security from Mostar came to the meeting with the chief of police, and it was then that political and police organizations from higher levels of the government decided to take the lead in the events at Medjugorje. In fact, Criminal Investigator Ivan Turudić recalled that it was decided that they would begin a wide range of police activities, which, in such a system, would lead to a drastic restriction of human rights and freedoms. Shortly after, the persecution of believers, priests, and even children began in Medjugorje, and special police units came from Sarajevo. Many believers were detained and questioned. Some were even beaten and others were imprisoned, including Ivan Ivanković, whose fateful day came on August 11th. At that time, guards were stationed below Podbrdo to prevent pilgrims from climbing the hill, and the children were hiding from the police in the neighborhood and fleeing through the fields.

“There was a meeting at the school,” Ivan Ivanković said. “They called the heads of the families, and as my dad and mom were in Germany and I was already married, I was the head of our family. I was in a dilemma; would I go, wouldn’t I go... I went and came back four times. But, I did go. There was talk about the system, about Tito as if he were a god, and everything in me kind of boiled. I knew what I had experienced and what the people had experienced. They always organized meetings at the same time Mass began. After two hours, I got up. The people were already starting to come out when they heard the bells; half of them remained, about a hundred. I asked to say only a few words. The mayor gave me the floor. ‘So that we do not quarrel and recount one way or another, Our Lady has come here, to Medjugorje, to the parish and is even now in the school and listening to what you are saying.’ At that moment, it was as if a fire broke out: ‘Enough, Ivan, enough, enough!’ I told them what I had experienced, [there were] 50 people at 11 p.m. when the light came, the turning of the cross, the Sun... The next day, they came to the company that I worked for, arrested me, and I was given two months in prison.”

Ivan Ivanković remembers the humiliation in prison—from the haircut to the too-wide trousers and constant provocations, like those from a female doctor who regularly used to heckle him, “Where are you, son of Our Lady? Is it spinning? Is it shining?”

“I met an acquaintance, a police officer with whom I used to play soccer, who warned me that two prisoners were always following us and that I had to be alert. That’s how I acted,” he said.

He recounted one particular Saturday:

“Saturday was a day we didn’t work; we read newspapers and watched television,” he began. “There was the Yugoslav League. Something knocked me down around 6 p.m. Something seemed strange to me; I didn’t feel good. I was aware of everything, but something was happening to me. A colleague kept me from falling. I laid down early and slept until morning. It was Sunday morning. We didn't [have to] work. We had a walk in the yard; Fr. Jozo was walking alone."

Ivan Ivanković worked near the Mostar hospital on a construction site building a police canteen. He shared that Saturday, and then on Monday, his sister saw him there for the first time.

"I waved at her, and a cop behind the building was watching," he recalled. "As she started approaching, the cop disappeared and peeked out. My sister asked me how I was. She looked at how they had cut my hair. She asked me how I had felt on Saturday night. I said that I hadn't felt very good, and she told me what had happened. On the Saturday night before the apparition began, someone reported the police were coming, so they [the six visionaries] fled to my house. My wife had already gone to Mass across the field. When Our Lady came, all of them jumped up and said, 'We see Ivan!' They saw me in the prison room! Jakov, as the youngest, went to tell my wife, Janja, who was someone important to them because she came to the village as a bride. He went halfway through the field and waited for her—who was pregnant and waddling—to come. 'Janja, we saw Ivan!' 'Thank you, Jesus!' she said, thinking that I came back from prison. 'Well, he is still in prison. But Our Lady showed him alive in the room,' said Jakov, who came running to inform her."

FROM THE CONVERSATION OF FR. JANKO BUBALO WITH VICKA

FR. JANKO: "Here we are, entering the fifth day of Our Lady's apparitions. I feel we will proceed a bit faster and more easily."

VICKA: "I hope so, too."

FR. JANKO: "Now, tell me briefly how that day unfolded."

VICKA: "All right. But, I'll try to be as short as possible. We'll never finish otherwise."

FR. JANKO: "All right! So, go ahead and start."

VICKA: "Well, we know that the day was Sunday. We got a little better sleep. We got ready and set out to Mass."

FR. JANKO: "And, from church back home?"

VICKA: "Lord! Had we done so, my friar!"

FR. JANKO: "But, where else?"

VICKA: "After church, Fr. Jozo called us into the parish office and began to question and question each of us individually. It really began to bore us."

FR. JANKO: "And, what did he ask you?"

VICKA: "Everything. Everything, and that's it. Whatever popped into his head."

FR. JANKO: "I suppose about your encounters with Our Lady?"

VICKA: "What else! But, there was no end to it."

FR. JANKO: "And, did he question you?"

VICKA: "Well, of course! But, I was the last to enter and, by then, he was exhausted, too."

FR. JANKO: "And, what did he ask, do you recall?"

VICKA: "Yes, I do, but let's leave that alone. We spoke of that already when we spoke of the fourth day. He asked us everything about that."

FR. JANKO: "All right, Vicka. As you will."

VICKA: "Not as I will, but so that we don't repeat the same thing again."

FR. JANKO: "Then, ultimately, you arrived home and waited for the afternoon?"

VICKA: "It was hot and crowded, but we could hardly wait for it."

FR. JANKO: "Naturally, people began to gather?"

VICKA: "What else? There was already a crowd of people at noon at Podbrdo and around our houses."

FR. JANKO: "Why so early?"

VICKA: "How would I know? Some of them asked for something, others questioned. Others looked for a more favorable spot and the like. Not many knew when we would arrive. A crowd just like a crowd! Who can figure them out?"

FR. JANKO: "What do you think, how many people—all in all—were there?"

VICKA: "How would I know, my friar? We weren't able to even see them all on the hill. They said that there were at least fifteen thousand of them. When we went to the site, we could hardly squeeze through."

FR. JANKO: "Who, 'we'?"

VICKA: "Well, we, the visionaries. Well, if our men hadn't made a path for us, we simply would not have gotten to the site."

FR. JANKO: "And, you set out at your appointed time?"

VICKA: "Yes, somehow, a bit after 5:30 p.m."

FR. JANKO: "Who all went?"

VICKA: "Well, the six of us."

FR. JANKO: "What six?"

VICKA: "The six of us who at the time were seeing Our Lady."

FR. JANKO: "All right. But, something else just popped into my head."

VICKA: "What is it now?"

FR. JANKO: "Well, nothing special. I wondered, did little Milka and Ivan—the son of the late Jozo—ever go with you again?"

VICKA: "Yes, yes, they did. Well, of course they did! They went on more than one occasion, but they no longer saw Our Lady."

FR. JANKO: "And, why not?"

VICKA: "How would I know? I only know who didn't see her the second day."

FR. JANKO: "That's the 25th of June?"

VICKA: "Yes, those who weren't there that day and did not see Our Lady that day, they did not see her ever again."

FR. JANKO: "According to that, Our Lady chose the six of you on that day as her visionaries?"

VICKA: "Well, I guess it turned out that way."

FR. JANKO: "All right. You arrived at Podbrdo, and then what?"

VICKA: "The crowd somehow made a bit of room for us, and we began to pray with the people."

FR. JANKO: "And, there was no Our Lady?"

VICKA: "What do you mean, no Our Lady? She quickly appeared."

FR. JANKO: "And, then what?"

VICKA: "We continued to pray and sing. We asked her some things."

FR. JANKO: "What did you ask her?"

VICKA: "Who's going to remember all that now? I know we asked her what she wished of all the people."

FR. JANKO: "And she?"

VICKA: "She said that the people should pray and believe firmly."

FR. JANKO: "Anything else?"

VICKA: "We asked again what she wished of our priests. Our Lady said the priests should be firm in their faith and that they should help us in that regard."

FR. JANKO: "And that was, I suppose, the way it ended?"

VICKA: "No, no! We asked her a lot that day, but who can remember it all? She appeared and disappeared many times."

FR. JANKO: "Go on. At least tell a bit more!"

VICKA: "We also asked her why she didn't appear in the church so that everyone could see her."

FR. JANKO: "And, Our Lady?"

VICKA: "Our Lady said, 'Blessed are they that do not see, but believe.'"

FR. JANKO: "Anything else?"

VICKA: "We also asked if she would come to us again."

FR. JANKO: "And her response?"

VICKA: "She said she would. Again, at the same place. Oh, yes! We also asked her if she preferred that we sing or that we pray."

FR. JANKO: "And, Our Lady?"

VICKA: "She said, 'Both.'"

FR. JANKO: "You see, you do remember! Go on, tell me more."

VICKA: "I again asked her before all the people, 'My Lady, what do you wish of the people gathered here?'"

FR. JANKO: "And, Our Lady?"

VICKA: "Our Lady said nothing, and she departed. But, she did not say goodbye to us. That was a sign to us that she would reappear."

FR. JANKO: "And?"

VICKA: "We prayed again, and she appeared again."

FR. JANKO: "Perhaps you were not to ask her anything more?"

VICKA: "Why, of course we did! I again—and three times at that—asked, 'My Lady, what do you wish of these people?'"

FR. JANKO: "And, Our Lady again disappeared as she did when you asked that the first time?"

VICKA: "You missed the target! This time, she stated even more clearly that the people who do not see her should believe just as the six of us who do see her. And I! I asked her again, will she leave us a sign here on Earth so that we can convince the people that we are not deceitful—that we are not lying and that we are not joking about her."

FR. JANKO: "And, Our Lady?"

VICKA: "Our Lady again did not respond, and she departed."

FR. JANKO: "And then, you went to your homes, where else?"

VICKA: "Where else, indeed."

FR. JANKO: "And, at home, a crowd, noise, turmoil… I can well imagine. And so. But, if you aren't too tired, would you listen to a live tape taken at one of the apparitions. To help you recall how it was."

VICKA: "Well, of course. Where did you get it?"

FR. JANKO: "That is not important at this point. The tape isn't the best. You know how it was to record in the midst of all the thornbushes. But, nevertheless, listen…"

. . .

RECORDING:

GRGO KOZINA: "The wind is blowing…The thornbushes sway… There they are, the six of them…They stand up…They pray the Hail Mary…

VICKA: "My Lady, what do you wish of us? My Lady, what do you wish of our priests?" (Vicka repeats this three times.)

"She said they should be firm of faith…My Lady, why don't you appear in the church so that all can see you?...Blessed are they who do not see, but believe…My Lady, will you come to us again?...I will at the same

place...My Lady, do you prefer that we sing or that we pray?...She said both...My Lady, what do you wish of the people gathered here?...She left...We will pray again...She did not respond."

GRGO KOZINA: "Vicka makes the sign of the cross and prays—they all pray—the Our Father, Hail Mary, Glory Be (twice). Our Lady appears again, and the visionaries said in one voice: 'Here she is!' They sing, 'Mary, O Mary,' and other songs.

VICKA: "She says we are her angels. Dear angels, she says to us...My Lady, what do you wish of the people here? (Vicka repeats this three times)

"She said, she gave the response, that the people here who do not see her should believe just as the six of us who do see her...My Lady, will you leave us some sign here on Earth so that we can convince the people that we are not deceitful; that we are not lying; that we are not fooling around with you?...Our Lady disappears..."

GRGO KOZINA: "Will she come again?... Make a little room for passage...The road is full...Cars lined up all the way to Beljina's store... Everything is full..."

...

VICKA: "So, you see, my friar, how it was! No one knows how it was for us! But, we were like in paradise."

THE SIXTH DAY – JUNE 29

The visionaries in psychiatry

Monday was a working day and the feast of Sts. Peter and Paul, or simply St. Peter's Day, as it was referred to locally. At that time in the Catholic communities, just like in Medjugorje, the feast day was a non-working day, so the children slept longer and dressed nicely to attend Mass in church. However, shock ensued as an ambulance, accompanied by police, came to pick them up first thing in the morning to take them to the Mostar hospital for a psychiatric exam.

"They were gathered like firewood in front of the house," Fr. Jozo remembered.

That day was also strongly imprinted in the memory of the visionary Mirjana because they were detained in the Čitluk police station before departure.

"One of the officers glared at me angrily," she wrote of the drama surrounding that morning. "'Where's that little shit?' he said, referring to Jakov. It seemed unthinkable to subject a child his age to so much hostility. The police were like artists when it came to cursing, as if they were competing to see who could be the most offensive. 'Jakov is only ten years old,' I said. 'Leave him alone. He's too little.' 'You lying bitch,' growled the policeman. 'He's not little when he can climb that hill in two minutes.' I closed my eyes and asked God to give the policeman peace, but the interrogation went on like that for hours."

Unable to compel them to deny their claims, the police crammed them in a small ambulance and took them to a clinic for an examination by Dr. Darinka Glamuzina, a local pediatrician.

"A confident and intelligent woman with short, dark hair, Dr. Glamuzina indicated to us that she was an atheist," Mirjana continued. "Certain there had to be a logical explanation for our story, she began spouting questions as fast as we could answer them: *What did you see? Where did it happen? How did you feel? Have you ever been hypnotized?* Her last question seemed particularly outlandish, but we answered everything with patience and honesty. At the end of the meeting, Dr. Glamuzina said, 'My colleague and I will come to Bijakovići later to observe you.' 'Observe us?' I thought. 'Does she think we're wild animals?'"

Once again, the children were in an ambulance. This time, they were taken to the neuropsychiatric department in Mostar.

"The police put us in the ambulance again," Mirjana remembered. "Packed together with nowhere to sit, every bump in the road was excruciating. After an hour, we finally arrived at Mostar Hospital. 'Get used to this place,' said the driver. 'It might be your new home when the doctors declare you insane.' The police first took us to a dark, windowless room and locked the door behind us. The air inside was damp and cold and foul. I saw what I thought was someone sleeping on a table. But, as my vision adjusted, I realized the person was dead. Scanning the room, I saw more bodies. 'The morgue,' I whispered."

Naturally, all six of the children were horrified with the place and asked themselves how they could do this to children. It was obvious that they wanted to frighten them—first with the morgue and then by keeping them in the neuropsychiatric department among mentally ill patients.

"After they finally released us from the morgue, we were taken to be examined by a doctor," Mirjana wrote. "His questions were similar to Dr. Glamuzina's, but his demeanor was noticeably colder. 'You know,' he said, 'we have a special place for the insane.' Tricking us into thinking it was a waiting room, he locked us in a ward filled with mentally ill patients. The people moved around aimlessly, shouting and making strange noises. One patient approached us. 'I'm a soldier,' he said, and he started marching around the room. We huddled together, terrified. Were they planning to lock us away in there forever? Thankfully, a nurse pulled us out. 'You don't belong in here,' she said. She led us through a dim corridor and into a room where other nurses had gathered. 'Tell us about seeing Our Lady,' said the nurse. 'Everyone is talking about it.'"

The children told the staff what they had seen and answered countless questions. By the end of their testimony, some of the nurses—about 50 nurses and doctors were there—were even crying.

"Their interest and reactions surprised me," Mirjana recalled. "Next, the head of the neuropsychiatric department of Mostar Hospital, Dr. Mulija Džudža, examined us. We were told later that she found us to be healthy, balanced children, adding, 'Whoever brought them here are the ones who should be declared insane!' What struck me the most—and confirmed to me that I should never be afraid to speak about Our Lady to anyone—was that Dr. Džudža was a Muslim. Even though the police released us that day, the experience of visiting the morgue and psychiatric ward left me traumatized. Disturbing images kept popping into my mind: A corpse on a stainless-steel table; the disturbed 'soldier' marching around; the patients babbling and wandering. But, I knew that if a time ever came when I had to choose between being locked away in an asylum or denying that I had seen Our Lady, I would choose the asylum without question. Nothing could make me forsake her—not incarceration, not even death."

"They took us to the doctors, too," Vicka added. "First, they took us to the police station in Čitluk, then they took us to psychiatrists in Mostar, where they immediately questioned us to see if we were okay. The people [doctors] immediately replied that, as far as they were concerned, the children were fine, but that they were told by police officers from Čitluk that six children wanted to overthrow Tito's Yugoslavia. I immediately told them, 'You tell me what was overthrown; we will immediately fix it.' They told me that if I continued like that, they would lock me in the basement where there were mice, while the rest of them would be released to go home. I told them, 'They're [mice] no bigger than me; no problem.' They threatened us a little with guns to scare us like children, and then they said that they would take my dad's passport away from him; that he would come home and would no longer be able to go to Germany. And I said, 'If others can survive here, so will we.' I wouldn't allow anybody to threaten me, to be greater than Our Lady—never!"

Ivan Dragicevic shared that they were driven to the psychiatry unit by his uncle, who worked as a driver in the Emergency Service at the Health Center in Čitluk.

"Dr. Ante Bošnjak accompanied us," he said. "At that time, he was the head of the Health Center in Čitluk. They took us to psychiatrists named Džudža, a married couple. We were sitting, talking to them normally, and then they asked, 'Why have you brought these children? They are healthy.' The meeting with them didn't last too long—about 20 minutes—and then they led us through the insane asylum; I would say through the part where people with mental disabilities were treated. I remember well. Jakov was nine years old at the time. He clung to us because he was scared, because they were leading us along those paths, and they [patients] were in the park and they started jumping at us. But, it was all okay. It was only for a short time. They simply asked us a few questions and that is how we ended it."

Jakov added that, on the way back from Mostar, the people who drove them stopped at a restaurant along the way to have something to drink, but they left the children in the car waiting for them in the high heat.

. . .

The children, shaken by the events, carried the weight of all that had happened to them in the first part of the day with them to the apparition. So, when Our Lady appeared to them, they all began to cry.

"Her vast love seemed to bring out our emotions," Mirjana wrote. "But, my fears and worries all disappeared as Our Lady showed me a series of vivid scenes from her earthly life. It was like watching a movie. The conditions in which Mary lived were nothing like the romanticized versions of her life that I had seen in religious art. From the time she was a little girl, I saw that she lived a humble and modest life—difficult, but beautiful in its simplicity. I saw glimpses of her most important moments, like the angel approaching her and the birth of Jesus. I realized that Mary was once a girl who endured many of the same pains and joys that everyone does, but with one profound exception: She became the mother of God."

One of the visionaries expressed her anguish about the day's events to Our Lady, asking her if they would be able to endure all of this.

"You will, my angels," Our Lady said to them in the most motherly way. "Do not fear."

"The heavenly blueness behind Our Lady dimmed as an unfamiliar form appeared above her right shoulder—the figure of a bloodied and bruised man with brown eyes, long hair, and a beard," Mirjana wrote. "I could only see the man's shoulders and head, and his face was locked in an expression of intense suffering. Unlike Our Lady—who always appeared to us like a human being—the man looked more like the bust of a statue. I realized who it was when I saw the thorny crown on his head. 'Look at the one who gave everything for faith,' said Our Lady, 'so that what you are going through might not seem like too much.' The figure melded back into the blueness behind Our Lady. I was thankful to have seen a glimpse of Jesus, but also a little ashamed that I ever thought of my suffering as too much. The experience made me careful to never give myself too much importance or think of myself as some kind of victim."

Dr. Darinka Glamuzina, the pediatrician from Čitluk, came to the apparition, as she had promised that morning that she would.

"Witnesses said that her look of skepticism changed to fascination when she saw our faces," Mirjana wrote. "She asked Vicka to present a few questions to Our Lady and Vicka agreed to do so. 'Ask her who she is,' Dr. Glamuzina said. Vicka presented the question and Our Lady replied, 'I am the Queen of Peace.' 'How can we have peace when there are so many different religions?' asked the doctor. Vicka relayed the question and Our Lady answered, 'There is but one faith and one God.' Dr. Glamuzina asked why Our Lady chose to appear in Bijakovići of all places. 'I came here because people pray and have strong faith,' she answered. The doctor then asked if she could try to touch what we were looking at and we presented the question. 'She may,' said Our Lady. We directed Dr. Glamuzina to Our Lady. The doctor reached out, but Our Lady suddenly ascended and disappeared. Dr. Glamuzina immediately turned to us with a look of distress on her face and said, 'She's gone, hasn't she?' 'Yes,' said Vicka, 'she's gone.' 'Did she say anything?' 'She said, "There have always been doubting Judases," and then she left.' Dr. Glamuzina's face filled with sadness. She descended the hill with an astonished look on her face."

. . .

"I worked as a GP [general practitioner] for just a few months when the event that completely changed my spiritual worldview happened," Dr. Glamuzina said in her testimony in December 2008, as quoted by Darija Škunca Klanac in the book, *Understanding Medjugorje*. "I was new in the neighborhood and didn't know either people or customs well. With all the ruggedness that I sensed in their mentality, I felt that the seeming external rudeness was a product of the centuries-long suffering, and that people were emotionally warm and compassionate."

"One day in June 1981, an ambulance driver from Medjugorje excitedly told us that 'some children' saw Our Lady and that the people began to gather around them. I ignored this story because I had heard that some girls in the villages claimed to have visions of Our Lady and that it was usually a type of psychological problem that they were trying to solve with fictional stories. Although, as a girl in Đakovo, I received a proper religious education, my years of medical studies have made me skeptical and critical of anything that cannot be measured, weighed, tested, and scientifically verified. As a very ambitious physician brought up in the spirit of exactitude and materialism, I thought that any unfounded story must be unmasked and the problem illuminated and discussed. I found this story funny and frivolous."

"As in the theater, [I] awaited the outcome of the events in the village, which stirred up the people and all the spirits in this region and in the country. It was almost unbelievable that a small group of children with some 'fantastic story' would excite so many people and, after a few days, I was surprised that the 'thing' was not calming down but was even 'getting worse.' I was thinking to myself, it was about the primitivism of the ordinary people, but the government—that was trying to control it—seemed to be incompetent and incapable of coping with the problem."

This is how Dr. Glamuzina was thinking when the visionaries were brought to the Health Center in Čitluk, and when the director of the Health Center invited several doctors to talk to the children in order to form an impression of them.

"I entered the conversation very interested, like a detective with the desire to find the weak points of such a 'fantastic story' and to end the farce in a medically expert and scientific manner," she testified. "We asked the children questions about how, where, and what they had seen. The children answered. They were convinced of what they were saying, the story was complete, it was obvious that they had had the same experience, and, in a way—for me, at the time, [a] very unusual way, because, of course, I did not expect it—they were persistent in conveying their experience, courageous, and unbending. We, of course, tried to confuse them! I was surprised by the answers because they seemed unusually mature and complete considering the level of education they had."

Dr. Glamuzina added that she remained quite confused by what she had heard. At the time, she thought that a procedural error in a scientific sense might have been made, that the children should have been examined separately, and then their story and emotions compared after that. But, she explained that, at that time and under such circumstances, it could not have been done differently. That is, that everything else would be strange and exaggerated.

"I knew then of another psychiatric phenomenon," she testified. "Hypnosis can lead to conditions such that the manipulated person has real somatic symptoms suggested by the manipulator. I had a dilemma: It's either the kind of hypnosis with which someone manipulates children, or it's really some physical alien phenomenon (many sci-fi novels read in my head). While thinking like this, the director came and invited me to be with him during the apparition in Bijakovići to perform a field examination as a medical team. He, as an important man in the village, probably had a task to, at least, conduct a formal medical supervision of an event that slowly started escaping the control of the entire community. I didn't get any binding assignments; I just needed to be formally present—that's how I understood it at the time—as a doctor."

So, she and the director of the Health Center went together to Bijakovići and went to Vicka's house first.

"Both the street and the house were full of people," Dr. Glamuzina testified. "The director knew the family and they knew him, as well. He introduced us and said that we needed to be there while it was happening. The family didn't mind. Everyone prayed with rosary in hand; I was also given a rosary. At one point, Vicka and everyone else hurried up the hill. The director and I followed them, too; we were almost running. I had the impression that there were already several thousand people on the hill and that shocked me. It was an extremely hot late June afternoon and the sun was still high. We came to a small clearing and, all of a sudden, I saw all the children line up and start to pray the rosary. Holding my rosary only formally (to be close to them), I watched them behave, expecting to quickly see what kind of state of consciousness it was and discover a possible manipulation or some parapsychological phenomenon conditioned by cosmic, until-then unidentified, phenomena."

However, Dr. Glamuzina admitted that what was happening at the time was beyond all her assumptions, and that it completely confused her.

"After they prayed the rosary, at one point, all the children knelt and shouted, 'Here she is!'" the doctor continued. "It was so unanimous that I got confused. The children started listening to the 'vision.' I saw that all of them communicated with that 'vision.' Their eyes were aglow. They also asked questions and nodded (they were getting answers). I was suddenly overwhelmed with the excitement of a researcher. I wanted to fully explore the nature of the 'appearance.' Up to that point, my attitude toward God could, at the very least, be called agnosticism, and I did not believe at all that it was Our Lady. Moreover, I wanted the matter to be completed as soon as possible and that my finding would be the crucial one. In order to confirm my doubts about manipulation or something else, I had to expose myself to some kind of my own experience. I wanted to check everything myself."

Therefore, Dr. Glamuzina asked the children if she could also ask questions regarding the appearance. To her astonishment, the children first turned to Our Lady to ask permission from her.

"Then, I asked a few questions, including who is she and why she appeared in Bijakovići (at the time, it seemed to me as if it was in some God-forsaken place)," she testified. "The appearance said she was the 'Queen of Peace.' I know this by my own astonishment after that answer. What kind of peace? We had peace in the world and why such an emphasis on peace? For Bijakovići, the answer was that she was there because the people here had a strong faith. After a few questions, I wanted to fully experience the presence of the vision, so I asked if I could touch her. I still didn't believe in the appearance of Our Lady, and I wanted to find a way to, somehow, professionally expose the visionaries. The visionaries asked Our Lady again if I could approach her and she agreed. They showed me where I should come and where Our Lady was. I started approaching and now I was already scared, but there was no going back. The desire to examine the appearance—ego!—was stronger than a weak faith in the possibility of this kind of truth. I tried to feel something from the 'appearance' with my hand, but nothing."

Dr. Glamuzina added that, at the same time, the children shouted, 'She's gone!' With shame, she thought that Our Lady had left because of her, which later turned out to be true.

"I came to Vicka; she was a little scared (because of me), and she said that Our Lady had said that, 'There have always been doubting Judases,'" the doctor continued. "I was stunned by such a statement. I couldn't believe that it applied to me; it was only later that I realized the depth and the truthfulness of it. At first, I was hurt. I pulled aside and watched the further happenings and behavior of the visionaries and of the people around them. The people were asking for help for this or that person; it was all too dramatic for me. The more I was with the visionaries, the more they seemed to me to be immersed in the event, each one of them in their own distinctive way. They were full of inner joy and elation that no external manipulation could cause. Suddenly, I was overwhelmed by a confident, firm, and clear feeling: The children do see; they do see the same. This is truly Our Lady! I was really an unfaithful—I didn't believe them!—Judas. I wanted to unmask them; I wanted to betray them—how true it was! Instead of unmasking them, I was unmasked. I am my own Judas! Even though this statement of Our Lady was almost devastating for me as a public figure, at the same time, I was overwhelmed by the greatest possible, inexplicably deep happiness—indescribable in human vocabulary—referring to a deep realization: 'God is here; she is truly here, and the children do see her indeed.' Not being ready for such an appearance was my personal problem, but also a challenge for a new life in a completely different attire."

It turned out to be one of the most dramatic experiences in Dr. Darinka Glamuzina's life. She added that she felt as though there was a difficult and fascinating task in front of her: to become a new person. She said she felt that she had been given a mother's slap by which she was trying to bring a bad child to reason and to the right path.

"I was ashamed and deeply humbled by the greatness of the appearance, which read me, but which also gave me warning and guidance (that is a good mother!)," she testified. "What followed later was my spiritual transformation, which was fully carried out by Our Lady in her own way—and she continues doing today—but that is a different story for some other time."

On her way back down the hill, together with the visionaries, Dr. Glamuzina continued her research—even though she felt like she had become a completely different person through a metamorphosis, after which nothing in her life was the same anymore.

"I kept questioning the children about the vision of that day," she testified. "They were very cheerful and pleased with what they had heard from Our Lady. I again asked—I think it was Mirjana—why they see Our Lady and I don't. She responded so innocently and honestly—and only fully honest and confident visionaries who are not manipulated by anyone can say so—'Oh, well, you also can see Our Lady only if you want to!' Such a thing can be said only by those who truly see what they see and who, in their innocence, think that others can also experience the same. What did Our Lady say when I wanted to touch her? 'Well, there have always been the faithful, the unfaithful, and Judases.' Why did Our Lady come to this small village in the middle of nowhere? 'Faith is firm here.' What does it take for us to see Our Lady as well? 'To believe, to fast, and to pray.' Who is she? 'She's the Queen of Peace!' Why? 'We don't know, but that is what she says about herself.'"

Dr. Glamuzina explained that, at the base of the hill, she had met with her director, who was watching her maneuvers from afar and was stunned.

"My behavior went beyond what was required at such a moment in the line of an official duty," she testified. "I briefly told him my experience during the ride to Čitluk. I told him that I thought the children did see what they claimed to see. I told him that, on the hill, at the moment when Our Lady was leaving and while I was trying to touch her, I had the incredible feeling of knowing that she was leaving and in what direction. Later, I also confirmed this with the visionaries. I just knew: It was Our Lady. I also knew that this realization was worth living and dying for."

The doctor reported that, when she returned to her apartment in Čitluk, she asked her aunt—who was babysitting her child—to pray the rosary together that evening.

"We prayed for a long time," she said. "Because of the excitement, I did not sleep all night. In the following days, I was exposed to various—mostly negative—comments about my action. I knew that what I personally had experienced in such a turbulent time, I could not talk normally about without being misunderstood—from all sides. And there were comments that I was a communist spy, though I had no political involvement at the time. No one even tried to understand my true motives; they were covered by political turbulence. I felt it was best to change myself spiritually and talk about myself through my acts."

Dr. Glamuzina added that, in the next few days, she talked about everything with one public figure, thinking, at first, that it was a friendly conversation on the then-most common topic. After a few years, she realized that it was an "official conversation."

"He came to my office and we talked about the events in Medjugorje," she testified. "I told him that I believe that the children see what they [claim to] see. He was confused and said that the event should be seriously examined. After a while, a representative from the 'church commission' for investigating the case also came. We talked about the event. He asked me if I had seen anything. I said that I hadn't, but that the children did see 'something.' No one asked me anything more. I knew that most people embellished their own story of my hike to the hill. But, in a strange way, nothing but my deep knowledge mattered to me and, somehow, it doesn't matter to me now, either."

In her testimony, Dr. Glamuzina said that the visionaries live their own lives, which are a great sacrifice on Our Lady's altar. And, knowing what a delicate job she was doing, she decided to talk all the less and act all the more in the world, demonstrating that spiritual transformation was possible—despite everything that others had intended for her spiritually and mentally—and that it was possible to break the bonds of one's own prejudices and ignorance.

"As an important part of this journey, I find that learning and working on myself is an irreplaceable part of this formation," she explained. "Our Lady is my most important guide along the way. My life with Our Lady is different than it would be without her. And, if I had not been on that hill that day and hour, my spiritual life would have been poor and unimaginably empty. That is why I am grateful for every word Our Lady said to me. It's true, there have been many ups and downs along the way. But, as on some ascending spiral, I know that I'm climbing guided by Our Lady's hand. All this [that happened] on Apparition Hill was not the end, but the beginning of my communication with Our Lady. It has continued through more significant dreams and messages that, later in life, have proved to be accurate and prophetic for my personal growth in God."

Dr. Glamuzina added that she is still [being] filled with divine words and messages coming from Our Lady and the visionaries.

"I respect the visionaries as modern apostles who have a difficult role to play in this spiritually exhausted time," she testified shortly before Christmas 2008, more than two and a half decades after the wonderful experience on Podbrdo on the sixth day of the apparitions. "They are people who—with all their human weaknesses, but with fascinating virtues nurtured by God's providence—have the strength and courage to continue to bear witness of Our Lady's figure and her word. As a humble person (I'm humble before the splendor of Our Lady's figure), still ashamed because of my human weaknesses, at this Christmastime, I pray to Our Lady for compassion toward me and all of humanity exhausted from unbelief."

. . .

Marinko Ivanković, who was with the children almost constantly, also remembers that day:

"A multitude of people—about 30,000 of them—were there," he said. "I got home from work early and went to Vicka. I found five visionaries and Ante Bošnjak, the director of the Health Center, and Dara Glamuzina."

During the apparition, Marinko stood to the right of one visionary. When they began to pray, Our Lady came, so he knelt, as well.

"They spoke to Our Lady very briefly," he recalled. "Our Lady said that everyone should kneel. I stood up, looked at the people, and waved my hand, 'Our Lady told the visionaries that you all should kneel down!' There were also Muslims, Orthodox, and others there. I knew some of them; they worked with me. I saw: The people knelt! Dara [Dr. Darinka Glamuzina] knelt, too. While we were still at Vicka's house, she said that her parents were not really good believers. She asked a hundred questions: How tall is Our Lady? What do her eyes look like? What language she communicates with? How is she dressed? Her shoes...She knelt and asked the visionaries, 'Ask Our Lady, I would like to touch her.' The visionaries asked and Our Lady said, 'She may touch me, but there are many Judases here.' She asked, 'Where is Our Lady?' The visionaries said, 'Over there.' And they pointed with their hands. She stood up, took two steps, and started waving her hands when the visionaries said, 'Our Lady left!' How she managed to remain standing on her feet without falling on her back, I do not know. She only said, 'I just saw a bright cloud go from the spot where I was into the sky. That's enough for me.' After that, she sang with the nun every night in the choir."

Interestingly, not all events left the same mark on all of the visionaries. At the time, the visionary Ivan Dragičević did not seem particularly impressed with what had happened to Dr. Glamuzina.

"I remember her a little," he said. "In those first days of apparitions, we were mostly with our people, and as soon as an apparition ended, we were always accompanied by someone to protect us and to be close to us. After each encounter with Our Lady, we had to withdraw as soon as possible, so that we would not experience any inconvenience or cause discomfort to the elderly people who were with us. We were underage, and as soon as the police saw that someone was protecting us, they would start to put pressure on them."

However, something very important happened that day. It was the first case of healing!

Marinko Ivanković explained how the children had come as they had every other day before. They made the sign of the cross, knelt down, and prayed the Our Father. When Our Lady came, a man came to them and said, "Ask Our Lady if my son Danijel will be healed."

"Afterward, the visionaries told him, 'Our Lady said that you must believe firmly, that you must pray every day, and your son Danijel will be healed,'" Marinko recounted. "I only saw him then; I didn't even know what was wrong with the child. His child and his wife were with him. In October or November—I am no longer sure—this family came to me because my house is the first when you come down from the hill, so the people used to come to ask me for water to drink. I recognized them and asked if they were that family. 'What happened to your child, has anything changed?' I asked them. And they said, 'He was completely healed!' 'What happened?' I asked, and they said that, 'He was not stable on his feet, nor did he speak purely.' This boy now works in Germany and, every year for a vacation, he comes to Medjugorje for a month. What a miracle! He is now 40 years old."

Mirjana similarly documented the first case of healing:

"That apparition was also memorable because a man brought his severely disabled three-year-old son to the hill. The boy's name was Danijel Šetka, and he had been paralyzed and unable to talk from the time he was a baby. His parents came hoping for a healing. 'Blessed Mother,' we said, 'will this child ever speak? Heal him so that everyone will believe us.' Our Lady turned toward Danijel and looked at him for a long time with an expression of compassion and love. Finally, she said, 'Let them believe strongly that he will get well.' We were, perhaps, a little disappointed that there was no immediate change visible in Danijel's condition, but later his parents returned to the hill to give thanks to God. That night, Danijel had started walking and talking."

"Danijel Šetka excited the public about a three-year-old child," wrote Fr. Ljudevit Rupčić. "Our Lady conveyed through the visionaries on June 29, 1981, that he would be healed if his parents would firmly believe. The child—according to the parents as they had been told by the doctors—developed sepsis on the fourth day after birth and was rigid between the fourth and twentieth day. The rigidity relented, but one side of his body did not develop normally. The child couldn't walk by himself. He fell all the time. He couldn't even speak, but could only mutter one or two words.

"His mother used to come often to Medjugorje to pray. She used to take soil from Apparition Hill. The child was prayed over at the church. In early November 1981, the mother reported that the child was healthy. She said that he was progressively being healed. She stated that she would be satisfied to have the child stay this way, but that his hand could be even more mobile. The child was treated in Mostar and was getting medication from Germany. All these were of no use."

It is interesting to note that some visionaries, like Ivan Dragičević, didn't notice that the boy was healed.

"I did not see that child, but I only heard about it when I got home, when I got down from the hill," he said.

Vicka testified that little Danijel Šetka was very close to them and that she had the opportunity to observe it all.

"The little one was close to us," she explained. "His parents recommended him in our prayers; it wasn't anything special to us. Then, later, they told us that the little one was healed, and that it was the first healing. And then, that the old man from Vasilji [part of the village where all the Vasilj families live] got his sight back."

The healing of "the old man Vasilj" was even more miraculous than the healing of little Danijel Šetka because Jozo Vasilj (born in Medjugorje in 1896) was not even on Apparition Hill. Father Ljudevit Rupčić quoted the "old man's" statement that was given to Fr. Stanko Vasilj on September 14, 1981:

"It's been eight years since I had a stroke," Jozo Vasilj said. "That is when my left eye completely died. For the last four years, I have not seen with the other eye, either. I asked Vicka Vasilj to bring me some immortelle and sage from the hill of Crnica [the former name of Apparition Hill]. I put that under my head in the evening. In the morning, I asked my wife to bring me some water. I mixed it and washed my face with it. When I was drying my face, I said to my wife, 'Here, I see!' She said, 'Come on, what do you see?' 'Well, I do see,' I told her, 'that you have no socks on!' That way, my wife was also convinced that I got my sight back. While I was washing my face, I prayed the Creed. The last time I was at our church was when Jure Ivanković came from America. God gave me another great gift on that occasion. I had scabs on my hands for some time. Then, the scabs disappeared."

However, with these healings and the increasing number of people coming to Medjugorje every day, the authorities and the police increased the pressure on the visionaries and the locals.

"It was getting harder day by day," visionary Ivan Dragičević recalled. "Soldiers from Sarajevo arrived; they pitched their tents above the area where Cenacolo is now. All the men had to keep watch for 24 hours a day so that no one would be allowed to go up the hill. That was later... We went to the hill on the third, fourth, fifth, and sixth day with the people. This was very difficult because there were a lot of police. People were also physically deterred. People from our village were especially harassed and taken for questioning to the police station in Čitluk. Like Ivan Ivanković, Marinko Ivanković, and some other people from the village."

Ivan added that, in those days, they were "together all the time" and gathered in isolated places where they could talk together about everything that had happened to them.

"Those were the days," he remembered. "I was not afraid of anything after the third day. I was ready to lay down my life."

The fact that the children were ready to die for what they saw—as well as that they were not afraid at all and that even their own lives did not matter to them—proved to Fr. Jozo that it was something extraordinary because the children could not be intimidated or bribed in any way. However, he was still quite suspicious of everything that was going on in his parish.

"I didn't believe the children," the priest said. "I couldn't keep track of everything then. I was very tired. I couldn't sleep because people came day and night. They used to set out from Roško Polje, Duvno, Livno, Sinj, Zadar, from everywhere...I had to get up. I couldn't do it; I was so tired and they asked me to talk to them. Well, what will I tell you, my people, let's pray. I remember, one Sunday afternoon, a group of priests came to talk with me about my experience, and I asked them why they were so curious and without faith. We held Jesus in Mass shortly before and now they asked me to talk to them. 'Let us all go together as priests and have one hour of adoration before Jesus in the church.' Not one of them said he would go! No one! Just curiosity, to see, to hear...And, at night, as I would listen to those children and our conversations, it all would become harder for me. These were simple answers. A child responds with such language. One almost cannot understand what it means for us in our language, in the language of the time, when a peasant says a word or when he confirms something."

Next, Fr. Jozo described when he began to believe the children.

"It all went slowly," he reported about his relationship with the children. "It cannot be said—[to] them. They were on one side and Our Lady was on the other. She did not leave me hanging, to be pulled in different directions by this or that information. It bothered me when some of the friars came and said, 'There will be an information.' I came from prison and I heard them calling Our Lady's messages 'information.' That's not an information, man! It is a formation, not an information. That is a call, an interpretation of that call, so it was painful to me to hear that...When? There is no such a thing like when! That's growth. You can't tell when you've grown out of baby clothes. There is no such day. All this was slow."

However, one event, in particular, was crucial, and that was a voice he heard in the church while he was praying there.

"This was when Our Lady called for the rosary," Fr. Jozo remembered. "They did not come to prayer until the hill was blocked. It was at 3 p.m. They were here around 5:30 p.m. or a little earlier. I heard a murmur; something rumbled, I turned around and the people were leaving—I was left alone. I was sad, I have nothing to tell you—as if curiosity overcame prayer—and I was sorry. I was sorry from the bottom of my soul. Oh, I comforted myself…My God. I sat in the third row of benches, those old benches where [the statue of] Our Lady of Lourdes used to be. (And St. Anthony was there where Our Lady is now.) I found these two statues in the steeple. The church without Our Lady's statue!? Starčević, who built the church, said that only the patron should be emphasized and nothing else. Well, who is the patron! I finely washed that statue, invited an Italian artist to paint it, had a pedestal made, and brought Our Lady in. It was as if I had won—I don't know what—but there was not even a mention of apparitions yet. I did it for the May devotions to the Blessed Virgin Mary.

"I read from the Bible," he continued. "The thoughts teemed within me, the anguish...I opened the Bible—Exodus. Moses and the people went through the desert. They were given water; God was leading them. So, in my heart I said, 'God, it was easy for Moses. He knew he was not alone. And here the multitude of the people knows nothing, neither do I.' And after my thoughts and complaint—I would say a conversation with God—I heard a voice: 'Go out and protect the children!' I was alone in the church. I bowed down. I left the Bible and headed out when I saw—on the left-hand side from the old school direction—children running through the vineyards and, panting, they said, 'Save us! The police are chasing us!' They went up to the hill from the church and now they were being persecuted. I ran quickly, opened the rectory and my room, which was first to the right, and I locked it up and told them, 'You have to be quiet and don't talk.' They had the apparition there and later they were seen by friars who stopped by to visit me. I offered them something to drink and eat and a chance to rest a little, so that we could talk about what Our Lady had said."

In this crucial moment, Fr. Jozo stood completely with the visionaries and, as a result, ended up in prison as the number one enemy of the state on August 17, 1981.

FROM THE CONVERSATION OF FR. JANKO BUBALO WITH VICKA

FR. JANKO: "Here we are already at the sixth day. So, let's continue."

VICKA: "We can, we can. But, don't you try to drag everything out of me as though I'm going to confession."

FR. JANKO: "Exactly! Just as though you were going to confession. Remember, that was the feast day of St. Peter."

VICKA: "Well, I know that! I will never forget it. But if I drag it out, don't let me do so..."

FR. JANKO: "Just go ahead and tell me."

VICKA: "Well, it was like this: Since it was a feast day, we all slept a bit longer. We arose, ate a bit, and then prepared for church."

FR. JANKO: "All right, then, you went to church, and..."

VICKA: "Lord, what kind of church! Two vehicles appeared before our houses. The ambulance from Čitluk and some other vehicle."

FR. JANKO: "And now, what was that all about?"

VICKA: "What? Agony and grief, my dear friar! They opened the door of the ambulance and told us to get in."

FR. JANKO: "To whom?"

VICKA: "Well, to us, visionaries."

FR. JANKO: "And you?"

VICKA: "What can you do? 'Might does not ask God for permission'— an expression I heard many times from my grandmother. Get in and that was it!"

FR. JANKO: "All six of you in the ambulance?"

VICKA: "They crammed those who were going to accompany us in the other vehicle. And off..."

FR. JANKO: "Who accompanied you?"

VICKA: "Well, our parents, or whoever happened to have gone with us that day, and the director of the Čitluk Health Center accompanied us, also."

FR. JANKO: "Who accompanied you?"

VICKA: "My mother, who else? My father was in Germany at the time."

FR. JANKO: "And, did they inform you where you were headed?"

VICKA: "They said to see the doctors in Mostar."

FR. JANKO: "And, you set out."

VICKA: "We were off. What else could we do?"

FR. JANKO: "And, ultimately?"

VICKA: "They brought us to some psychiatric place. Well, until then, I barely heard of such a thing. When we arrived, they told us to get out, and the examination began."

FR. JANKO: "And, the referral cards for the examination?"

VICKA: "What referral cards?"

FR. JANKO: "And, who was called first for the examination?"

VICKA: "They took all of us into a room at one time."

FR. JANKO: "And, who examined you?"

VICKA: "Some lady doctor."

FR. JANKO: "Did she examine each of you individually?"

VICKA: "No, no! All at the same time. Well, there really wasn't any sort of examination to speak of. She kept making inquiries and aggravating us."

FR. JANKO: "And, what did this look like?"

VICKA: "She attempted to make of us some kind of sickies that we were imagining things; that we were some kind of addicts; that we were fooling people, and the like. She attacked me for being dressed in the latest style, and as if I pretended to be Our Lady's girl. Lord! Who could recall it all! We just wanted to get out of there as fast as possible so that we could go home to look after our own business."

FR. JANKO: "Someone said that they also took you into a morgue?"

VICKA: "Yes, they did that, too. I suppose they wanted to scare us with something, whatever it was."

FR. JANKO: "And, for example, did they frighten you with anything?"

VICKA: "Not at all, not with anything!"

FR. JANKO: "Really, with nothing?"

VICKA: "Well, I told you—they didn't frighten me at all. What could they do to me? Someone is dying all the time. So, let them die! I only wanted to get into the vehicle and get back home as quickly as possible."

FR. JANKO: "And, the drivers?"

VICKA: "What choice did the men have? All of this seemed strange and crazy to them, also, but what can you do?"

FR. JANKO: "The director of the clinic—the one who accompanied you—what was his attitude?"

VICKA: "Good. Fine. What could the man do?"

FR. JANKO: "Did he accompany you on your return?"

VICKA: "Yes, yes, what else?"

FR. JANKO: "And thus, they returned you to your homes?"

VICKA: "Somewhere about two in the afternoon."

FR. JANKO: "You didn't tell me what the lady doctor had to say to you?"

VICKA: "She said whoever brought us there was crazy, and that we were completely normal children. What else could she say?"

FR. JANKO: "Well, at least she was honest, then."

VICKA: "Let it go! Let's forget this already."

FR. JANKO: "All right, Vicka. You arrived home, rested a bit, and then?"

VICKA: "Well, there was no rest. The people gathered around us. We could hardly move. Everyone wanted to know... And we weren't exactly too eager to talk. We were just waiting for our moment, for Our Lady."

FR. JANKO: "It's a bit strange! Heat, weariness, stress, but you again went to Our Lady?"

VICKA: "Where else? Nothing could stop us."

FR. JANKO: "And, the people at Podbrdo?"

VICKA: "So many of them! It was overflowing. One on top of the other. We couldn't stand upright anywhere. Some were shouting, some crying... Well, that was amazing."

FR. JANKO: "And, how did you poor things manage to get to the top?"

VICKA: "Just barely! Some of our men went before us to make a pathway for us, while others held hands in a circle at the top of the hill to make space for us. We could not have done it without them."

FR. JANKO: "All right. Somehow, you managed to get to the top. And then?"

VICKA: "We knelt and began to pray."

FR. JANKO: "And, Our Lady?"

VICKA: "Our Lady appeared almost instantly."

FR. JANKO: "And then?"

VICKA: "We all began to sing and pray in unison...and ask Our Lady something."

FR. JANKO: "Do you recall what you asked her?"

VICKA: "Yes, I do. We asked her, 'Dear Our Lady, are you happy at the size of the crowd here today?'"

FR. JANKO: "And, Our Lady?"

VICKA: "She smiled greatly. It was beautiful! And, she was happy. Well, it's inadequate to say she was happy. It can't be described. She gazed at the people below, over the fields, at Križevac [Cross Mountain] and..."

FR. JANKO: "And then?"

VICKA: "I remember well, we asked her, 'My Lady, how long will you remain with us?'"

FR. JANKO: "And she?"

VICKA: "She responded, 'As long as you wish, my angels!'—Just think, 'As long as you wish!' Well, forever! But, we couldn't say that, my dear friar. Well, no one knows how that comforted us. And, wouldn't I go to jail for her? Well, I would die for her. I'd go anywhere!"

FR. JANKO: "And, with that, it ended that afternoon?"

VICKA: "No, no! Only, then, we became bold enough to ask her."

FR. JANKO: "And, what else did you ask her?"

VICKA: "We again asked her what she wished of the people, who were hungry and thirsty, who struggled and perspired surrounded by the thornbushes."

FR. JANKO: "Vicka, I believe you, but did Our Lady answer?"

VICKA: "Yes, of course she did! She said there is but one God and one faith. Let the people believe firmly and have no fear."

FR. JANKO: "And then, anything else?"

VICKA: "We asked her something for ourselves, too. We asked whether we would be able to endure all of this because some were persecuting us for saying that we saw her."

FR. JANKO: "And, Our Lady?"

VICKA: "She said, two, three times, 'You will, my angels. Don't be afraid! You will endure it all!'—only to believe and to trust in her."

FR. JANKO: "Anything else?"

VICKA: "At the time, we asked and prayed for a sick person for the first time."

FR. JANKO: "Can you recall who that was?"

VICKA: "I can. Well, of course I can! I'll never forget it. A little boy. His father held him in his arms. The little boy looked half dead. He hung his head on his father's left shoulder. Really, he looked miserable."

FR. JANKO: "And then?"

VICKA: "The father pleaded and prayed to Our Lady to cure him, and he asked us to pray and ask Our Lady to help the little boy."

FR. JANKO: "To ask what?"

VICKA: "To ask if the boy would be healed."

FR. JANKO: "And you?"

VICKA: "We asked. In fact, I was the one who asked."

FR. JANKO: "Perhaps Our Lady said nothing?"

VICKA: "What, nothing? She looked upon the boy. Tenderly, tenderly… And, she said the parents should pray much and believe firmly."

FR. JANKO: "I heard that one of you said that the boy was sure to get well."

VICKA: "I know that. I think that little Jakov said that. Only, in the press of the crowd, he forgot to say that the parents need to pray much, fast, and be firm in faith."

FR. JANKO: "Good. And, what happened with the boy?"

VICKA: "I know only this: His parents thanked us and I later saw the boy. He was playing around us whereas before he was unable to stand on his feet. I don't know anything further."

FR. JANKO: "All right, Vicka. However, we still did not say who the little boy was?"

VICKA: "I really don't remember such things, but I did remember this, for it was a special case. The boy's name was Danijel Šetka and he was from Podgorje."

FR. JANKO: "Did that day then end with that?"

VICKA: "I don't know why you are suddenly in such a hurry—usually you ask that I talk at length."

FR. JANKO: "So, go on, talk!"

VICKA: "At the time, there was an interesting situation with some lady doctor."

FR. JANKO: "What's that all about?"

VICKA: "Well, at the time, there was also a lady doctor at Podbrdo."

FR. JANKO: "And?"

VICKA: "She wanted to touch Our Lady."

FR. JANKO: "What then?"

VICKA: "We asked Our Lady, and Our Lady said, 'There have always been unfaithful Judases, but she may. Let her approach.'"

FR. JANKO: "And then?"

VICKA: "The doctor approached and touched Our Lady."

FR. JANKO: "How did she know where to touch, since she could not see Our Lady?"

VICKA: "I directed her."

FR. JANKO: "And, she really touched Our Lady?"

VICKA: "Really, certainly!"

FR. JANKO: "And, where did she touch her?"

VICKA: "On the right shoulder. That was most convenient."

FR. JANKO: "And, what did the doctor do then?"

VICKA: "What could she do? She stepped back, and who knows what she was thinking to herself."

FR. JANKO: "Did she say anything?"

VICKA: "She said nothing in front of the people. Later, she stopped at our house and, before everyone, declared that, when she touched her, she felt some sort of tingling (goose pimples, as she said) through her hand, but she didn't say anything else."

FR. JANKO: "Did she ever come again to the apparitions?"

VICKA: "I never saw her again. But, you know how that is with them. They are intelligent, so..."

THE SEVENTH DAY – JUNE 30

The apparition outside Medjugorje

"Were you in Mostar yesterday?" Fr. Jozo asked Ivanka. "I looked; you were not at Mass."

Fr. Jozo's conversation with the visionary Ivanka on the seventh day of the apparitions began rather provocatively and sarcastically. He did not see the children in church at the Eucharistic celebration on the feast of Saints Peter and Paul; she replied that they were not at Mass because somebody suddenly came for them and took them to the Health Center in Čitluk for a medical examination.

"At six o'clock, they came and told us about the medical examination," Ivanka explained. "We left by bus at half past six. We were in Čitluk and then we left. We came to Mostar—to the old hospital—to see Džudža, and she said if we go again, we would go to the hospital. And, they wanted, she said, to pay for us to go to the coast, to separate us."

"Well, split up," Fr. Jozo said.

"Tell me about it!"

"Why didn't you want to split up?" the priest asked.

"Because Our Lady is here," she replied to him.

"I know, but do you know that the apparitions could take place in America and here, both at sea and on land," he said. "It doesn't matter; Our Lady is not bound to space."

Fr. Jozo explained to Ivanka that the apparitions were not tied solely to one place, and that they had also previously taken place around the world.

"But, Marinko told us to accept it and, when we return, she would come again," Ivanka responded. "She said she would come as long as we wanted."

Fr. Jozo inquired whether it meant that they "were commanding Our Lady in some way", which Ivanka decisively denied. He was also interested in what Marinko Ivanković, who was closest to the children in those days, said about everything.

"He told us not to be afraid of anything, that nothing would happen to us," Ivanka said.

"You were in the hospital a lot because of your mom," Fr. Jozo continued. "You went to visit her, so you were scared, right?

"Ouch, if we had stayed a little longer, I would have died there," Ivanka spoke honestly about the situation in which they went to the psychiatry unit and met with mentally ill patients.

"For what?" Fr. Jozo asked.

"I have no idea," the girl responded. "A woman entered saying that her daughter was ill, to give her a place in the hospital. They told her that there was no room. How would there be a place for us when we are healthy. She [the doctor] told us that she hadn't seen smarter children than us."

"So, why did you deceive Fr. Zrinko when you said...?"

"I was so scared of that hospital," Ivanka interrupted. "But, when it was about 5:30 p.m., I had to go. Everything was pulling me up and I had to go."

Ivanka described the feeling she had as the time of the apparition was approaching. Meanwhile, Fr. Jozo was most interested in what the visionaries would tell the people on that day, that is, as he tried to steer them from Podbrdo to the church and persuade the children to do the same.

"What do you think you should do today so the people won't be fooled?" he asked. "What would be the easiest way to deal with the people today? What do you think that the people should be told today regarding what Our Lady is telling them?"

"Like this," she said. "We would tell them not to come anymore."

"That Our Lady tells them so, right?" he clarified.

"That's right," Ivanka replied, explaining why she was not in favor of people continuing to come to the hill. "Not to gather so that the police would not come here. They dressed in civilian clothes."

"And what else will you tell them today?" Fr. Jozo asked.

"I don't know," Ivanka said.

"Not to come, and...what else?"

"I don't know."

"How shall you tell them this?" he wondered.

"Not to come because Our Lady said so," she said. "They have picked up all the soil from the place where Our Lady came…"

Ivanka explained what the place of the apparition on Podbrdo looked like—the place where people grabbed everything they could reach, tearing out both thornbushes and their roots, and taking the soil and stones with them from the spot of the apparition.

"Tell me this, how shall you say that to people if Our Lady doesn't say so?" Fr. Jozo continued.

"Marinko told me what to say, that they shouldn't come anymore," Ivanka replied. "Everybody says, my children are sick, ask about them…"

She then spoke to Fr. Jozo about the pressure they were experiencing from all sides.

"This is what interests me," the priest began. "You said today that Our Lady would not come again. You already know that?"

"We said so," the girl confirmed.

"And who said so? Marinko?" Fr. Jozo clarified.

"Yes," Ivanka responded. "To tell the people not to gather."

"Are you afraid to put words into Our Lady's mouth, when you have not spoken to Our Lady?" Fr. Jozo asked. "Claiming that Our Lady said something if she did not say it?"

Ivanka said that they would ask her "if they could do so."

"And we asked her if we would endure the constant persecution. She said, 'You will, my dear angels,'" Ivanka added.

"To whom did she say that?" Fr. Jozo asked.

"To all of us."

"You all heard it?" he continued.

"Yes, we did," she replied.

"Seriously?"

"Yes."

Fr. Jozo asked her how it was possible that she had not changed at all, that she had remained the same, "although she saw Our Lady."

"How is it possible that none of it affects you—neither fear, nor what you do, nor what she tells you?" he inquired. "She wasn't the first to talk to you until now, right?"

Ivanka replied that she had only told them, "My dear angels."

Fr. Jozo was also interested in what the children would ask Our Lady today and how she would answer them.

"If she does not have the power, as Marinko said, to give a sign, [then she should] ask Jesus to help her," Ivanka answered.

The children were insisting that Our Lady leave them some sign so that the people would know that they weren't lying. However, they had some doubt as to whether she *could* leave a sign—if she had enough "power" to do so. Therefore, Marinko Ivanković suggested that they tell her that if she couldn't leave a sign, that she should ask Jesus—who might be "stronger" than Our Lady—to do it for her.

"All right, Marinko thinks so. But, what do others think? What do you think?" Fr. Jozo asked.

"That it's right to ask her because she might not have the power," Ivanka confirmed.

"All right. If she speaks to you and you cannot remember what she said to you—you don't remember it, do you?" Fr. Jozo asked, provoking her slightly with this question.

"I can," Ivanka responded briefly.

"You can remember it? What did she say last night?"

"Like this, we asked her…"

Fr. Jozo interrupted, "Who asked her?"

"It seems to me that Mirjana asked her if we would endure it."

"And, who told Mirjana to ask her that? Was it Marinko?"

"He gave us all these questions, so I asked how long she would stay with us," Ivanka explained. "We asked about that little boy, then what did she want from us."

"I know, but she didn't tell you anything!" Fr. Jozo replied, slightly disappointed.

"She answered everything," Ivanka claimed.

"What answers did she give? What was the first question?"

"Shall we endure it. She said, 'You will, my dear angels.'"

Fr. Jozo wanted to know what the second question was.

"I asked how long she would stay with us and she said, 'As long as you want, as long as you want.' Something like that."

"Go on."

"Then, she said about the little boy that they should firmly believe that he would be healed."

"She didn't say anything else? That she would come today?"

"She did, she did," the girl confirmed. "The doctor also asked if she could touch her. We asked her and she said, 'There have always been unfaithful Judases. Let her approach.'"

"Well, Judas was not without faith," Fr. Jozo retorted.

"He was a traitor," Ivanka replied.

"I know, but the traitor doesn't have to be an unbeliever if he has received the gift of faith," the priest explained. "Thomas was an unbeliever. How did it occur to you to say Judas? Was it because he betrayed Jesus?"

Fr. Jozo was suspicious because it seemed illogical to answer that Judas—qualified as a traitor—now became "unfaithful," that is, the characteristic associated with the apostle Thomas.

"Well, that's what she said," Ivanka defended herself.

"Who?"

"Well, Our Lady did."

"To whom did she say that?"

"To us," Ivanka said. "Mirjana asked that, as well."

"Did she say that to you?"

"I heard that, too," Ivanka explained. "We all heard that."

"And why would she say something like Judas when she knows that Judas had faith as an apostle?" Fr. Jozo wondered aloud as he returned to Our Lady's answer.

"How would I know?" Ivanka admitted. "When she [Dr. Glamuzina] touched her, Our Lady left. She [Dr. Glamuzina] saw the cloud when she left."

Fr. Jozo then wondered if anyone besides them saw something.

"It seems to me that Jana saw something," Ivanka said.

"I didn't mean something, but Our Lady or...Why can't you bring some of your colleagues or friends to show them?" the priest inquired. "How can you not sway him [a colleague or friend] to see?"

"I don't know that," the girl said honestly. "I wonder how I can even see her."

Fr. Jozo wondered if she was ever first to see her and if she would inform the others by stating, "There she is!"

"I did," Ivanka said. "Sometimes, they didn't look up, but down, so I did show them."

"How can they not see her if they look at her and can see her?" Fr. Jozo asked. "Why do you have to say, 'There she is'?"

"They say the same, 'There she is, there she is,'" Ivanka recalled. "First, we see the light and then Our Lady. This morning, we ran up there. There was light."

Ivanka disclosed that other people also saw the light in the morning, so the visionaries went up the hill, but that there was no apparition then.

"Did anyone see this light besides you?" Fr. Jozo asked.

The girl told him they did not see the light, but "some woman told them."

"Did she teach you to pray any prayer?" he continued.

"Nothing."

"But, how? So far, she taught everyone with whom she spoke," Fr. Jozo continued. "She taught the children in Fatima to pray the rosary and she told them to pray for the conversion of sinners."

Ivanka replied that she had not said anything like that to them and that, whatever they asked, she simply answered and said nothing else.

"Why doesn't she answer with something new for you, but always answers the same?" Fr. Jozo asked a little angrily.

Ivanka, not knowing how to answer, remained silent.

"What are you going to ask her today? Not to come anymore?" Fr. Jozo continued.

"I don't know," Ivanka replied.

"You have to think of something," the priest said. "How did you think of what you were going to say to the people yesterday? When did Marinko write that yesterday, [the] questions and answers?"

"In the evening," she responded. "But, he did not write the answers, only the questions."

Ivanka avoided Fr. Jozo's trap about supposedly pre-written answers.

"What you said to the people yesterday—with Marinko—have you gotten ready for today?" he continued.

"We haven't," Ivanka said. "Only Mirjana will ask if Our Lady has the power to give us a sign. Yesterday, the doctor asked if the people of the same faith or of another faith should be reconciled. She said there was only one faith and one God."

Next, Fr. Jozo wondered when the children had seen the cross.

"Twice. Once Marija, once me," Ivanka said.

"And, why doesn't Ivan see or hear anymore?" Fr. Jozo asked, referring to Ivan Dragičević as if he had not experienced any more apparitions.

"Ivan does see!" Ivanka replied.

Then, Fr. Jozo wanted to know if Ivan had also been at the apparition the day before. Ivanka told him that he hadn't been.

"Isn't he interested anymore?" Fr. Jozo wondered.

"Ask him," Ivanka said, before changing the subject. "He said he would never fall behind again. I was afraid of the hospital and of those doctors."

"What is there to fear when Our Lady is with you?"

"I don't know," the girl admitted. "When that time comes…"

Clearly, Ivanka was thinking about the time when the apparition approaches and when no one can stop the children from seeing Our Lady.

"You are now the most popular," Fr. Jozo teased.

"Cameras record us, and we ask them why they record and take pictures of us because, wherever we go, they take pictures of us," she replied. "Why do they take pictures of us? To sell them to some people there."

Ivanka was dissatisfied with the sudden popularity. Fr. Jozo asked her if she would like him to come to Podbrdo today for the apparition.

"Come," Ivanka answered briefly.

"What do you think, should I go?" Fr. Jozo continued, although Ivanka did not offer a specific answer.

"Come if you want," she said.

"But, I don't feel the need at all," Fr. Jozo told her, disclosing his suspicious attitude about apparitions and private revelations.

"Well, then don't," Ivanka responded, accepting Fr. Jozo's opinion.

"Why not, if it's Our Lady?" Fr. Jozo wanted to know. "And, why doesn't Our Lady appear in the church?"

"How would I know? We didn't ask her this," Ivanka admitted.

Fr. Jozo was also interested in how Our Lady was dressed the day before.

"Exactly the same," Ivanka said. "Always the same."

"And, does she always speak in the same way?" Fr. Jozo inquired.

"As if she were singing," Ivanka replied.

Fr. Jozo wanted to know if she had said what the children should pray and sing yesterday.

"Nothing," the girl said.

"Do you know that the people are terribly upset?" he asked. "They do not see any sign. You are not changing. The people feel that they are terribly deceived by you, that they are tricked. How do you interpret this?"

"I believe in it. I see her," Ivanka explained, defending herself. "And, even if the people saw her, I certainly would not doubt that I see her."

"You didn't believe before that Our Lady existed?" he asked.

"I did, I always did," she said.

"You've never seen her before, but you believed?"

"Yes."

"Okay, so why are you seeking to see her again now?"

"Because..." Ivanka replied vaguely.

"Why do you say because?" he asked. "For example, Iva [Ivanka], you see Our Lady and you are happy and joyful, but she does not say anything about what you should do. You just asked her about your mom and nothing else."

"Nothing else," Ivanka said.

"Well, why don't you ask her about someone else?" he wondered. "Or, are you not interested in anyone else?"

"We did ask," she explained. "How many people came to me this morning to ask about some blind people, and then about a child. And, this man that we asked for, he took his child and came to ask if he should buy us a gift. Gift, no way!"

Ivanka shared that the children didn't want to receive any gifts from the people who asked them to speak to Our Lady on their behalf.

"Did you ask for the child?" Fr. Jozo inquired regarding little Danijel Šetka.

"Little Jakov did ask," she said.

"And, where did Our Lady look when he asked that?"

"Straight into the child, like this," Ivanka showed him what it was like.

"Why didn't she heal him?"

"She said, 'Let the parents firmly believe,' and he would be healed," the girl responded.

"Well, why didn't you tell them that?"

"We told them that and they thanked us," she replied. "They wanted to buy some gifts for us."

Again, Ivanka talked about people wanting to give them gifts.

Fr. Jozo commented, "What a funny thing—why presents when the child wasn't even healed?"

"I have no idea, they wanted to do so," she said.

Then, Fr. Jozo told her in a serious tone that she should not joke about God.

"Iva [Ivanka], you are here before God and before the cross," he began. "It's terrible to joke about faith, you know?"

"I know," she answered.

"It is terrible to joke about faith, and God cannot let you get away with it," Fr. Jozo spoke in a reprimanding voice.

Ivanka told him that she knew it well, but that she couldn't help herself because she truly saw Our Lady.

"It's not a lie," she defended herself. "I see her as I see you here."

"But, you have to tell the people not only what you see, but…" Fr. Jozo said, assuring her that people also need to receive some sort of sign to trust that the children really do see Our Lady.

"She will undoubtedly leave a sign one day," Ivanka replied confidently. "For sure. I am convinced of this."

Fr. Jozo wondered where she would leave it.

"On the hill up there," she said. "That's for sure."

"What kind of a sign do you expect?"

"Whatever it is," she replied.

"Do you have an idea—an image—of that sign?" Fr. Jozo continued.

"I don't know," Ivanka admitted. "I would most like the people to see her. That everyone may see her. That she tells them something. She can leave something on Earth. People are talking about water."

Within her answer were the speculations of others about the kind of sign that it might be. At one time, the talk was about water—most likely because it was the most incredible possibility that water could begin to flow from a gray stone and a hill overgrown with thornbushes.

"Do you think she could leave water?" Fr. Jozo asked.

"Why not?"

"What would be your favorite, water or…?"

"That all the people may see her."

"What do you think, can people see that?"

"If that's what Our Lady wants, they can," she responded. "But, how shall she show herself to them when they curse there!"

"Don't you see that it is Satan present there, not Our Lady?" Fr. Jozo explained. "No swearing is supposed to be done on the hill, my Iva [Ivanka]. Where Our Lady is appearing, people do not curse and that is something that is misleading you. That's not Our Lady, my Iva!"

"What else is it but Our Lady?" Ivanka questioned, defensively.

"You can't imagine how awful it is to hear it through this open window," Fr. Jozo said, as he told her about the curses he heard through the window of his parish house when people passed by swearing.

"None of us curse," Ivanka told him, certainly thinking of the other visionaries and the people who helped and accompanied them.

"The people curse on the way back," Fr. Jozo shared, and he described the people who cursed as they were descending from the hill and passing by him.

"I do not know that," she admitted. "How shall she show herself to them when they curse?! We ask, but nothing is heard."

Fr. Jozo wondered whether she heard people speak at the time of the apparition.

"I have heard from others that some had cursed," Ivanka said. Apparently, the visionaries couldn't hear it during the apparitions.

"Then, how did you hear the doctor ask Our Lady?" Fr. Jozo inquired, looking for any inconsistencies in the story—that the children had not heard the people around them cursing, but that they had heard Dr. Glamuzina asking them to ask questions of Our Lady on her behalf.

"She pulled me and said, 'Ask this, ask this,'" Ivanka told him. "It was tiring. I'll ask Our Lady if she can touch her. And she did touch her."

Then, Ivanka told him what happened to Dr. Glamuzina, and Fr. Jozo asked, "What did the doctor say?"

"Nothing," Ivanka replied. "She just saw the cloud leave, and she said she would come again today."

Next, Fr. Jozo asked Ivanka to grant his wish and do something important for him.

"Will you obey something I ask you, Iva?" he said.

"I will," she replied.

"Go ahead, tell the people today..." he began his plea. Ivanka begged him to write it down because she thought she would forget by the time she got up there.

"How shall you forget!?"

"I don't know," she said. "Marinko also wrote it down."

"Did Marinko write down everything?" the priest asked.

"He did," Ivanka said. "I read until I got up there and I remembered everything."

"But, I have to write down what you will say, and not the question. I have to write down an answer for you, not a question," Fr. Jozo told her, which provoked her reaction.

"What do you mean, an answer?" she asked. "Well, Our Lady gives the answers, not us."

"No, no," Fr. Jozo continued. "You have to know what you are going to say to the people. I'll write it down for you."

He wanted the children to convey his words to the people, but certainly not in a way that they would know that he had told them that.

"All right. Write it down, go ahead," Ivanka agreed.

"Will you say it?" Fr. Jozo checked, once again.

"I will," she confirmed.

"How will you say it?" he asked. "Will you say that Our Lady said that?"

"First, I will ask Our Lady if this is ok," Ivanka explained.

"Will you say that Our Lady speaks like this..." Fr. Jozo suggested. On the recording, he can be heard writing something on paper.

"No, I'll first ask Our Lady if I can say this," Ivanka was determined not to allow any manipulation either in questions or answers.

"Ouch," Fr. Jozo sighed.

"I can't lie," Ivanka said.

Fr. Jozo explained to her that it wasn't a lie.

"I thought you should tell the people to come to pray in the church," he explained. "That you go before them and come to church. We would bring out a statue of Our Lady in the church and pray to God the rosary."

"All right," Ivanka agreed.

"As if it's something bad…How are you going to say it then?" Fr. Jozo clarified, wanting to get another confirmation from Ivanka that she would convey it to the people.

"I will say, 'Our Lady said, if you can, we should go to church and pray there. Those who want to pray.' Is that right?" she asked.

"Our Lady said…" Fr. Jozo can be heard writing something down on paper in the recording.

"But first, let's ask Our Lady if I can say that," Ivanka corrected him.

"Well, how are you going to say it? 'Our Lady said to us…'" Fr Jozo persisted.

"… to go to church and that we all pray there," Ivanka finished his sentence.

"But, beware that the unbelievers would not go to church," Fr. Jozo warned.

"Only believers who believe in Our Lady," Ivanka added.

"Those who believe in God! Let them come and we will pray the rosary. Come on, write it down."

"You write it down," Ivanka replied, pushing his idea away from herself.

"What shall I write?" Fr. Jozo continued. "Come on, tell me."

"Well, write that down," Ivanka said.

"To write what?" Fr. Jozo laughed, as he began to write again. "Our Lady says…"

"Write it down," Ivanka repeated.

"And, what if she doesn't speak?" Fr. Jozo interrupted.

"That's what I'm going to ask," the girl explained. "I can't tell you. And then, we will tell the people not to come anymore and we will be alone with her again up there every night. That's what I think is best. Our Lady says that…"

The two were silent for a few minutes, and only the sound of a pen writing on paper could be heard. Fr. Jozo was most likely writing questions for Ivanka.

"I have one more question," Ivanka said.

"Which question? How shall you ask this question?" Fr. Jozo asked.

"Our Lady, can I say this to the people?" she began. "I will read it and say, let's all go to church and pray. And, tomorrow, we will come up again without anyone knowing."

Ivanka revealed that the children would still go up the hill alone without the accompaniment of so many people.

"Aha," Fr. Jozo said. "When, in the morning?"

"Not in the morning! Also at six, at the time of the apparition," she replied.

"Aha, up there on the hill," Fr. Jozo said aloud as he wrote. "Like this, to pray the rosary and the chaplet up there."

"Let only believers come," Ivanka added.

"Or those who venerate me [Our Lady]…How shall we put it?" Fr Jozo asked her.

"Believers," Ivanka confirmed.

"That's number one. And you also have to come, you know?" he said.

"We will come."

"You will stand in front," Fr. Jozo began, as he explained the children's new role to her. "I will give you a microphone and you will pray the rosary. I will give you rosaries and you will pray. I'll give you a text on how to pray the rosary."

"Good. We will be up at the altar?" Ivanka questioned him about where exactly the children would stand in the church.

"You can kneel in front of the altar, down in the front," Fr. Jozo told her.

Ivanka replied that "the first bench" was a better choice and that it was "better in the bench"—obviously not wanting to stand out.

"Where would you put the statue of Our Lady, in your opinion? In the middle of the church?"

"Something like that," she said.

"What else shall we ask, Iva?" Fr. Jozo pleaded. "Come on, tell me."

"I don't know. You say something," Ivanka replied.

"Let's ask her, let's ask her...What could we ask her, please?" Fr. Jozo continued.

"I don't know," she said.

"How shall you ask that question?"

"Mary, teach us to pray something."

"What have we just spoken about, please? What is your favorite prayer...and song?" Fr. Jozo suggested. "Fourth question: Where have you appeared to people so far?"

"Write it down," Ivanka said.

"Tonight, we will pray in the church…" Fr. Jozo wrote.

"Tonight?"

"Yes, just let the believers come, and let's give some order to it," he explained. "Then, we will pray the rosary and the like."

Ivanka then ended their conversation by simply saying "good."

…

Meanwhile, on that day, the pastor, Fr. Jozo Zovko, and his chaplain, Fr. Zrinko Čuvalo, were at the first meeting with government officials in Čitluk, during which it was revealed that both the authorities and Fr. Jozo wanted people to move from Podbrdo into the church. Strangely, although they had opposite attitudes and interests, both the priests and the communists really didn't want people to gather up on the hill, but rather to stay in the church. Fr. Čuvalo described that meeting to Fr. Svetozar Kraljević:

"The government officials from Čitluk wanted to warn us that a lot of people were gathering up there on the hill," he began. "That, politically, it was becoming very dangerous; that various elements were coming there; that anything might happen; that it might bring harm to the region and to the people and that it should be stopped as soon as possible. In short, it ended with their plea: 'Look, if they want to go to the church, if they are in the church, we wouldn't mind them never coming out of it.' Then, we priests said that we had nothing against them being in the church, for if there is anything religious about it, it shall remain and end as such. However, when Mass was to be celebrated in the church the next day, they came and asked for the Mass to be cancelled. The Mass became an even bigger problem for them than the hill itself."

Fr. Zrinko also noted that the communists wanted to prohibit celebrating Mass in the evening, explaining that Masses are celebrated in the morning. But, he responded that Jesus did not celebrate the last breakfast, but rather the Last Supper!

The government authorities didn't talk to the friars about the medical examination performed on the children or about their health.

"We didn't bring the subject up at all, but only set forth our difficulties and tried to assure them somehow that they had nothing to be afraid of since we bore the brunt, rather than them," Fr. Zrinko related. "We tried to assure them that the matter was purely religious, one which might have bad effects only on the faith. I said plainly, 'What negative could there be for you in all this? Should there be anything negative, it will only befall us. We will sully the honor of the Church and the parish priest and not that of the sociopolitical organizations. Therefore, we are more upset and concerned about this matter than you are and, therefore, we are going to inquire into this matter, for we do not know what it is about.'"

Fr. Zrinko described that the basic difference between them and the communists was that the communists did not allow for the possibility of revelation or supernatural intervention, whereas the friars believed the possibility existed.

"We refuted their 'Church teaching' of 'no miracles after Jesus,'" Fr. Zrinko said. "We said that there have always been and that there will always be miracles. 'But,' we said, 'we don't know what this is. We'll see.' We told them to open their eyes and see what the children are like, to examine the children; the experts will examine the children to determine whether they are hereditarily encumbered, whether they are sick, whether they are drugged—which is not excluded—whether they are being manipulated. I also asked—I do not know whether directly or indirectly—this question: 'Does the state security service have any information or indication that it could be manipulation from a third party?'"

He asked for the communists' help and if that was even possible. In fact, he wanted to warn of the fear that Fr. Jozo expressed when he returned from Zagreb.

"First, I warned about the possibility of drugs because, in a conversation with one of the visionaries, I found out that they had smoked," Fr. Zrinko began. "Second, suddenly a girl from Sarajevo came. Was she unknowingly manipulated? Was she sent by someone? The latter concerned Fr. Jozo even more than the drugs. As to drugs, Dr. Vukšić told me that it was out of [the] question. I concluded: If it is not drugs, then it must be something else. I thought that the enemies of the faith had a hand in this. Well, I also wanted to warn the authorities of it so that they would also open their eyes."

Fr. Zrinko explained the motives for asking for help from the authorities. He added that they were also saying that the children should be examined in order to determine what they were really like and that they were unqualified to pass judgment on the children.

"We wanted to point out that neither we, as priests, nor they, as politicians, could judge at that exact moment whether the children were sane or not, whether they were drugged or not," the priest explained. "In this respect, we were laymen—both us and them."

Fr. Zrinko recounted an event from which one could see their attitude toward the children and all these events: One day, the visionaries' parents came in tears to the parish office and said that their children had been taken to the doctor for examination. Fr. Zrinko tried to comfort them with the words, "Do not worry about anything, they should go to the doctor."

"I was also in favor of that," he recalled. "I even told Dr. Vukšić that the children should be examined. Jure Jerkić brought the children back from the examination. I immediately asked him if the children had been examined and whether their blood and urine samples had been taken, and he replied that the children had only been examined and that the latter was not necessary. He guessed the doctors knew what they were doing. 'It is necessary,' I shouted.

First, we heard that one of the girls had brought drugs (I heard it from the authorities) and, second, that one of them—I don't know which one—was an epileptic and hysterical. I couldn't judge whether someone was ill or not; the experts needed to examine and determine this. So, I attacked Jure for not performing a complete examination."

However, Fr. Zrinko could not remember what day it was because he didn't "deal so much with the children or remember the chronology of events." Rather, he left the children to Fr. Jozo and he no longer took care of them. Then, when Fr. Zrinko needed to talk or listen to them, he would bring them in and say, "Here they are, Jozo, listen to them." He talked to them only occasionally to entertain them and to assist Fr. Jozo, although this was very rare.

"So, at the meeting in Čitluk, you didn't ask them to take the children for an examination?" Fr. Svetozar Kraljević clarified. "You just recommended something like that?"

"I did not recommend that, but I—if you will—expressed our wish that the children should be examined," Fr. Zrinko answered. "I said, 'Whether the children are normal or not, what makes these children problematic, and what this is all about—we laymen cannot decide; neither we priests nor you politicians, but experts and doctors. And we will take care of that.' That is why we asked them to leave the children to us—to make it comfortable, not rude. Fr. Jozo told them nicely that the children should be treated carefully [but] their police methods produced the opposite effect with them: The children shut down and no results can be obtained. He wanted to say that rudeness should not be used, but that everything should be done in a nice way, and to summarize everything we requested: 'Leave the children to us because we will be more rigorous in our research and in our view on this appearance. We will surely be stricter in this than you.'"

Fr. Zrinko added that, regarding a common fear of manipulation, they said to the policemen, "This is your job. You open your eyes to it; you are paid for it. And let us do our job."

That was the entirety of the meeting, which lasted about two and a half hours. The municipal authorities listened to them carefully, and their impression was that the priests were not enthusiastic about it, did not approve it *á priori*, and did not claim that it was really Our Lady's apparition. The authorities also accepted their misgivings and fears (drugs, manipulations, and illnesses) as their conviction. So, the next day at local community meetings, they said, "Fr. Zrinko said, Fr. Umberto said, Fr. Ante said, 'The children are sick, the children are on drugs, the children are lying, the children are being manipulated, etc.'"

"Therefore, what we said it could have been—drugs, manipulation, lies, etc.—they accepted as our final judgment," Fr. Zrinko said. "We mentioned this as a possibility and we demanded that we all had to be calm; that we all should position ourselves as educators; that we should comb through it all, find out what it was about and then act—and not to hit the wrong nail or be reckless. We used to say that one should first understand the nature of things, then make judgment and take measures. Until then, we should leave the children alone, let the people go, and act without tension and trouble. But, behold, they got the impression: The friars do not see anything there."

In fact, the authorities actually wanted to give the impression that the friars were not enthusiastic about the apparition; that they did't see anything there; and that, as such, they would easily get on with everything.

"Later, because of the incorrect understanding of our attitudes, they kept saying, 'Fr Jozo deceived us. Fr. Jozo deceived us,'" Fr. Zrinko said, describing the tensions between the priests and the authorities, which were not at all easy or pleasant for a priest at that time in the communist environment. "The authorities actually elected to take just what suited them from our statements in that meeting. They didn't even pay attention to the fact that the apparitions were possible and that we allowed the possibility that what was allegedly happening in Medjugorje might have been true. They adopted that curious standpoint, claiming it as a teaching: 'No miracles after Jesus.' Fr. Jozo had been giving them a lesson in catechism on the matter for at least 45 minutes. Finally, one of the officials cut him short and replied with a blasphemy, adding sharply, 'We have had enough of catechism. We haven't come here for you to give us a lesson in Church teaching. We have come here to reach an agreement with you.' Then, I interposed, 'What can we agree upon? We aren't gods to tell God what to do. If it is from God, neither you, nor we—nobody—will be able to prevent what is happening. If it comes from the devil, it will only fall on our heads and then you will have nothing to be afraid of, for you can cheer for joy over our dilemma.' This was exactly what I told them."

Fr. Zrinko added that, in this meeting and all the meetings that followed, events began to take "strange turns" that always surprised them.

"Actually, it seemed that we were all actors—the SUP [Secretariat for Internal Affairs], the municipality, the sociopolitical organizations, and those of us who were priests—and that we all somehow acted against our plan, our desires, and our point of view," Fr. Zrinko said. "Everything went differently, and what is so interesting is that it tended to do so all the time. It seemed that everything was somehow acting contrary to our plans, wishes, and attitudes. Not only that meeting, but all the meetings which followed and all those events. I once told the government officials that we were all harnessed to the cart we had to tow; someone is a donkey, someone is a horse, and someone is a coachman."

"It seems that all of you, in a certain way, were only in service to all those events?" Fr. Svetozar Kraljević asked.

"It simply looked as though we were all being duped—all of us," Fr. Zrinko replied. "For the first few days, everybody seemed—in some way or another—to have accepted or at least allowed for the possibility except for us, the parish priests. Dragica, Marinko's wife, finally came and fired away at me. She told me to my face and with much honesty that everybody was up there—from the police to the mayor, doctors, priests, friars, the bishop's secretary, and all sorts of people. She asked pointedly, 'Only you are holding back. You, who should be first! No sign of you. Shame on you! What are you here for, anyway? You unbeliever! You should be chased away!' I only patted her on the shoulders and said, 'Dragica, calm down, you will see one day and you will know, too, why we had to be the last.'"

Fr. Zrinko added that, for the first few days, everybody seemed—in some way or another—to have accepted or at least allowed for the possibility that it was real. On the other hand, it seemed that the local priests of the parish appeared to be absolutely against the visions and were even ignoring the events as much as possible.

In the meantime, Fr. Jozo was trying to get to the heart of everything that was going on and the children were the most important source of information for him, so that's why he decided to talk to them. That day, he had individual conversations with them, which he recorded. After Ivanka, he spoke with Mirjana Dragičević, who told him after her arrival that she had met some friars who were not from the parish. They had attacked the children saying that the children did not see Our Lady, that they had lied, that nothing they said was true, and that it could not be Our Lady because she "did not speak for herself" until the children questioned her. However, Fr. Jozo wanted the same thing from Mirjana as he did from Ivanka, and that was to formulate questions to ask Our Lady.

"Here, ask her this today," he began. "Do you want me to write a question for you?"

"No need, I'll remember," Mirjana said. "I should ask Our Lady if she cannot do a miracle on her own, to ask God to help her?"

Fr. Jozo asked the girl if Marinko had told them this, which Mirjana confirmed. Mirjana then told him what the examination at the Mostar hospital was like.

"If I had stayed there for just another half hour, I would have gone crazy," she admitted. "All kinds of lunatics were walking, shouting."

"Were those people alive?"

"Well, yes."

"For God's sake!"

"And, you know what else?" she said. "As we were waiting for our parents—who went there to talk—to come out of the hospital, a nurse came and asked me to go with her and to talk to the nurses. That was so moving. I came in and fifty of them gathered. Nurses or doctors, I don't know what they were. I was talking and they were all crying. I begged to stay longer, but their director came in and I had to leave."

Fr. Jozo was again interested in what those priests had told her.

"They told us not to go to the hill, but to come to church," Mirjana said. "Our Lady told us to go up the hill."

"She said that?"

"Yes, she always tells us in the same spot."

"I thought that, when you saw the light, that this was why you went up the hill, and not because she told you to go up the hill?" Fr. Jozo said.

"No, she always tells us [to come to] the same place," Mirjana recounted, sharing the same event that Ivanka had mentioned previously. "Even this morning, when you left, we climbed the hill. The people from the fields saw the light on the hill."

"And, you didn't see it?"

"I just finished eating when they came for us and we ran up the hill," she explained. "We prayed and she did not come to us."

Fr. Jozo wondered if she had ever before "cheated on them in such a way that she did not come."

"Last night, was she there?" he asked.

"Yes, she was," Mirjana answered.

"What do you think, will she be there tonight?"

Mirjana replied that she surely would because Our Lady announced this to them during the farewell.

"Today, I will also ask how many days she will stay with us," the girl stated. "Just to tell us how many days she can stay with us because this is the seventh evening tonight."

Mirjana explained that everything that was happening was touching, especially being in contact with some people who couldn't hide their emotions and compassion in meeting with them.

"Then, you are extremely popular," Fr. Jozo joked.

"But, it bothers us," Mirjana confided, describing how they had climbed the hill that morning when people saw the light. "We would prefer it if there was no one else there. Today, when we climbed the hill, it was just us and some women. If she had appeared, it would have been much nicer. Just us, without many people, with no one swearing."

"Maybe the people even help you to see her better," Fr. Jozo suggested, as if he wanted to attribute what was happening during the apparition to the people—to the throng and to the mass effect. "The tension that the people create and the like..."

"We heard some swearing while we were waiting," Mirjana complained about the people around them, paying no attention to Fr. Jozo's intention. "They were really rude. They said, 'The first part [of the drama] was held, now the second is about to start.' So, really…"

"People have started to despise and reject you because you don't give them anything, no sign," Fr. Jozo warned. "And, they keep coming, more and more? How will you justify yourselves before the people? God severely punishes those who deceive the people. Are you familiar with that?"

"Yes, I am," Mirjana replied briefly and, at that moment, the sound of the church bells ringing can be heard on the recording, most likely for the noon Angelus prayer.

"How are you going to deal with this, tell me, please?" Fr. Jozo continued as the bells rang in the background.

"What can I do about it when I see her and they do not see her?" Mirjana defended herself.

Fr. Jozo wanted to know her thoughts on how many more days they would see her.

"Something keeps telling me that she'll appear for another two, three days," the girl replied. "I was just thinking about that, as if she's telling me so. In the evening, when I lie down, I think like that. And Vicka, while sleeping, she's saying in her dream, 'Leave some sign, leave some sign!' Her cousin said so. They didn't sleep all night because of her. She scared them."

"And, tell me, did you pray last night? You didn't?" Fr. Jozo asked.

"I did. Until 11:00 p.m., we were sitting and singing the holy songs," Mirjana replied.

The priest asked her for an example of what she had prayed that morning.

"This morning, I prayed 'Our Father,' 'Hail Mary,' and 'Glory Be.'"

"Has Our Lady taught you to pray anything else?"

"We learned to sing all these songs by heart. We learned the entire 'Hear us Mother, Our Hope' because we had only known the first stanza before," Mirjana shared. "We have learned 'How Beautiful You Are.' We have learned everything."

Then, Fr. Jozo asked—almost pleading—what would happen to the people who were coming in increasing numbers.

"Oh, my people [Oh, my God], what shall we do with the people, you tell me?! I am tormented by that," he said.

"First, let's ask Our Lady what she would do," Mirjana replied. "It all depends on her. If she would say…"

But, Fr. Jozo interrupted her, "Did you ask Marinko what should be said to the people?"

"Marinko said that we should tell the people that Our Lady said that they should no longer come, that she would no longer be coming," Mirjana said, before Fr. Jozo interrupted her again.

"And, that's what you're going to say today?"

"Not that she will no longer come," Mirjana told him. "I do not know how to say it, that people will no longer come. Then, the people would come."

"They wouldn't," Fr. Jozo responded decisively.

"Let's just say that she said the people should no longer come?" Mirjana said. "If she agrees…"

"Who?"

"Our Lady."

"Well, there is nothing for her to agree about. If you agree, ha?"

Then, Mirjana said that they "don't need the people" and that they are "just disturbed by them."

"You are disturbed by the people because one of them takes a photo of you, afterwards the other one talks to you, the one does this, the other does that," he said, alluding to their sudden popularity among the people.

"We don't care for it," Mirjana admitted. "But, [we just want] to talk normally to Our Lady, to go back home and that's it."

"What else did Marinko think should be said to the people?"

"Last night, he said the people were not behaving nicely," Mirjana related. "When we go out, everyone is pushing us."

"Do you feel that this is exactly the sign that it is not Our Lady?"

"No, but everyone wants to hear," she explained.

"I know, but if they swear, it cannot be Our Lady when they swear," Fr. Jozo persisted in disputing what was going on in those moments on the hill.

"There have always been unbelievers," Mirjana replied briefly.

"How you imagine this, I don't know," Fr. Jozo warned. "That's a big problem, you know? I know that those who tricked the people or delivered false messages were chastised harshly. Among the Israelites, in the early Church, they were excluded from the community. God rebuked them severely. Are you afraid of anything like that? I'm terribly afraid of that."

"I'm not," Mirjana replied confidently.

"I know, but what if God punishes the five, the six of you tomorrow…" he said.

"I don't think He will."

"Why do you think He won't?"

"Because we are not lying," Mirjana said, determined.

"I know, if you're not lying, then He can't," Fr. Jozo said. "But, if it seems to you, and the message is not for all the people, then... Look, you can have it, but if she doesn't tell us anything and doesn't tell the people, you shouldn't have made it public, you understand. What should be done here?"

"I don't know, the cars from Belgrade, Makarska...who told them all of it? We only told our people in the village, and no one else," Mirjana explained to him how word of the apparitions spread because the news was conveyed from one person to another with incredible speed.

"Why did you speak?" Fr. Jozo wondered.

"You know, when you are pleased with something and you have to share it with someone," Mirjana explained.

Fr. Jozo then turned his questions in another direction and asked Mirjana if she slept "alone or with Iva [Ivanka, in a room]."

"No, I sleep with my cousin," Mirjana said.

"I can't imagine that you can't see her in the room, ha?"

"I don't see her in the room," Mirjana replied calmly.

"Let's say, when you kneel down and pray, and you can't see her. I can't imagine why or how that is?"

"I can't see her."

Next, Fr. Jozo wanted to know why she hadn't brought her cousins with her to the apparition.

"They do go," Mirjana said.

"Do they see her?"

"No."

The priest was interested in why they couldn't see her.

"I don't know," Mirjana responded honestly. "Well, she can't appear to everyone."

"Why can't she?" Fr. Jozo persisted. "You said that it would be the nicest sign if she appeared to everyone. Why couldn't she appear to your cousin, too?"

"I don't know."

"Why did she appear to you, and not to her?" the priest continued. "Do you think you're better than her?"

"Well, no, but I don't know. Such was a choice," Mirjana replied, but he nevertheless persisted and asked her if it occurred to her that she was better than others.

"No, I'm like everyone else," she replied humbly.

"I know, but how is it that Our Lady appears to some people and not to others?" Fr. Jozo continued his focus. "Do you think that you should be different from others now?"

"I should have become even better, believe even more," Mirjana told him.

"Do you feel you have?"

"I do feel. Faith is..." she began, before he interrupted her.

"What does your faith make you do, please, sincerely and friendly?"

"I simply want to do good deeds."

"And, what would these good deeds consist of?"

"I'd like to help everyone wherever I can. Whoever would ask me, I would do," she replied.

"Go on," Fr. Jozo prompted her for a more detailed answer, but Mirjana was silent.

"Do you feel sorry for the people when they don't see Our Lady and you do?" Fr. Jozo asked, breaking the silence with a new question.

"I do," she confided. "I want everybody to see her. The people agonize, they climb up the hill barefoot. Some even walk for six hours to be there. Wouldn't it be nice if she appeared to them, too?"

"Nice," he agreed. "But, do you sense, when Our Lady will not appear and become visible, did you pray for this intention, did you fast or do anything today to ask God for Our Lady to appear or to perform some kind of miracle—let's say, to heal someone? Were you sure last night that the child would be healed?"

"She looked at him for two to three minutes with an expression of compassion with a firm faith that he would be healed," Mirjana replied.

"Why wasn't he healed?" Fr. Jozo asked, wanting to know why the healing of Danijel Šetka did not happen immediately and in front of everybody.

"Well, not immediately," Mirjana responded.

Then, Fr. Jozo asked when she thought the little boy would be healed.

"She said let them believe strongly that he would get well," Mirjana said, which caused Fr. Jozo to wonder how the little boy should believe.

"Let them believe strongly that he will get well," Mirjana repeated, interpreting the words she heard Our Lady speak. "I think that this refers to him and his parents."

"And, what do you think, will that boy ever get well?"

"I think that he will because she looked at him in such a way."

"And, when could he get well?"

"In a year, I think so..." Mirjana replied.

Next, Fr. Jozo asked her where the boy was from and Mirjana answered that his name was Danijel Šetka because his father had told them so.

"The little boy is called Danijel. And, how old is he? Is he Jakov's age?" Fr. Jozo continued, trying to get additional details.

"He's younger. I think that he is four years old," Mirjana estimated.

Fr. Jozo wanted to know if even little Danijel was on the hill.

"Yes, he was," Mirjana told him. "His dad found us. We were sitting in a room and he asked us for our addresses to send us some gifts. We said that he should just believe in God even more, and we didn't need anything."

"What do you think, will some healing take place up there today?" Fr. Jozo went on.

Mirjana replied that she didn't know, and that people shouldn't demand only miracles from Our Lady, but that "one must also pray."

Fr. Jozo then asked her if she would have liked to have prayed the rosary on the hill yesterday, to which Mirjana said that she would, and that she would also like people to pray with them.

"Tonight, invite the people to church. Okay?" Fr. Jozo said, reinitiating his favorite subject of the day.

"Not to go to the hill?" Mirjana clarified.

"I don't know," he responded. "Do you feel that people don't need to go up the hill anymore?"

Mirjana told him that she thought that "it would be the same in the church or on the hill," although she preferred to go to the hill because it was "a little harder, like some kind of a vow." But, "if we need to, we can go to church. The church is the temple of God."

"Absolutely, but this is what I'm interested in, Mirjana," the priest began, suspiciously. "If Our Lady does not appear in the church, can you oblige her to appear to you in the church? Maybe you can, right? What do you think about that?"

To this, Mirjana said that she didn't know because they hadn't thought about it until now. Fr. Jozo seemed to be persuading her and said that she could "oblige" Our Lady to appear to them in the church. Because, as he said, everything would be easier in the church than on the hill because there were loudspeakers and a sound system, so people could hear better.

Mirjana shared that some people had promised to bring loudspeakers to the hill, but that has not yet happened. At this point, there is a short pause in their conversation, after which Mirjana's voice is heard.

"We are not afraid now, just so they do not take us to a hospital," she said.

"Aha, you are afraid of the hospital?"

"Yes, because I would really go crazy there," she began. "One man was marching around like a soldier and the morgue smelled horrible. You can imagine when Marija, the skinniest one, she didn't dare to lean on a tree, but first she put on a handkerchief and then leaned. You can imagine how scared she was, poor girl."

Fr. Jozo brought her back to the main topic of the conversation, which was the possibility of holding apparitions in the church, which he strongly supported.

"Oh, my God…And, tell me, will you invite people to church?" he asked. "Will you go up the hill then? "

"How will I invite people to church when, at 3 p.m., they are already climbing the hill? I think some have already left," Mirjana explained, to which Fr. Jozo assured her that no one had gone to the hill yet.

"They did. Seriously, Reverend."

"Now? At noon?"

"Yeah," she replied. "We ask them how long they've been there, and they say that some of them have been there since 1 p.m. or 2 p.m. just to get to the best spot. We can only climb the hill and then tell the people. We will go earlier and then tell the people."

"Namely, people will go down anyway, right?" the priest clarified. "You will wait down there for a while and then say 'Let's go to church.'"

"I'd rather say..." Mirjana began, but Fr. Jozo kept talking.

"And then, you would set out with the people toward here, and then you would pray here," he said. "Then, at church, you would ask Our Lady..."

"If she showed up, we would ask her," Mirjana interrupted in a serious tone.

"If she doesn't show up, what shall we do with the questions?" Fr. Jozo asked.

Mirjana replied that she didn't know and that she thought "that there is little chance of her appearing in church."

"Why? Jesus is there and her statue, too."

"I heard that Our Lady appeared in the church, as well, but no one saw her," Mirjana replied.

"Who did you hear that from?"

"I read a story," she said.

"She does show up at church, why not? I think there is no problem here," Fr. Jozo assured her.

Next, Mirjana asked him if he would like the visionaries to tell people to go to church.

"I would like the believers to come to the church and to pray to God in the church," he said.

"That would be better because then the police would not chase us, either," Mirjana said.

"Not only that, but we would pray to God for Our Lady to come and leave a sign, because God says pray and you will be given," Fr. Jozo said. "God says that we [should] believe and persevere in our heart and everything we ask will be given to us. So, we need to persevere in prayer and firmly believe and we will receive. So, we're going to pray, right? How are you going to do it today, tell me?"

Mirjana explained that they would climb the hill around 6 p.m. and that "all the people will already be up there," so they would ask people to come with them and pray in the church.

"But, let only Christians—true believers—come to church with us," Mirjana added.

"We will not wait until 6:30 p.m., right?" Fr. Jozo clarified, and Mirjana agreed.

"Great," he said.

Mirjana replied that they should agree with Marinko Ivanković about that beforehand because he had helped them a lot with everything.

"What if Marinko doesn't agree with this?" the priest asked. "Because it would be important to say a rosary in the church. That all the people pray and not swear. And, if Marinko disagrees, you will obey Marinko, will you?"

"I don't know, we should discuss that," she said. "Marinko arrives around 3 p.m. and if he doesn't agree and if he thinks differently, then we will come here to you."

Fr. Jozo told her to come with Marinko later and let him bring them by car so they would see each other together.

That day, Fr. Jozo had marathon conversations with the visionaries and, after Mirjana, an interview with Vicka ensued. As soon as she entered the room where they were talking, Fr. Jozo asked her if they had agreed about what they would say to Our Lady today.

"We didn't," she replied. "There are some questions…"

Vicka tried to tell him, but Fr. Jozo wanted to know what they discussed with Marinko, so Vicka explained that Marinko had instructed them to ask Our Lady if she had the power to leave a sign so that people would believe the visionaries—that she really had been appearing to them—because that was a growing problem for them day by day.

"If she cannot, let the Savior Jesus help her. So, we'll ask," Vicka said.

"And, what else do you have to ask her today?" Fr. Jozo asked.

Vicka repeated that she would ask Our Lady if she would leave them a sign and how many days she would be with them.

"We will find five or six questions, which I will ask," Vicka said.

Then, Fr. Jozo wanted to know if she was the one who asked Our Lady all the questions; if she asked questions on behalf of all the visionaries.

"I will not ask all the questions," Vicka said, adding that she would ask only what she herself was interested in.

"Did you ask anything last night?"

"I did."

"And, she didn't reply to you?"

"No, she didn't."

Fr. Jozo then asked if it was a problem for her because she didn't answer her.

"It was. She didn't answer me; what can I do?"

"It means you didn't see her then, my Vicka?" Fr. Jozo questioned, suspiciously.

Vicka told him that she asked her first question and that Our Lady did answer her.

"I asked her the second question, then she didn't [answer]," she clarified. "As if she was hesitating. Somehow, she starts, I can see that she is answering, but…"

Fr. Jozo wanted to know what her question was.

"What does she desire here in this place?" Vicka replied.

"And she didn't know how to answer?" Fr. Jozo wondered.

"She didn't know."

"What kind of Our Lady is it who doesn't know? Then, she is less than a child!" he replied sarcastically.

But Vicka explained to him that Our Lady started answering her question and they wanted to hear what she was saying, but people suddenly pushed them and the children fell.

"And I didn't remember to ask her that question again," Vicka explained.

"What did she start to say, please?" Fr. Jozo wanted to know every detail.

"She started saying, 'Angels…' Because, from below, all the people pushed us and bowled us over. Later, I remembered to repeat the question because I was sure she would start telling me again."

"Vicka, last night you were willing to not go up the hill, right?"

"No. I immediately said I'd go."

"Why didn't you come to pray to God on Sunday?" Fr. Jozo asked, obviously referring to the afternoon prayer in the church.

"On Sunday? I couldn't come because we came home at 2:15 p.m. and my two sisters came…" Vicka began, justifying herself.

"Why don't you bring your sisters to see her, too?" Fr. Jozo interrupted again.

Vicka told him that she had taken them, as well as another cousin, and one of them told her that "it was as if something were walking on her back."

"And one of the sisters said, 'I'll be behind you tonight, but I've seen the stars and the cloud and everything, but I won't say it until I'm sure.' Ankica told us so," Vicka narrated.

"So, she wants to say that so as not to be as uncertain as you were?" Fr. Jozo asked.

"Normally, we are not uncertain. We are really certain! We know what we're talking about," the girl stood firm. In the group, she constantly stood out for her boldness.

"When you haven't yet figured out what you will say to the people, the people come up there and you have not yet agreed," Fr. Jozo stated. "That's a torment now. People get angry, you know. What are you going to say to the people today? You are brave, you speak the strongest. I wonder, what are you going to say to the people today?"

Vicka told him that she would tell the people "let no one come anymore."

"What will you tell them if they need to come?" he asked her.

"If they really need to come, let the people come," she said. "We will nicely ask Our Lady if we—and if she—can do it without the people. It would all have been different, they brought a cassette player and listened to music, and later they took the tape to record. What believers they are!"

Fr. Jozo also asked if she would invite the people to come to church to pray today.

"Well, I don't know that," she admitted.

"So we could pray the rosary...Do you think that's smart? Our Lady would like that, wouldn't she?"

"I don't think so. I don't know, we can come, but..." Vicka began.

Then, Fr. Jozo asked if Our Lady "doesn't love when people pray."

"She does, she does. I didn't say anything [like that]," Vicka defended herself.

"But?"

"She loves both when we pray and when we sing," she explained.

"Why don't you want us to come to church?" Fr. Jozo inquired.

"Something is drawing me to go up there more," she replied. "In the church, I pray to God and everything, but I have a special experience [there]."

"No, but when it's over up there, then we continue to pray to God here," he interrupted.

"And, what about up there?" she asked. "Then, why would she be up there on Podbrdo?"

"Yes, so that we continue to pray to God here," Fr. Jozo tried to explain his plan to her. However, the plan was not entirely clear, except for his clear desire for people to come to church and stop going to the hill.

"Oh, yes, I agree," she responded. "Because I thought that, as soon as people came up there, to go to church from there, to go to church immediately. I wouldn't agree with that."

"Let the apparition begin at six o'clock, and then after that..." Fr. Jozo began.

"But, last night, it started in a split second," Vicka interrupted.

"What started?"

"She came in a split second."

Then, Fr. Jozo wondered if Vicka had been dressed during the apparition as she was now before him.

"Like this? I wasn't [dressed] like this."

The priest then asked what she did "have on up there," or what was she wearing.

"Some shirt, T-shirt," Vicka replied.

"Are you properly dressed?"

"Sometimes I am, sometimes I'm not," she admitted. "I really don't look at what I'm going to wear."

Vicka was sincere, acknowledging that, as the time of the apparition approaches, it is only important to arrive at the agreed upon location on Podbrdo as soon as possible to meet with Our Lady.

Fr. Jozo then turned the conversation toward the popularity that the children had acquired in just a few days.

"Now, you have become popular in the village, the most popular," he said. "Everyone is talking about you in Herzegovina and everywhere. Everyone wants to see you."

"We were asked by that friar from Čapljina when we would come to Čapljina," Vicka shared. "I told him I had no idea when we would come. What can I do"

"Why would you go to Čapljina?"

"I don't know," she replied. "He said he would like us to come to him [to his parish]. The nuns asked us to tell them the day, and I didn't say anything, since I don't know. To say and then to lie, I won't."

Next, Fr. Jozo asked her when she thought the apparitions would cease.

"I think if we said we wouldn't be coming again, if she left us an exact sign, it would stop," Vicka opined. "And we won't say that until she leaves us something so that we would not lead such a crowd behind us, as they say, by the nose . We will not! Because when we're on the right path, let's show it. Let's show them that we're not lying."

Vicka was determined to prove that the children had not invented what was happening to them.

"And what does Jesus say: Pray and believe firmly, and it will be given to you," Fr. Jozo said.

"Normally," she agreed. "And no one can force you to go anywhere and you will succeed with everything. And no one can do anything to you, as we know that no one can. We are not afraid of anything."

"You never invited me up the hill so far?"

"When we went, we thought you would come with Fr. Zrinko," Vicka responded. "When he came, we asked him where Fr. Jozo was, and he said, 'He is praying in the church.'"

. . .

The children understood the pastor of Medjugorje, who wanted people to come to pray in the church and to stop going to the hill. Similarly, at the end of her conversation with Fr. Jozo, visionary Mirjana also testified that he was concerned that "so many people were going to the hill—which the pilgrims now call Apparition Hill—instead of praying in the church of St. James."

"The increasing police presence also concerned him," Mirjana reported. "The government prohibited large gatherings and the crowds grew every day. Fr. Jozo wanted us to come to the church at the time of the apparitions and to invite the faithful there. It sounded safer and more comfortable than dealing with the crowds, police, and oppressive heat on the hill every afternoon, but would Our Lady appear to us in a different place?"

Mirjana shared that, shortly after the meeting with Fr. Jozo, they were approached by two women named Mica and Ljubica, who identified themselves as social workers.

"I had never seen Ljubica before, but I recognized Mica," Mirjana said. "She lived in Bijakovići at the base of the hill and had been present during at least one of the apparitions."

Mirjana also noted that Mica told them with urgency that "the secret police were planning to come for them," and Ljubica added that "they had orders from Belgrade."

The children told the women that they would lock themselves in their rooms and not come out, but Ljubica asked if they really thought they could hide from the secret police in their rooms. That's why the women suggested they go off somewhere with them outside of Medjugorje—on an excursion. Ljubica suggested they go to nearby Čapljina to get some ice cream, which caused Jakov's eyes to widen. The children just couldn't imagine that the two social workers wanted to take them away from Medjugorje so they wouldn't be back in time for the apparition.

"Vicka knew and trusted Mica, so I felt comfortable about her, but I was a little skeptical of Ljubica," Mirjana continued. "Still, the thought of the Internal Secret Police coming for me sent chills through my body. They were like the gestapo of the Yugoslav government, notorious for violent interrogations, beatings, and even executions. The crowds were growing exponentially so it was not far-fetched to think that they would soon intervene. After quickly discussing it amongst ourselves, the five of us piled into the back seat of Mica's car. Ivan was not with us that day. As we were leaving

Bijakovići, however, the local police commander, Zdravko, waved us down. We rolled to a stop and he came to our window. Peering into the back seat, he seemed both surprised and concerned to see us."

"Mica," he said. "What's going on here?"

"We're in a hurry," said Mica.

"I need to ask you something, Mica," Zdravko spoke in a hushed, but stern tone.

Mica looked out at all the people streaming into the village. Some of them had stopped to gawk at the children in the car.

"Crowds will form around the children if we stay here," Mica said to Zdravko.

"Mica, wait just a minute," he replied.

"We can't wait," she said, as more onlookers stopped near the car.

Zdravko looked at them, and then back at the children.

"All right," he said, and he got into his car and followed them.

They soon came to a *milicija* car parked sideways to prevent anyone from driving into the village—or, in their case, out of it. Several policemen stood near the car. They stared at them, seemingly confused about what they should do.

"Move! We're in a hurry," Mica yelled out the window. Her assertiveness surprised the children, but the policemen stayed put—that is, until they saw Zdravko pull up behind them in his car. Thinking he was with them, they quickly moved their car out of the way.

"We waved at the confused policemen as we drove past the checkpoint, and Mica sped away fast enough to lose Zdravko," Mirjana remembered. "Soon, we were zooming down the road, windows open, savoring the wind in our hair, and laughing. Our first stop was Počitelj, an ancient, walled city with a historic mosque and the crumbling remnants of a medieval fortress. As we climbed the stone walls and explored the ruins, our worries disappeared. I gazed at the emerald-colored Neretva River that flowed through the valley below Počitelj. The moving water made me think of all the pilgrims streaming into Medjugorje. Like the mighty Neretva, it seemed like nothing could stop them. After Počitelj, we drove to Čapljina, one of the larger and more modern towns in the local area. Mica and Ljubica took us to a café. I had been to cafés before in Sarajevo, but it was a novelty for the others."

"Do they have juice in bottles?" asked Jakov.

"Of course they do," Mica replied with a smile, and the rest of the children also laughed.

Mica and Ljubica ordered them cake and ice cream, and juice in bottles, of course. They sat there eating and talking until a young man approached them.

"Are you from Medjugorje?" he asked.

"Where's Medjugorje?" Mica said, but the young man looked at Jakov.

"But, I recognize some of you. Aren't you the ones who see Our Lady? I was there on the hill last night," the young man said, looking at them one by one.

Ljubica said that they did not know him, but the young man looked at Mirjana's wrist and asked her where her watch was.

"Don't you remember how I asked to see it?" he asked Mirjana, who told him that perhaps he did, but there was no watch on her wrist because the police had taken it from her after word spread about how it had changed.

"They never gave it back to me, but later I heard that the police took it to a watchmaker who examined it and said it was impossible for the watch to have changed like that and still be working," Mirjana narrated.

Meanwhile, other people in the café overheard the young man and soon everyone was watching the children. An older woman came up and asked if they were going to be "up there on the hill" today. Eventually, the attention became too much and they had to leave.

"I realized then that my privacy was a thing of the past," Mirjana wrote. "Even people who lived outside of Medjugorje were treating me differently and looking at me as if I were some kind of holy person when, in truth, I was the same girl I had always been."

After leaving the café, the children's next destination was Kravice, a magnificent waterfall on the Trebižat River.

"On the way there, we expressed our worry that we would not make it back to Medjugorje in time for the apparition, which had been taking place at around 6:40 p.m. every day," Mirjana remembered. "Mica and Ljubica assured us that we needn't worry. When we reached Kravice, we were so captivated by the torrent of water, lush foliage, and cool mist in the air that we stopped paying attention to the time altogether. I did not have my watch, anyway. It was not until the sun descended below the trees and shade filled the river valley that we suddenly realized how late it had gotten. We implored Mica and Ljubica to take us back to Medjugorje. They finally agreed, although it seemed like they drove the car slower than they had all day. It was starting to appear like Mica and Ljubica had not exactly come to save us."

As the car approached Medjugorje, the children could see Apparition Hill in the distance—as well as the immense crowd of people waiting there. They felt a tinge of guilt; they should have been there among the people, but reaching the hill in time seemed impossible. Their anxiety increased moment by moment, as it became increasingly certain that they would not arrive at the place of the daily apparitions on time.

"Just as I was about to cry, the intense anticipation I always felt before the apparition suddenly washed over me," Mirjana testified.

"Pull over," Mirjana said decisively to Mica.

"Where?" said Mica.

"Anywhere!"

Mica pulled the car off the road onto a rocky trail, and the children hopped out and knelt in a barren wasteland of karst and briars. The tranquility of the surrounding wilderness was a welcome change from the chaotic crowds to which they had become accustomed. Mica and Ljubica stood by the car and watched as they began to pray.

"Ask the Virgin what she's going to do to me for stealing you this way," joked Ljubica.

Mica laughed, but then suddenly pointed at Apparition Hill.

"Do you see that?" she said excitedly.

"My God," said Ljubica with fear in her voice. "What is that?"

"Some kind of mist," Mica said, as she made the sign of the cross.

"Or like a light," Ljubica said.

The children also looked toward the hill and saw a glowing shape in the air above all the people.

"That's her," said Vicka.

Mirjana reported that, in that moment, sadness gripped her. Our Lady and thousands of faithful pilgrims were waiting for them on the hill and they were stuck on the side of a road. How could they have let this happen? But then, the light that they saw above Podbrdo began gliding toward them in Cerno. As it approached, they could see Our Lady within it.

"She's coming!" Ivanka shouted.

"Upon reaching us, Our Lady said 'Praised be Jesus,' which had become her standard greeting," Mirjana recalled. "Thinking back on my conversation with Fr. Jozo, I realized that my question was now being answered—it *was* possible for Our Lady to appear somewhere other than the hillside. As always, her radiance and beauty rendered me momentarily speechless, but I wanted to make sure she was not disappointed."

"Are you upset that we were not on the hill?" Mirjana asked her, to which Our Lady replied that "it did not matter."

"Would you be upset if we did not return to the hill," Mirjana asked, "but instead waited for you in the church?"

Our Lady smiled in a gentle, motherly way and said, "Always at the same time."

The children asked her if she would leave a sign but, as always, she did not answer. She moved slowly away until her light was, once again, shining on all the people who had gathered on the hill.

"We heard her saying, 'Go in the peace of God,' and the light faded away," Mirjana remembered.

Mica and Ljubica took the children to the parish office and then headed with them inside to Fr. Jozo, who, at first, did not know that the children had not had the apparition on the hill—that Our Lady appeared to them in Cerno.

"Upon arriving back in Medjugorje, Fr. Jozo asked all of us—including Mica and Ljubica—to come to the rectory and tell him everything," Mirjana continued. "He was initially concerned that the people on the hill would feel deceived since we were not among them, but when we told him that Our Lady said she would appear in the church, he became joyful. He was also eager to know what Mica and Ljubica had experienced."

"The woman who worked for the Executive Council came..." he began. "She had a task. Her family name was Vasilj [one of the family names in Medjugorje]. She had betrayed her family; I didn't want to greet her. That was terrible. And they took the children away. I didn't know that. They were at their houses, and there was also Mica, who had to accompany Vasiljusha [the nickname for a woman from the Vasilj family] as a social worker because the children knew her. They went to Čapljina and, when they came back, they said, 'Imagine that, friar, everybody knows us down there! All the people know us. How lucky we are! Are you from Medjugorje? Yes, I am. Wow, everyone knows us!' It was a reaction of naivety, and simple, but humanly genuine."

Fr. Jozo continued, "As soon as she got out of the car in Cerno... Ljubica...saw the light and wanted to tell the other [Mica], but she couldn't speak. They stood petrified. Later, they couldn't even get in the car because they couldn't even drive. I am the only one to know it because they came to me to tell me that. The children told them to leave them 'at friar.' I wanted to seize the opportunity and talk to them first, so that this experience would not be lost."

The priest then asked them what happened.

"'Be silent. Don't talk. I won't do this job anymore, there is no such money [no matter how much money]. No way,' Ljubica responded to me," Fr. Jozo recalled. "And Mica said, 'I have decided to flee to Switzerland.' Ljubica returned to Sarajevo. My dear, it wasn't really...They got the sign and began respecting the children and not chasing them anymore. When the local policemen—who saw so many signs—gave up and withdrew, others were brought from Mostar, Sarajevo, Belgrade."

Again, there was a tape recorder between him and the children, with everyone talking together this time, not individually like earlier that day.

"You were the first one to see her? What did you say when you saw her?" Fr. Jozo asked Ivanka.

"I didn't say anything," Ivanka told him.

Fr. Jozo wondered if Our Lady greeted her or if Ivanka greeted Our Lady.

"We knelt down and sang," she replied.

"Mirjana, did you speak with Our Lady?" Fr. Jozo asked.

"I asked how many days she would stay with us and she said three more days," Mirjana replied. "So, it means until Friday. Was she angry that we went from Podbrdo to another place... We asked if she would be angry if we didn't go to Podbrdo anymore but to church, and she was kind of hesitant when we asked this, as if she wasn't very pleased with it, but she said she would not be angry, that she would be in the church at the same time. And she asked about Ivan, 'Where is the other boy?'"

The other boy, Ivan, was not with them at the time.

"Wait, did she say she would be at church at 6:30 p.m.?" Fr. Jozo asked.

"Yes, she said she would appear at the church at 6:30 p.m. Wednesday, Thursday, Friday," Mirjana confirmed.

"This means you will come to church tomorrow?" the priest asked.

"Yes."

"And, did you read the questions?" he asked.

"No, we didn't have them with us," Mirjana admitted. "Mica said that some investigators—the police—would be coming; that it would be better if we went to another place; that she would appear to us somewhere else. And then, in a hurry, we put on some clothes, and so the questions remained in my other pants. We ran until we got in the car and then we left. I just asked her about the church."

Ivanka added that they had asked if she would leave them a sign.

"Again, she told us, 'Go in the peace of God,'" Mirjana said.

"Did anyone explain to the people that she would be in the church tomorrow?" Fr. Jozo asked.

"No, no one did," they replied.

"Why didn't you tell the people that she would be in the church tomorrow?" Fr. Jozo wanted to know.

"But, Reverend, something pulls me up to the hill, I can't resist it anymore and I have to go up the hill," Mirjana said, explaining what she feels before the apparition begins.

"What would drag you up the hill if she had left?" he asked.

"I don't know, I just want to go up there," she responded.

"Jakov, what else did she say when she came this evening?" the priest continued. "You didn't see her when she was coming…"

"I did, everything shone like this when she was coming. Light," the boy said excitedly. "We all asked her the same—if she would come to the church."

"And, what did you say to the people?" Fr. Jozo persisted.

"Nothing, we have just arrived," Jakov said.

Fr. Jozo seemed to be losing his temper a bit and the children explained to him that they did not ask her anything on the hill because they were actually in Cerno.

"What? Weren't you up there? You were in Cerno? How could the people be here, man!?" Fr. Jozo asked in surprise.

Vicka explained that they had been told that "some investigators" would be coming and that it was best for them to leave Medjugorje, so that is how they found themselves in Cerno.

"It was around 2 p.m.," the children said to him in unison.

"They took us to some other place to see if we could still see her," Mirjana clarified.

Fr. Jozo then wondered if the apparition in that other place was the same as it had been on Podbrdo. The children told him that it was exactly the same.

"So, it would be the same if you were in Sarajevo or in Čapljina because she would find you," he stated. "Then, this is not a problem."

The children agreed and said that they would show him the exact place in nearby Cerno where Our Lady had appeared to them because they marked it. They also told him that they wanted to stop in Cerno because "their hill" could be seen from there. When asked if there were "some people" there, they said no one was there but them, Mica, and Ljubica, and that they saw the light shining on the people on Apparition Hill.

"Wait, I still don't understand that light and that with Cerno [what happened in Cerno]," Fr. Jozo said, trying to reconstruct the story in detail. He asked them who was in that "commission" that came to examine the children and, because of which, they left Medjugorje. The children said that several police cars were there and that the police commander arrived, as well.

"So, the people didn't see anything this evening?" Fr. Jozo inquired.

The children answered that they didn't know and that they guessed that the people "must have seen the light."

Then, when asked if they felt the need to say something to the people, one of the visionaries said that she felt that they should tell people that Our Lady could appear elsewhere and they should go to church.

"Go ahead, go and say it," Fr. Jozo urged her.

However, the children told him that they couldn't do it because all the people would rush to them and that they were told to go to their homes only when all the people had left—about 9 or 10 p.m., but not before—because they could be caught by "the commission" from which they had escaped.

"We need to tell Marinko, let him tell the people," little Jakov suggested.

Vicka added that, if they showed up before the people, they would not "get rid of them" until midnight. Nevertheless, Fr. Jozo insisted that someone go tell the people, but the children refused. Mirjana said that they would "suffocate" her if she went among the people, because many of them came on foot, left work early.

"If Our Lady requires you to say something to the people, then you have a duty to go," Fr. Jozo persisted. Now, he invoked the authority of Our Lady because he realized that he would not be able to persuade the children to go among the people. But, the children said that Our Lady did not explicitly ask them to do this, rather that it should only be "conveyed to the people."

"Mirjana, do you feel that this should be said to the people?" Fr. Jozo redirected his pressure toward her.

Mirjana said that she felt that the people should be told that they "no longer gather on the hill" and that Our Lady told them "to come to the church."

"As true Christians, to follow us to church," Mirjana explained.

Vicka then mentioned that they were also told by the "commission" that it would be good if they experienced the apparition in the church alone—without people—because "the people leave their work early, nobody wants to work."

"Do they speak on behalf of Our Lady or on your behalf?" Fr. Jozo asked.

"On our behalf," Vicka answered.

Fr. Jozo persisted that, if that was what Our Lady had told them, how could they deceive her?

"I don't deceive anyone," Vicka said determinedly. She said she would tell everyone she met that night and the word would go from person to person and people would come.

"They will not! They will not!" Fr. Jozo exclaimed. "Because, today, the people were not up there where you were."

Yet, the children claimed that they would. So, he asked again for support from Mirjana. She said that the people would not come because only true Christians would follow them to church and that, on the hill, there were certainly those who had come to "fake" a little and to see what Our Lady was doing, but that unbelievers would certainly not go to church.

Jakov said that they should tell someone to tell people, but Fr. Jozo insisted that the visionaries should be the ones to tell them because they were the ones who had always addressed the people so far. Yet, the children were uncomfortable because people would gather around them. But, Fr. Jozo explained to them that neither he nor anyone else couldn't get involved in this because they had not seen anything. So, the children thought about how to do it and Mirjana suggested climbing up on the concrete "patio" of Marija's house and, from there, addressing the people so that "whoever hears them, ought to hear."

"Reverend, you didn't understand us," Vicka began. "Last night, we yelled at the top of our voice from Marinko's terrace and repeated everything that Our Lady had said. We couldn't be happier because we are always cheerful, but the people didn't leave us alone until 11 p.m. We told them everything, but it was in vain. It was in vain!"

Mirjana added that they could tell them and return to the parish office again, so that people would not keep them until midnight that evening, as well. The children also told him that they thought Our Lady would prefer the apparitions be in the church, although they didn't exactly know how to verify it because she "looked at them hesitantly."

Then, in the middle of the conversation, one of the visionaries went out from the parish house and immediately came back in saying that there were so many people out there. In fact, the children thought they would not be able to pass, and that the only thing they could do was to "run to their houses." But, the others were not in favor of it because not everyone could run that far. And, while Fr. Jozo assured them that the people would not recognize them, the children claimed the opposite—that they were already recognized and stopped everywhere. As people were passing by, they looked through the window and suggested that they could talk to them from the parish house and tell them that Our Lady would appear to them tomorrow at 6:30 p.m. in the church. But, Fr. Jozo wanted to know whether people would believe them. The children assured him that the information would be spread among the people.

"As it first spread among the people, I think it will continue to be the same now," Vicka said, adding that it didn't matter if there weren't any people in the church; there would be six of them at the apparition and they would actually prefer not to have anyone there and to be alone with Our Lady.

"Does she appear for you or for the people?" Fr. Jozo asked.

The children responded that they thought it was for them because she could have found someone else, but she had just found them. Mirjana and Vicka said they thought it was both for them and for the people, and then Jakov, Marija, and Ivanka agreed.

The conversation then went back to whether and how to tell people to come to church the next day. The visionaries said that, now, people must have thought that someone had taken them somewhere, and that the people might even get angry because it was said that the children could have been taken to psychiatry at the hospital.

"Let's not say anything, so we'll see tomorrow if people come spontaneously to the church," Fr. Jozo suggested, and the children said they could try it.

At that moment, Mica and Ljubica entered the room.

"Go ahead, sit down," Fr. Jozo said. "Don't be afraid of anything. What's your name?"

"Mirjana, Mica," Mica introduced herself. "Well, I'm not afraid."

"I'm Ljubica," the other woman said. "We've been with them all afternoon, since 3 p.m. We went to cafes in Počitelj, in Čapljina, Trebižat..."

"Ivan was not with you?" the priest asked.

"No, he wasn't," Ljubica replied. "We were at the waterfall on Kravica and, at 6:10 p.m., we left from there and stopped in Cerno."

Next, Fr. Jozo asked where they had lunch, to which they said that they didn't. Rather, they ate ice cream and pastries in Čapljina, where they were recognized and people asked if they were from Medjugorje. In Cerno, they reported that they stopped the car "in a bramble" and watched people on Podbrdo. The children were still with them, and the two women said neither of them saw nor heard anything.

"They asked two or three questions independently of us," Mica shared. "When I asked them if the Blessed Virgin Mary would appear at church, they said that she smiled and said she would. Then, Mirjana asked at what time—I didn't tell her this—and she told her at the same time. She also asked her how many more times she would appear to them. They unanimously said three times. And, when Jakov asked her to leave a sign, she just smiled at them and, as she disappeared, she just told them, 'Go in the peace of God.' They said to me, 'Do you see? Do you see, Mica? Do you see the light?' And I didn't see any special light. Maybe, at the moment, it seemed to me that I did see the light, something like a sunset. I don't even know if that was it. They asked me how it was possible that I didn't see it going toward the crowd and entering the sky. We sat on the stone for another five minutes, and Ljubica kept asking me how it was possible that I could not see that light."

"And you, Ljubica, saw the light?" Fr. Jozo asked.

"There was something," she began. "They were saying that it was leaving. And, when she was coming, they said, 'Here she is! Here she is! She is coming! She's descending!' We stood in front of them. We saw or heard nothing. We asked where she was, and they said, 'Here she is, in front of us.' They asked a few questions."

Ljubica added that she had not been afraid, but that she "got chills" and that they had been uncomfortable that the Blessed Virgin Mary was in front of them.

"A person can't be indifferent, but I was not afraid," Mica explained. "I wouldn't be with them otherwise."

Mica then recounted that, until 6 p.m., they were driving in the car; listening to music; laughing and joking; singing songs—including the holy songs. She emphasized that Ljubica was an atheist and that she worked for the Federal Executive Council in Sarajevo.

Fr. Jozo said that Ljubica was not an atheist, and Mica told him that she worked as a social worker in the municipality of Čitluk. He asked the children if they were uncomfortable with the two being present at the apparition.

"Not at all," the children answered.

Fr. Jozo skillfully led the conversation. Suddenly, he asked when they had decided to leave Medjugorje and why they had chosen another place when a “crowd of people” were already on Podbrdo and they had known that thousands of people would come to the apparition at the same time.

Mica said that she had been in meetings all day, but confirmed that she wasn’t involved in socio-political work in the municipality; that she was not a member of the League of Communists; and that everyone knew that she was with the visionaries every day because she lived in the neighborhood. She added that, in the meetings, she didn’t say anything about the events in Medjugorje. She could hear people saying that there were workers from the municipality who were in socio-political functions and were spreading some rumors, which she perceived to be related to her.

“Later, I was asked to talk to the parents and the children,” Mica narrated. “I told them that I talked to them every day. I sat with Vicka yesterday for an hour in my room when I got home from work. They asked me if I would like to go with them to talk to the parents and I said I was going home, anyway, and I would talk. They went, but without a doctor because they said they had done their duty. The president of the union and the chairman of the executive board insisted on going. There was not a word about the children going somewhere; no one told me that. Along the way, we met a national security officer who was going because of our workers working abroad. I went to Vicka’s mother, Zlata, knowing how she felt those days. She was crying; Vicka was sleeping. Mirjana came and we woke her. They immediately said they were not going. I asked what they were going to do, and Mirjana said they would lock themselves in her room. And then, it occurred to me and I asked them what they thought of going somewhere. They said no problem. They called Marija and Jakov.”

“You went with two cars?” Fr. Jozo inquired.

“Well, with one car!” she clarified. “We even waved at the police, ha ha. He knew me well, so he wanted to ask me something, but it was an awkward moment, so I told them to move aside because we were in a hurry. They told their parents who they would go with and when they knew it was me, they said no problem."

Mica described how they first went "to the walls" at Počitelj because they had never been to Počitelj. Then, they had a drink, went for pastries, and...

"Had a good time," Fr. Jozo interrupted.

"When we got to Cerno, it was 6:15 p.m., so we stopped," Mica continued. "We stopped somewhere in the woods. We looked for stones to set for them to stand on to be able to see. We let them go forward. The two of us were standing in the back."

Mica explained that it was 200 meters (220 yards) from the inn, toward Ljubuški, and on a hill, where there was also an old road.

"We left the car by the road, but we went 50 meters [55 yards] into the woods so that people would not see us, so that they would not start gathering," Ljubica explained. "But, the car had Sarajevo registration plates, so no one would even think it was something [out of the ordinary]."

Mica asked how she could go home now because everyone would condemn her for taking the children and say that someone persuaded her to do it.

"I rarely swear to anything," she admitted. "I trust people and let them trust me. No one persuaded me, but I wanted to do it myself—because I also studied psychology at school—to see how the children behave in a different place. It really interested me. I was up there in the crowd every time and I could see their reactions from afar."

Mica also noted that, one night—when the children were returning from the hill and suddenly knelt at a thornbush—she ducked under that bush to see if there was any force or anything else below it, as she put it, "to repel or to attract."

Then, the group teased Ljubica, saying that she had been afraid and she was from the Executive Council, but she said she had not been afraid. Mica—who said her hands had been shaking with excitement—was also not afraid. She said that Mirjana had asked how many more times Our Lady would appear and Our Lady had said three more times.

"When does that end?" Fr. Jozo asked.

"They said on Friday," Mica replied.

At that point, one of the visionaries (either Mirjana or Ivanka) can be heard adding that this would be the case unless Our Lady told them that she still wanted to come—which is important for understanding what would happen later for the continuation of the apparitions in subsequent years.

Mirjana said that it would end on Friday so she could travel on Saturday, and joked that Our Lady had decided so because of her. They said they had not eaten anything today, and Fr. Jozo asked for sandwiches and drinks. He then asked Mica and Ljubica which of the visionaries were the most active, according to them.

"Vicka seems to me, somehow, blissful," Mica said, because of the way Vicka prayed the Our Father prayers, the way she held her hands, and the way she looked. But, it seemed to her that Mirjana was the most actively following, probably because of her position.

Mica was very talkative the whole time, as if she were processing Fr. Jozo a little, or as if she were philosophizing, as she turned out to be somewhat pretentious.

Fr. Jozo wondered why Our Lady had asked where Ivan was because, as Our Lady, she should know where he was and be able to find him as she had found them.

"She might have found him," replied Jakov who, at that moment, could not have known that Ivan had had an apparition that day at the same time as they did.

"How about asking Ivan?" Vicka suggested. "He'll tell you the same thing as we did: That he saw her. It doesn't matter where he was. If I were in Split or Dubrovnik, all the same. They would tell me that they also saw her. One hundred percent."

Likewise, Vicka also didn't know that Ivan had had an apparition because they had not met with him yet.

By now, Fr. Jozo was trying to decide whether it would be good for them to withdraw—if Our Lady desired so. Perhaps it was a private matter and the apparitions were only meant for the children and not for the people. Maybe that they pray more to God; the children didn't know. He asked them why they had to tell the people, but they said that they had not—that they had only told their loved ones and then it spread.

"You can see for yourself how far it has reached," one of the visionaries said.

"A long way, a long way," Fr. Jozo agreed, before asking Ivanka what their duty was that day, after the "people have been deceived."

"Let's see if she will also come to some other place," Ivanka responded.

"But, the people are furious," Fr. Jozo said, following them out and speaking more with Mica. Unfortunately, the conversation was no longer recorded clearly because the tape recorder was on the table and everyone can be heard leaving the parish office.

. . .

There was another surprise waiting for the children that day. While Fr. Jozo was chatting with the children, a real drama took place in Čitluk with Marinko Ivanković, which neither the children nor Fr. Jozo knew about: The police detained Marinko.

"The police had already come to Vicka's house on that Saturday," Marinko remembered. "I was doing something in the vineyard when I saw them. Vicka wasn't home, but they found Ivanka. I asked her what they had talked about, and she told me that they had told her that if she kept talking about Our Lady, that she would never finish school, that she would never have a job, that she would never marry."

Marinko described the initial arrival of the police in Medjugorje and how they took him on the seventh day.

"Around noon, I was driving my car from Mostar and when I came to Čitluk, I saw a police car following me," he continued. "I stopped in front of the old house and the police commander came up behind me and said, 'Marinko, you have to come to the SUP at once. Will you come with me or will you drive your car?' I told him that he was free to go and that I would drive my car. I knew him and I knew the other policemen because I used to service their cars for them without ever taking a dime. I really knew every one of them. I just went to tell my father that when my wife, Dragica, came home from work, to tell her I had to go to SUP."

Upon arriving at the police station, Marinko immediately went upstairs to the commander's office.

"We talked for sure, two, three hours," he recalled. "He wanted to know everything about every visionary; how many brothers and sisters each one of them had; how old they were; what they said about Our Lady; where their fathers worked; everything possible. He left, another policeman came in and asked me to tell him the same thing. He also left; a third man came in to ask me the same thing. It was already dark outside, around 9:30 p.m. or 10 p.m."

Marinko stated that the authorities obviously had a plan to bring him to the police station that day and keep him there until late at night—as well as to take the children out of Medjugorje for a supposed excursion—to stop everything.

"They took the children, the police took me, and they wanted it to stop," he remembered. "Since my father had been in Rome in exile, they thought that my father told me to take the children and train them and to make a commotion in the communist system with them."

The communists had marked Marinko's family past with the label of the Ustasha (the Croatian Revolutionary Movement) and the "anti-state element." Even so, Marinko reported that he actually felt quite free in the police station because he knew the policemen and because he hadn't said anything that was not true.

"I spoke openly and without any fear," he continued, "everything I had heard from the children and what they had conveyed to us."

At one point, Marinko heard the children's voices in the adjacent room because, on their return home from the parish office, they had heard that Marinko had been arrested and immediately went to Čitluk to release him.

"When the children came, one policeman remained with me," Marinko said. "He was rolling his eyes and I didn't know what was going on outside. Namely, when the children came home, someone told them that I had been taken, so they came to SUP in Čitluk. There was a loud noise in the other room. Later, I was told that they [the children] were threatened with guns, as well, and after ten minutes, those three police officers who talked to me—and another one—swore at me profusely...What kind of system did I think I lived in and what am I doing? But, what am I going to do, man of God? I do my job in Mostar, maintain their police vehicles, have many vines. I told them I knew that these were the children of my relatives, but I had never stopped and talked to them, neither had I played nor had [I] done anything else with them. After that, one of them hit me twice under my eye. If I were standing, maybe he would have knocked me down, but I was sitting, so I just felt a little dizzy.

"Just as Jesus said when he took up the cross, when he hit me, I lowered my head, closed my eyes, and said, 'Dear Lady, thank you for coming to us. They can slaughter me right away, but I won't lie to them.' I didn't want to say anything to them or look at them anymore. They saw that I had lowered my head and remained silent, so they gave me a pen and paper to write down everything I had said before. They let me go home around 1:00 a.m. and told me to wait for them at home because maybe they would need me again."

Marinko also recalled that Our Lady had told the children that "she would come to church for the next three nights."

FROM THE CONVERSATION OF FR. JANKO BUBALO WITH VICKA

FR. JANKO: "Mainly, Vicka, we know that on Tuesday, the 30th of June, you weren't at Podbrdo for a meeting with the Virgin."

VICKA: "We weren't, we weren't."

FR. JANKO: "Why and how was that?"

VICKA: "They took us on some sort of excursion. We came back late. And thus..."

FR. JANKO: "Who took you?"

VICKA: "Two girls came for us about two in the afternoon, and they offered to take us out for a bit in their car. Not suspecting anything, we got ready and went with them."

FR. JANKO: "Who all went?"

VICKA: "Well, the two of them and the five of us visionaries. All except Ivan."

FR. JANKO: "Why didn't he go, also?"

VICKA: "Well, we didn't encourage him too much, and he really didn't seem to want to."

FR. JANKO: "Did the two girls tell you where they planned to take you?"

VICKA: "No, no! They just said let's go out for a bit, and that was all."

FR. JANKO: "And, where did they take you?"

VICKA: "First off, to Čitluk."

FR. JANKO: "And then?"

VICKA: "Then to Žitomislić, then to Počitelj. We looked around a bit in Počitelj, and then off to Čapljina."

FR. JANKO: "And then?"

VICKA: "They treated us to some juice and pastries there, and then off again. . ."

FR. JANKO: "Where to?"

VICKA: "On to Kravica [a waterfall], then Ljubuški, and then home. . ."

FR. JANKO: "And, when did you arrive at home?"

VICKA: "I don't know exactly. Somewhere around nine at night."

FR. JANKO: "And, why so?"

VICKA: "Why! Well, it's a long story."

FR. JANKO: "So, tell it. You know I'm always eager for such stories."

VICKA: "Well, everyone knows the story, but here goes: While on the road, we already realized that we had made a mistake in going on the excursion, for, in the end, it seemed to us that they just took us so that we would not be present on Podbrdo with Our Lady."

FR. JANKO: "Who knows, perhaps."

VICKA: "I'm not sure myself, either. However, on the way through Cerno, we asked them to stop so that we could pray to Our Lady."

FR. JANKO: "What time of day was it?"

VICKA: "Somewhere around six in the afternoon when we usually meet with Our Lady."

FR. JANKO: "Did you tell them why you wished to stop?"

VICKA: "I'm not certain, but they must surely have known."

FR. JANKO: "And then?"

VICKA: "They were somewhat reluctant to stop. They pretended not to hear us. But, when we said we would jump out of the car if they didn't stop, they stopped. We then got out and went off the road a ways. We began to pray, and Our Lady came to us."

FR. JANKO: "Are you certain?"

VICKA: "Well, what else but certain?"

FR. JANKO: "What then?"

VICKA: "We prayed and sang with her, as usual."

FR. JANKO: "And, what were the two [girls] doing then?"

VICKA: "Who knows! God knows what they thought. That is their business. But, they told us that they thought they saw something, too, some sort of light, some shining cloud, or the like…"

FR. JANKO: "Did Our Lady scold you for what you did?"

VICKA: "She wasn't exactly happy but, nevertheless, she sang with us."

FR. JANKO: "Someone once told me that she asked you where Ivan was?

VICKA: "Yes, yes. She asked us, 'Where is the boy?'"

FR. JANKO: "And you?"

VICKA: "What could we do? Well, Our Lady knew where he was."

FR. JANKO: "Accordingly, Ivan did not see Our Lady that day?"

VICKA: "Well, of course he did! Since we were not there, the poor fellow didn't dare go to Podbrdo by himself. Rather, at about six o'clock, he went out a ways beyond his home. He began to pray, and Our Lady appeared to him. She spoke a bit with him, said goodbye, and departed…"

FR. JANKO: "All right. Good. And where, exactly, did this happen? Where did Our Lady appear to you?"

VICKA: "That was a bit before Kusina's restaurant, one or two hundred meters [110 to 220 yards] away."

FR. JANKO: "To the left or to the right of the road going from Ljubuški?"

VICKA: "To the right. Right where that bit of unpaved road merges with the road. The place, as I have heard, is called Bandurica."

FR. JANKO: "All right. When Our Lady—as you say—appeared to you, did she suddenly appear in front of you, or…?"

VICKA: "No, no—all of a sudden! From there, we could see Podbrdo and the people on it. And, when we began to pray, something cloudlike and shining appeared above the people, but we could see immediately that it was Our Lady. We quickly and clearly saw her. She was floating in the air. Her garments were swaying. She was floating straight toward us. It was beautiful. It can't be described."

FR. JANKO: "And, when she departed, was it suddenly, or…?"

VICKA: "The same as when she appeared. When we had prayed seven Our Fathers with her, sang a bit, and conversed with her, she said her farewells and departed."

FR. JANKO: "In what direction did she depart?"

VICKA: "Well, toward the place from where she came. She again slowly floated toward Podbrdo. She descended upon the people waiting there and disappeared. We were awfully sorry about the people, but what could we do?"

FR. JANKO: "And, did the two who took you for the excursion ever speak to you about the event?"

VICKA: "I already told you about that, and I know it was uncomfortable for them, for both of them got lost quickly. One went to Sarajevo, the other to Germany. They weren't back here for a long time."

FR. JANKO: "Good. Our Lady departed, and you?"

VICKA: "What could we do? We got back in the car, and..."

FR. JANKO: "And, off to home, where else?"

VICKA: "No, no. What do you mean 'to home'?"

FR. JANKO: "Where else?"

VICKA: "We all stopped at the parish house."

FR. JANKO: "And, what did you want there?"

VICKA: "Well, it was awful for us. A large crowd gathered on Podbrdo. They waited for us and Our Lady, and neither us nor Our Lady were there. The poor people! They waited and waited, but nothing. All kinds of rumors went around—that we ran off somewhere, that we were taken off to jail. Well, all kinds of things, all kinds of things, and that's it. You know the way people are."

FR. JANKO: "All right, then. And, what did you do in the parish house?"

VICKA: "We hid from the people. The people were just coming back from Podbrdo as we arrived at the church. Where could we go now? Quick, to the parish house."

FR. JANKO: "And then?"

VICKA: "That is how Fr. Jozo learned that we were not at Podbrdo, but on that miserable excursion. And, bang, the questions. Each of us individually, then all of us together. There was no end to it."

FR. JANKO: "All right. But, tell me, what did he say to you?"

VICKA: "He asked us how we could do such a thing; what to say to the people now; did Our Lady appear to us there; what did she say to us, and the like. Who's going to remember it all now?"

FR. JANKO: "Did Fr. Jozo make any suggestions or give you any advice?"

VICKA: "We all struggled. One suggested this, the other said that, but no one was wise enough."

FR. JANKO: "And, in the end?"

VICKA: "In the end, we left for home about nine in the evening, and that's how it ended."

FR. JANKO: "And, when you got home, what did your parents say?"

VICKA: "It was agony for them, too. They imagined all kinds of things. They thought we might have had an accident on the road or that we were put in jail. They imagined everything possible."

FR. JANKO: "All right, Vicka. You told me this at least twice already. The others told me the same, so I don't have any reason not to believe you. But, something is still bothering me."

VICKA: "And, what is that?"

FR. JANKO: "It's uncomfortable for me, but I must. Recently, I replayed some of the cassettes, including that conversation with Fr. Jozo, and I came across one of your assertions that does not agree with what we are talking about."

VICKA: "Well, what is it about?"

FR. JANKO: "About this: You told me here, and you've always maintained, that the girls tricked you into that excursion."

VICKA: "Well, they did! We quickly realized it, but what could we do? What happened, has happened."

FR. JANKO: "That's all right. But, one of you, in your conversation with Fr. Jozo, said that you went so as to see if Our Lady would appear in a different place. It seems to me that you also confirmed that point of view, and how is that? How could you test Our Lady to see if she would come wherever you went, or were you supposed to follow Our Lady?"

VICKA: "Fr. Janko, I don't recall that at all, but if it's on the tape, then we must have said something like that, talked nonsense. But, no one understands us! That was the day after our awful trip to the psychiatrist and the rest. We did wish to get away a bit, dash about a bit, but we never dreamed of not coming back in time. But, you know how it all turned out."

FR. JANKO: "All right. Why, then, did you have to say that you wished to test Our Lady?"

VICKA: "Well, I really don't know what all I said at the time. But, you need to understand us, too. We were children, not angels. You know that no one always speaks that which he thinks. Everyone thinks he will have his wits about him, and everyone thinks that he doesn't always have to say everything that he thinks. That misled us. Understand our position! We were not comfortable in front of those two..."

FR. JANKO: "Which two?"

VICKA: "Well, in front of those two girls. It wasn't easy to tell them to their face that they tricked us. And, thus, we..."

FR. JANKO: "You told a lie?"

VICKA: "Let it be that way. But, that isn't so awful. We didn't mean any harm by it."

FR. JANKO: "Did Our Lady later scold you about that?"

VICKA: "No, no. Our Lady is better than people are. She understands us."

FR. JANKO: "All right. Let it be. But, something else that is inaccurate broke through."

VICKA: "Like it's only one thing!"

FR. JANKO: "One of you said that Our Lady told you in Cerno that she would appear to you only three more days."

VICKA: "I really don't know that. I don't recall. Someone may have said that just so they would leave us in peace. Fr. Jozo really wore us out then. From here, from there. Ask this, then that, and then again. It makes you stop thinking!"

FR. JANKO: "And, what all did he ask you?"

VICKA: "All kind of things. Well, all kind of things! I already told you about that. A hundred combinations. Would Our Lady appear to us in the church? Would she do this, would she do that? Well, even now, an agony seizes me when I just think about it. We were tormented by it. Why did we allow ourselves to be deceived? Why did we leave the people—as the saying goes—in the lurch? How could we get back home without them seeing us, and a hundred other things. And, he got a hold of us. Perhaps someone said leave us alone, Our Lady will appear to us just three more days. Perhaps someone 'blurted' that, as though it was easy for us! It was awful for us! That's why I say, perhaps someone said..."

FR. JANKO: "Nonetheless, it didn't come out the best!"

VICKA: "True. And, it was the most difficult for us. And we won't, I suppose, go to hell because of that."

FR. JANKO: "Good. And then, you arrived at your homes?"

VICKA: "Where else? But, only a bit after nine o'clock."

FR. JANKO: "And then, I suppose, you were a bit more at ease?"

VICKA: "We were tormented there, too. Our parents were terribly worried about us. I already told you that. And, when we told them the whole story, it was late into the night."

FR. JANKO: "As I can see, the excursion didn't quite pay off."

VICKA: "Well, you heard the story!"

FR. JANKO: "I think, nonetheless, in the end, everyone went to sleep happy?"

VICKA: "If it were only so, my dear friar."

FR. JANKO: "And, what now?"

VICKA: "Just as we were getting ready to go to bed, someone came and told us that they had taken our Marinko."

FR. JANKO: "Where did they take him?"

VICKA: "To Čitluk, to the secret police."

FR. JANKO: "So, all right. Nothing to worry about! They took him and they will bring him back."

VICKA: "It isn't awful for you but, for us, it was awful. We knew that they took him because of us. Well, the man who wouldn't step on an ant, as my grandmother used to say."

FR. JANKO: "And, then what?"

VICKA: "We went to Čitluk to find him."

FR. JANKO: "It was difficult for you to find him!"

VICKA: "We didn't find him, but we surely said all kinds of things to the mayor and those who were there. We said all kinds of things. Arrest us, if necessary, but leave the man alone, and the like. Just all kinds of things."

FR. JANKO: "And they?"

VICKA: "They responded the same way to us. It was an ideal situation for them because when we arrived, they all yelled together, 'Perfect, just what we ordered.' And then, they said all kinds of things to us, also. Well, I don't even want to think about it or to talk about it. Well, let's drop it!"

FR. JANKO: "All right, Vicka. It's better that we do so. And then, you went home, where else?"

VICKA: "Where else! We arrived about two in the morning."

FR. JANKO: "On foot?"

VICKA: "No, no. We came back by car—one of ours, the same one that we had gone in."

FR. JANKO: "And, Marinko?"

VICKA: "He came home sometime in the morning."

FR. JANKO: "And then, you finally relaxed? Perhaps it wasn't necessary even to get so upset?"

VICKA: "All right. Let's say that it wasn't."

After the first week

The events in Medjugorje cannot be viewed in isolation and outside the context of the time in which they occurred. This was noted by journalist and publicist Žarko Ivković, one of the top experts on the Medjugorje phenomenon, who has documented it in several books.

Here is what Ivković wrote about the socio-political events in the world, Yugoslavia, and Bosnia and Herzegovina at the time the apparitions in Medjugorje began:

In 1981, the world was very turbulent: A state of emergency was declared in communist Poland due to mass labor protests; in China, Mao Zedong's widow and other members of the "four-member gang" were sentenced to death; U.S. President Ronald Reagan was wounded in a bizarre assassination attempt by a failed student who wanted to impress film actress Jodie Foster; 23-year-old Turk Mehmet Ali Agca severely wounded Pope John Paul II in St. Peter's Square at the Vatican; socialist François Mitterand became the French president; Muslim fundamentalists in Cairo killed Egyptian President Mohammed Anwar el-Sadat, and Hosni Mubarak was elected president; the USA and USSR—bloc enemies—began disarmament talks in Geneva; the Americans launched the first Columbia shuttle into space; Meryl Streep played a major role in the movie "The French Lieutenant's Woman"; Prince Charles and Lady Diana married; film actress Natalie Wood tragically passed away...

Communist Yugoslavia, which had been getting accustomed to life after Josip Broz Tito, was also restless. In the spring, mass protests erupted in Kosovo, [protests] by which Albanians were demanding that the province of Kosovo become the seventh republic of the SFRY [Socialist Federative Republic of Yugoslavia] and that the Albanians be granted the status of a constituent people. Yugoslav authorities declared a state of emergency and sent the army against the protesters, prompting the escalation of violence and the deaths of several dozen people, mostly Albanian students. These events—which had strained Serb-Albanian relations and awakened Greater Serbian nationalism—were seen as a catalyst for the political crisis in Yugoslavia that has resulted in the disintegration of the country.

At the beginning of June 1981, at the dawn of Medjugorje apparitions, Yugoslavia won the silver medal at the European Basketball Championship after being defeated by the USSR in the finals. And, in the shadow of a major sporting event, the political trial of Croatian intellectual Vlado Gotovac was nearing its end. He was sentenced by the Zagreb District Court to two years in prison for "hostile propaganda and inciting national hatred and discord." Gotovac ended up in prison because he had warned—in foreign media—about the subordination of Croats in Yugoslavia. The joint session on June 10, 1981, was held by the SFRY Presidency and the CK SKJ [Central Committee of the League of Communists of Yugoslavia] Presidency, who concluded that the "stable international position of Yugoslavia" could only be preserved by "further development of self-management, overcoming economic difficulties, and strengthening the unity and socialist communion of all peoples and nationalities." "Unity" was demonstrated at the July celebration of the 40th anniversary of the uprising and revolution of the peoples and nationalities of Yugoslavia and by laying of flowers at Tito's tomb.

The great Croatian writer Miroslav Krleža also died that year, Croatian pop-rock band *Prljavo Kazalište* released what was likely their most mature album, "Hero of the Street," and the movie "Do You Remember Dolly Bell?" screened in theaters...

On the day the visionaries first met with Our Lady— June 25, 1981—in the news broadcasts of Yugoslav radio and television that evening, there was no news about the unusual occurrence in Medjugorje, and there was nothing in the press the next day, either. In fact, the Yugoslav media remained silent about Medjugorje until Branko Mikulić—the most powerful politician in Bosnia and Herzegovina at the time—broke the silence. He spoke about Medjugorje on July 4, 1981, in Tjentište, Eastern Bosnia, at the Veterans Day celebration.

"The clerical nationalists have raised their heads and have especially pounced upon the youth," Mikulić stated. "By abusing religious freedoms in our country and their duties in the Catholic, Islamic, and Orthodox communities, some priests in BiH [Bosnia and Herzegovina] have acted from hostile positions. What the Clero-nationalists are capable of doing is demonstrated by the latest example from Čitluk, where—as in the first post-war years, when the remnants of a defeated class-enemy fought against young people's authority by all means—they have reinvented their Lady, by whom they intimidate people, trying to make fools of them, to manipulate them politically, and to harness them to the cart of those who work against the national interests of our peoples and nationalities."

Mikulić reminded [the listeners] that, some time ago, a bishop from Yugoslavia wrote in an Italian newspaper that the communists in Yugoslavia wanted to destroy the believers and the Church, that Stepinac was sinless, and that the Croats rejected communism.

"Which Croats?" he wondered. "Those who—together with members of our other peoples and nationalities—were in the first battle lines of Tito's fighters on the Neretva, Sutjeska, Kozara? Those who are engaged in the fight for socialism and defense of their country's independence, or those who have been in the service of fascist occupiers?"

Mikulić assessed that such behavior by clerical nationalists should be "qualified as a hostile activity." In fact, it was a call to the media for a campaign of persecution against Medjugorje, and his claim about the clerical nationalists who had invented Our Lady would soon become the basis for prosecutions.

Two days later, on July 6, the first articles about Medjugorje appeared, and the first official news item was published by Belgrade-based *Tanjug* on July 7. This Yugoslav news agency—and everyone else [referring to the news media]—reported that Our Lady had appeared to the children in the village of Bijakovići and that "the authoritative, priestly figures from this region had dissociated themselves from the credibility of the children's statements and declared them to be mere superstition." *Tanjug* also communicated that the socio-political organizations of the municipality of Čitluk and rural local communities "have initiated a broad and organized action to resolve and unmask the intentions and aspirations to manipulate people." The news agency also said that it [the appearance] had been most energetically condemned by working people and citizens, especially by believers.

Following the news, a brief media silence ensued, but it was interrupted again by *Tanjug* on August 17. *Tanjug* then announced that the SSRN Municipal Conference of Čitluk had concluded that "the resurrection of the Virgin Mary is the perfidious act of the clerical nationalists and a brutal attempt to toy with the religious sentiments of the faithful citizens, with the obvious intention of jeopardizing the achievements of the socialist revolution." *Tanjug* added that, at the same session, "the conduct of a number of the priests was vigorously condemned," and they were identified by name: Bishop Pavao Žanić, Fr. Jozo Zovko, and Fr. Ferdo Vlašić.

The media at the time then raced to see which one of them would bring out the most accusations and slanders against Medjugorje, as well as the people involved in the Medjugorje events. *Oslobodjenje* and *AS* from Sarajevo; *Sloboda* from Mostar; *Večernje Novosti*, *Borba*, *Politika* and *Duga* from Belgrade; *Arena* from Zagreb... took the lead in communist propaganda. All of the articles in radio and television broadcasts had common themes: Medjugorje events were viewed as the rapid development of clerical nationalism, clericalism, and clero-fascism; the Vatican was linked to the Ustasha regime; and everything, as it was written, was directed against the brotherhood and unity of the Yugoslav peoples. The basis of all of these texts and articles was atheism, which did not accept any possibility of the supernatural. As such, everything was proclaimed to be a fabrication of Fr. Jozo Zovko and other Franciscans. Moreover, they called the Mother of God "the Ustasha's Our Lady" and even "the cut-throat Our Lady" because they connected the apparitions with the alleged atrocities committed by Ustasha in that place during World War II.

"That Thursday, June 25, 1981," Ivković wrote, "there was real confusion in the Čitluk Committee, the main Communist Party body in the municipality. The situation was similar in the municipal government, the police, the youth organization SKJ...All were concerned with the seriousness and strength with which the news had spread. The question of whether all this would pass peacefully or whether they would have to act was hovering in the air. The story of the apparition was only ignored by the chief of the SUP of the municipality of Čitluk, Gojko Ivanković, who considered it all a child's fabrication. But, the next day, on June 26, he changed his opinion and, in the afternoon, called the police station commander Zdravko Bevanda and crime investigator Ivan Turudić to his office."

"He told us," Turudić remembered, "that there would be no joking with the events in Medjugorje because the people were gathering. Politicians and chiefs from Mostar and Sarajevo had been calling, and the State Security Service (SDB, the notorious secret police known as UDBA) demanded something be done to keep it from expanding. I said that there was nothing significant to me because it was not a criminal offense. We concluded that the child-visionaries were the most important figures in this event. As they were underage, nothing should be done to them without their parents' knowledge. The chief of police then said he would send word to the parents to bring their children for an interview that evening. Therefore, it was necessary for the commander of the police station and me to come in the evening to participate in it."

The children came to the chief's office in the evening, accompanied by their parents and the Medjugorje chaplain, Fr. Zrinko Čuvalo, and were interrogated by the chief, the police station commander, and Investigator Turudić. The conversation was actually initiated by the children. As soon as they entered the office, they began to ask, "Why have we been brought here? What are we supposed to do in a police station? What will happen to us?"

"We told them," Turudić said, "that they were invited only for a conversation and that they would go to their homes afterward. Fr. Zrinko was also telling them to calm down. As we did not make a plan or prepare for the interview, we randomly asked them what we were interested in: Where did they see Our Lady; whether Our Lady was old or young; would they see her again...To the claim of one of us, 'It's not Our Lady, it's just some girl tending the sheep,' the children answered unanimously, 'That was Our Lady! And she told us she would appear again.'"

Shortly before midnight, the children went home, and the three police officers remained to discuss their impressions.

"Afterward, we concluded that they were children with whom we should be cautious and avoid police activity," Turudić recalled. "But, that the next day, in agreement with their parents, they would be taken to the health center in Čitluk for examination. The children did not give me the impression that they were lying, but that they had experienced some illusion which they said that it was Our Lady. I didn't believe in it. I thought those might have been hallucinatory visions that came about because of puberty and summer heat, or—even worse—because of the use of narcotics, primarily LSD. But, the children looked quite normal and healthy."

However, the authorities declared a state of emergency. Crisis headquarters were established in the police station, numerous politicians, SDB staff...were coming. The police were ordered to regularly record the license plates of cars entering Medjugorje and to list the names of those going to Apparition Hill. And the communists organized numerous meetings in local communities to frighten the people, but also to present the apparitions as false and in the service of the enemy of the state. The meetings were held throughout Herzegovina, where political activists from Čitluk read information showing the friars as opponents of communism and about the pastor, Fr. Jozo Zovko, who seduced the people and the children. He soon became the number one enemy of the state.

...

After the first week, news of the apparitions spread all over former Yugoslavia. TV, radio, and newspapers started showing interest in the Medjugorje phenomenon, but skepticism, condemnation, and mockery were common amongst all of the reporting.

"Journalists ridiculed us and referred to the thousands of pilgrims coming to Medjugorje as 'religious fanatics' or worse," Mirjana wrote. "State-run news outlets accused us and the local priests of being Croat nationalists who had fabricated the apparitions to foment a counter-revolution. The national television news labeled us 'bitter enemies of the state,' and newspaper headlines referring to Medjugorje seemed like they had come from a tabloid: 'Religious Hoax Draws Thousands of Zealots,' 'Friars Suspected of Nationalist Plot,' 'Six Yokels Invent Visions of Mary'... The authorities held a community meeting at the elementary school and summoned our parents and relatives to attend. They said that if the 'nonsense' did not stop, then we would be expelled from school and locked away in a mental institution, and our parents would lose their jobs and passports."

...

When the police failed to break the children, they tried to intimidate their parents. The first to be attacked was Vicka's mother, Zlata, who was taken to Čitluk the following Wednesday, one week after the apparitions began. Because of Vicka's bold demeanor, the authorities thought that she could be the group's ringleader, so they demanded that her mother sway her daughter to stop all of it. Despite being interrogated until the afternoon, Zlata did not buckle under the pressure in any way.

Then, the authorities devised a plan to prevent the visionaries from going to Apparition Hill that day. First, they planned to persuade Zlata to make the children wait for Our Lady's apparition in her house and to have representatives of the authorities present at the apparition. The president of the Municipal Executive Council (Government) and the president of the Commission for

Relations with Religious Communities were designated for this event. Meanwhile, the police were supposed to be represented by the criminal investigator, Ivan Turudić, who was also assigned as the driver for that official delegation, which had departed Čitluk for Medjugorje that afternoon.

"I really liked that idea," Turudić testified some twenty years later. "It gave me an opportunity to participate directly and freely in the apparition. Others were prevented from doing so and some were also arrested."

But, not everything went as smoothly as planned. Namely, neighbor Draga Ivanković threatened the president of the Municipal Government with a stone and then he fled. Ivan Turudić and Jure Jerkić remained, and Zlata, kindly welcomed them and served them a drink. Then, both Ivanka's grandmother and Jakov's mother arrived for a chat, and Vicka, Ivanka, Marija, and Jakov occasionally entered the room.

"None of the adults objected to this idea, and I was burning with the desire for the apparition to begin," Turudić admitted.

However, Vicka's sister did not want the gathering to be at their house, so someone suggested that the children be taken to a secluded place other than Podbrdo. One of the adults could go with the children, Vicka's sister said. Then, they got into the car, but Jakov's mother pulled her son out of the car.

"We did nothing to get Jakov back in the car," Turudić remembered. "However, his mother's reaction provoked the faithful who were present against us. People started banging their fists on the roof of the car and started gathering around us. I was driving slowly and breaking through. We headed to Krstine, where we intended to attend the apparition."

Suddenly, a child's voice came from the back seat: "We must be with Our Lady!" Sighs and groans were heard.

The visionaries later said that they had experienced the apparition in the car. Specifically, Vicka later testified that, at that moment, she had not seen the car nor the people in it, but only Our Lady. According to the children, Our Lady simply appeared among them and told them not to be afraid of anything. (Although the people in the car had no ill intentions toward the children, the children didn't know, so they were afraid.) When she smiled at them and left, the children told Turudić and Jerkić that they needed to go to the church. And, after a brief discussion, the two decided to take them to the friars. They parked the car in front of the parish house and Jerkić went to see if any of the friars were there to take them in.

"At that moment, I turned to the children and told them that the friars would surely welcome them," Turudić recalled. "And I also said that now they could see that the two of us had no ill intention toward them and that I was sorry that we all were in such a situation. Soon, Jure waved at us to come, so the children got out of the car and ran to the rectory, and I parked the car and then also went to the rectory. There, we talked to the friars for an hour. It was pleasant; I was relaxed, relieved, and, in some ways, proud to be involved in all of this that day because I felt I had done something right, not worrying at all if any of my superiors would be angry about it and call me to account."

However, when Turudić and Jerkić returned to Čitluk and reported to their superiors what had happened, they grabbed their heads in frustration and cried out, "Could you have done anything worse to us?! Why did you take them right to the friars?"

. . .

That evening, the people gathered at the church shortly after 6 p.m. Most of them really believed that the children saw Our Lady, who called for fasting on this night.

Fr. Jozo placed Jakov up on the altar and said, "Today, we invite you to fast."

In response, someone from among the people replied, "All that Our Lady asks, we will do!"

In those days, the children also met with the Bishop of Mostar-Duvno, Monsignor Pavao Žanić, in Medugorje.

"He asked us questions for over an hour and recorded our answers on tape," Mirjana wrote. "He then told us to put our hands on a cross and swear that we were telling the truth, which we all did without hesitation. After our meeting, he told Fr. Jozo that he was certain Our Lady was appearing to us. Fr. Jozo urged the bishop to be prudent, but eventually a newspaper article quoted Bishop Žanić as saying, 'It is definite that the children were not incited by anyone, and especially not by the church, to lie.'"

She also shared about a time when Fr. Jozo heard a voice saying that he must protect the children and, after that, hid them from the police who persecuted them.

"His demeanor had changed so drastically that I wondered if he was being sarcastic," Mirjana remembered. "But, as he ushered us inside, I realized that his tenderness was genuine. That evening, Our Lady visited us in a small room near the church's altar, just opposite the sacristy. In the days ahead, she continued to visit us there, and Fr. Jozo never doubted us again. His support brought us momentary solace, but nothing could curb our fear and anxiety as what we thought might be Our Lady's final apparition approached. How would we go on without her? When that day came, we were full of emotion. The crowd—estimated at tens of thousands of people—was the biggest we had ever seen, and it seemed that many expected some sort of miracle to accompany the apparition. When Our Lady appeared, however, there was nothing out of the ordinary and no special message for the world. We asked again if she would leave a sign, but she only smiled. After she departed, we addressed the crowd. Many of them seemed disappointed that there had not been some magnificent conclusion to the events. Personally, more than anything, I was confused. I did not feel in my heart that the apparitions were over. The next day, we all tried to go back to our normal routines. I was at my uncle's house when I felt something within—a familiar flutter of expectation that rapidly became a cacophony of excitement. I felt like I would explode if Our Lady did not come at that moment."

She described how, as sudden as a breath of wind, Our Lady appeared in front of her. Mirjana fell to her knees enrapt, wanting nothing but to look at her.

"I cried profusely after she departed," Mirjana recalled. "The other visionaries saw her, too, and that's when we realized Medjugorje was not exactly like Lourdes. Our Lady continued to appear to us every day. Around the same time, the persecution rose to a dangerous new level when the Yugoslav government declared a state of emergency in Medjugorje. The effects of the apparitions had reverberated all the way to Belgrade, the capitol of Yugoslavia, and the communists—incensed by our unwillingness to bow to their pressures and afraid that they were losing control—became intent on squashing the problem as quickly as possible. Within days, the military pushed into the village. Soldiers with automatic rifles and snarling German Shepherd dogs took positions on the hill and in front of our homes. Military vehicles patrolled the streets. Helicopters buzzed over pilgrims as they tried to pray. It felt like we had disturbed a gigantic nest of hornets. The interrogations—now done by federal police instead of local ones—became lengthier and more intense. I was taken in one day and a foul-mouthed policeman became increasingly frustrated when I refused to deny the apparitions."

Mirjana remembers the conversation with the policeman:

"Confess," he said.

"I only confess to my priest," Mirjana responded calmly. His face turned a reddish-purple color and the veins in his neck bulged.

"Admit that you do not see Our Lady!"

"But, I do."

At this, he pulled his handgun out of its holster and laid it on the table between the two of them.

"Come clean," he said, glancing at the gun. "You didn't see *anything*."

"Help me, Gospa," Mirjana prayed silently. Afterward, she explained how, despite the deadly weapon on the table, she felt a strange sense of calm because, after seeing Our Lady and experiencing Heaven, it was nearly impossible for her to be afraid of anything.

"Time's up," the policeman said. "Now, give me the truth."

Mirjana looked him straight in the eyes. "The truth is that I see Our Lady, and I'm willing to die for her."

He slammed his fist on the table, holstered his gun, and stormed out of the room.

"If we had been adults, the communists would have surely locked us away in the deepest, darkest prison cell they could find, or we simply would have vanished in the same way that my grandfather did," she wrote. "But, as brutal as the government authorities could be, they knew they would face public outrage if they imprisoned children. In a way, our youth protected us, but nothing prevented them from trying to terrify us. Aside from all the frightening experiences, there was excitement, as well. Every morning brought the promise of a new surprise or adventure. Sometimes, we experienced multiple apparitions on the same evening. The police chased us and tried to disrupt our plans, so to evade them, we constantly changed the meeting place. In the woods behind one of our houses, in the middle of an unkempt field, beneath a grove of shade trees—it somehow felt appropriate to experience the apparition in the seclusion of nature, where the fresh air and starlight afforded a serenity befitting Our Lady. Years later, in one of her messages, she said, *'Today, I invite you to observe nature because there you will meet God,'* and in another, *'I call you to give glory to God the Creator in the colors of nature. Through even the smallest flower, He speaks to you about His beauty and the depth of His love.'*

"During one of these extraordinary visitations, Our Lady interacted with the villagers in a surprisingly intimate way," she continued. "On August 2, 1981, she appeared at the regular time and asked us to await her again that evening. My memories of this and other early apparitions are foggy, but Marija reported that Our Lady said, *'All of you together go to the meadow at Gumno. A great struggle is about to unfold—a struggle between my Son and Satan. Human souls are at stake.'*"

Mirjana explained that, later that evening, they went to the area known as Gumno near her uncle's house. In Croatian language, the word *gumno* means *threshing floor*—a large, circular area of hard ground where farmers separated grain by having cows or horses walk in circles over it.

"In the Bible, John the Baptist used the same word when he figuratively described Jesus' mission as a harvest of souls," she related. "'*His winnowing fork is in his hand, and he will clear his threshing floor and gather his wheat into the barn, but the chaff he will burn with unquenchable fire.*' About forty local people joined us at Gumno. Crickets chirped loudly and mosquitos flitted around our faces as we kneeled in the red clay. We prayed and waited and, suddenly, Our Lady appeared in front of us. Some of the people had asked us if they could touch Our Lady, and when we presented their request, she said that whoever wanted to could approach her. One by one, we took their hands and guided them to touch Our Lady's dress. The experience was strange for us visionaries—it was difficult to comprehend that only we could see Our Lady. From our perspective, guiding people to touch her was like leading the blind. Their reactions were lovely, especially the children. It seemed that most felt something. A few reported a sensation like electricity and others were overcome with emotion. But, as more people touched Our Lady, I noticed black spots forming on her dress, and the spots congealed into a large, coal-colored stain. I cried at the sight of it. 'Her dress!' yelled Marija, also crying. The stains, said Our Lady, represented sins that had never been confessed. She suddenly vanished. After praying for a while, we stood in the darkness and told the people what we saw. They were nearly as upset as we were. Someone suggested that everyone there should go to confession, and the next day repentant villagers inundated the priests."

Mirjana added that, during these daily encounters, Our Lady emphasized things like prayer, fasting, confession, reading the Bible, and going to Mass.

"Later, people identified these as Our Lady's 'main messages'—or, as Fr. Jozo called them, her 'five stones,' an allusion to the story of David and Goliath," Mirjana explained. "She was not asking us to pray or fast just for the sake of it. The fruit of living our faith, she said, was love. As she said in one of her messages, '*I come to you as a mother, who, above all, loves her children. My children, I want to teach you to love.*' Our Lady's ethereal beauty captivated us from the very beginning. One day during an apparition, we asked a childish question: 'How is it possible that you are so beautiful?' Our Lady gently smiled. '*I am beautiful because I love,*' she said. '*If you want to be beautiful, then love.*' After the apparition, Jakov—who was only ten years old—looked at us and said, 'I don't think she was telling the truth.' I reproached him. 'How can you say that the Blessed Mother didn't tell the truth?' 'Well, look at some of us,' he replied. 'Some of us can love our entire lives and we'd still never be beautiful like she said!' We all laughed. Jakov did not understand the type of beauty that she was talking about. Hers is eternal and comes from within, and she wants that kind of beauty for each of us. If you are clean inside, and if you are full of love, then you will be beautiful on the outside, as well."

Mirjana explained how, despite such lighthearted moments, the overall gravity of the apparitions was becoming clear to them.

"Through our daily encounters with the Blessed Virgin, we realized that her plans with Medjugorje were not merely for the village itself, nor were they limited to Yugoslavia," she said. "She had come to change the entire world. She revealed to us that God's plan would ultimately be realized through a series of future events. She began to relate these events to us with instructions to keep them secret until just before they were to take place."

. . .

Vicka's mother, Zlata, and her brother Franjo testified that the apparitions were preceded by a very unusual event.

"We were getting ready to go gather firewood that morning and I went to hook up the trailer for the cultivator, which towed it," Franjo began. "And, when I was cleaning it, I found two rosaries in one of its corners. I took them home wondering whose rosaries they were, but no one claimed to have left them there. They were kind of old-fashioned, and one of them had sacred relics in it."

"I thought one of the neighbors had left the rosaries," Zlata explained. "So, for a few days, I asked around the neighborhood whose rosaries those were, but everyone said they were not theirs. In fact, there were no such rosaries in our village. I also asked the friars and told them to ask further on, but no one answered."

Zlata saved the rosaries and remembered them when the apparitions began.

"I told Vicka one day to ask Our Lady from where those rosaries in the trailer were from," Zlata said. "And, when the apparition ended, Vicka said, 'Our Lady said that she had left them for us.'"

Vicka's mother carried the heavy burden of everything that went on in those days, months, and years. In fact, she took care of the family by herself because her husband worked in Germany and would take a short vacation twice a year. Zlata took care of eight children and a niece, who came to live with them when her parents went to work in Germany. Two grandmothers—Zlata's mother and her mother-in-law—also lived with Zlata and the nine children.

"I was alone to give birth to my children, to baptize them, to bring them to receive First Holy Communion, to get them confirmed..." Zlata remembered. "Pere [her husband] was in Germany. What times those were! The UDBA was constantly at our heels. They used to come at night and bang on the door and throw stones on the roof. The children would get scared, so we all slept in one room of ten square meters—me and eight of them! And, in the heat with the windows closed, we almost suffocated."

Franjo recalled how people began to come and literally besiege their house, wanting to see Vicka and the other visionaries, who most often stayed in their home.

"We'd get ready for school and open the door to see hundreds of people waiting outside the door!" he said. "We couldn't go out normally, so we went out through a window in back of the house, then went through the garden into the neighbor's yard and sneaked toward school. We couldn't even go downstairs to drink milk."

Zlata added that Fr. Slavko Barbarić wanted to organize the visits, so he attached a board to the front of the house with a schedule showing when people could speak with the visionaries.

"First thing in the morning, the police came and removed the board with a hammer and asked who had put it up," Franjo said. "Of course, we didn't say, and our grandmother—who was a little hard of hearing—kept on saying, 'I don't hear anything from you, son, I don't hear anything from you.'"

Zlata also recalled that, a few months before the first apparition on June 24, Ivanka and Vicka saw "a woman in white on the hill."

"Ivanka and Vicka were not aware of this," she stated. "We had a garden above the houses where we planted onions and some vegetables. The two of them took some bread and salt, intending to pick up onions. And, up that way, all the way up, the two of them sat to eat when they saw a woman in white. This was two months before the real apparition occurred. At the time, they didn't tell anyone. They were scared and, on their way down, Vicka fell and hit herself hard. But, they never told anyone anything. But, when the apparitions began, they started to talk about how they had been up there and had seen it."

Zlata added that the rosary was also found on the trailer around the same time. As expected, the shock and the surprise of the first day were overwhelming for her.

"When Vicka came on the first day, I was surprised and said, 'My God, my God, couldn't you give me any other possible penance in this world!'" she admitted. "I was saying all kinds of things, and Vicka didn't want to remain silent. The next day, we all went to pick tobacco. The kids were small, but everyone was picking tobacco, and she kept on saying how she had seen, how they had been there, and I told her, 'Be silent! You won't go out ever again! You will not!' But, she said she would go again today when the time was right. 'We will and that's it. Who will stop us? Nobody.'"

Notably, Zlata said that it was her idea for the social worker Mica to take the children outside Medjugorje on the seventh day of the apparitions.

"They came and asked us parents to let the children go with them for a little walk," Zlata shared. "Ivan Turudić, who worked for the police, and Ljubica from a committee in Sarajevo wanted to take them. But, one of ours, Mirjana [Mica], was working in the municipality in Čitluk and I told them to let Mica go rather than this man. She was not planning to go. That's why I feel sorry that they put her in the 'black book.' She shouldn't be in it because she was not part of the plan. She was not attached to the Communist Party or anything like that. She was just an ordinary girl as all our girls were, too. But, it was my fault for getting her into it. She would never have experienced what she had experienced in Cerno had she not gone."

Vicka's mother knew how to bravely resist the police when they wanted to achieve something by force.

"Someone named Barabić, a police officer, came," she continued. "I asked him to show me the warrant and he threatened that he would beat me."

She then noted that those who used to be the last were now the first.

"Those who persecuted us are now first in the church," she said. "I said I wouldn't mention anyone's names. Let the names remain secret. Whoever had done things, had done them."

Although Zlata did not want to mention the name of any persecutor, she recounted the case of a former official. Although he had been against Medjugorje during communism, after many years, he began to receive pilgrims at his guesthouse.

"On one occasion, he brought a bus of his guests [pilgrims] to the front of our house looking for Vicka, who was not in the house at the time," she remembered. "He leaned on the fence and wouldn't go inside, and I said to him, 'Good afternoon, sir. How are you? What are you doing? Come in for a drink.' He said he wouldn't, that he was waiting for some company [some people] because he remembered what he had done then."

Zlata admitted that, at first, she had begged Vicka not to tell anyone about the visions because she would "disgrace herself" and "what would the people say?" because we must not "toy with what is sacred."

The story of the apparitions even reached her husband, Pere, in Germany, who had just recently been home on vacation prior to these events.

"The post office was damaged, so he couldn't call," she explained. "He had a friend in Čitluk, Drago Stojić, so we arranged to talk through him. He asked me if Vicka was normal. I said she was and that he should not worry."

Zlata laughed because Vicka was causing the most headaches for the police, such as the police commander who said that he would like "only to get rid of this damn daughter of Pere."

"She was not afraid of anyone; she was one step ahead of everyone," Zlata said and described the incident when the police chief and commander came to their house. The authorities sat in the house, while the family, together with their children, were stringing tobacco in front of the house.

"They said that our children were crazy," she said. "They said this and that. That they would never marry. That they must not meet again. That some priests gave birth to children...They made up all kinds of things. When Vicka heard this, she told them, 'Get out, get out of here! You won't say that to me in my house. That is not true what you are saying, and the fact that I see Our Lady, that's something else. And you, get out!' She had so much strength. And they were off quickly and went out."

Franjo testified that their mother was under great pressure.

"Every day, the authorities would convene a meeting at the school and that was a real battle against us [they would say all kinds of things against us],” he explained. “On one occasion, a man from the committee stood up and said, ‘Pere is not here. Zlata should be taken to jail!’ And they all repeated, ‘Zlata should be taken to jail! Zlata should be taken to jail!’ After a month, she did receive a jail warrant, but, in the end, she didn’t go!”

Franjo noted that their friend Drago Stojić, who was a teacher, told them what the authorities were planning.

“He was among them, and when he would hear what they were planning, he would come to us at night—so that no one would see him—and would tell us everything,” Franjo recalled. “He informed my father they would take his passport. Daddy just arrived from Germany, we—his children—didn’t even see him the right way, and Drago Stojić told us to take him to Čapljina on a train and make him leave for Germany as soon as possible. The police came in the morning and asked where he was, and we said that he hadn’t even come, but they knew everything.”

“A police officer sat in front of our house the whole time, watching who came and went,” confirmed Zlata, who was never frightened nor hesitant in protecting her children and her family. “I’d secretly give them something to eat. They were ordinary police officers from the street.”

“I told Srećko Jelavić, the head of UDBA from Mostar—who interrogated me for an hour in Čitluk regarding whether my husband Pere brought something, did he do this, did he do that—I told him that no one would banish God from my house!” Zlata stated. “If He came, then He would stay in the house! Jelavić later told Drago Stojić that he had never encountered a more honest woman. I thought to myself, ‘Oh yeah, you did. You just came at an opportune time.’ I was not afraid. I had the strength. I accepted whatever someone said to me and I was not angry.”

Laughing, Zlata shared that often at dawn—about 4 a.m., while it was still dark—she used to go to the parish office to tell Fr. Jozo everything that was happening. Fr. Jozo wanted to bring people to the church. He feared that the communists would accuse him of organizing a religious rally outside of the church. All sorts of things ran through his mind. He was anxious for the people and visionaries to come to the church as soon as possible because he had heard that people on Apparition Hill did not pray and could not hear.

"I felt a responsibility as a pastor before God and the Church," Fr. Jozo admitted. "What to do?! We must pray! I will invite them all to prayer at three o'clock; until three o'clock, I will have catechesis and pray with the young people. Come to prayer because God will never let us down. He will always reveal His will, His way to those who pray. God will help and will reveal to us what His work is, what His plan is, what His will is, but also what is a fraud and what is from the evil one. We are in a great test. We need to pray a lot and to listen to the voice of God. That's a big responsibility for us. And it would also be a big, tragic, and scandalous issue for us and our faith and the Church to say and testify to something that is false. You have to understand me, you have to understand both the parents and the parish and come to this prayer with the intention that God may help us.

"They responded and the strength these people received from prayer was evident," he continued. "Because, up on the hill, they did not pray at all! The children only prayed the Our Father prayer. Those who were near them somehow participated in the prayer, while others down the hill were pushing, not knowing that those up the hill were praying. There was no one to say, 'Let's pray.' Now, people came to the church, I prayed in church, we had Mass, a sermon, confession...We started a program that continues to this day. Then, the sick would gather and I would pray over them. Then, the Adoration of the Blessed Sacrament of the Altar, the Veneration of the Cross on Friday...The whole program developed slowly. It was in that first week, in those seven days. Our Lady asked for all this and asked that the rosary be prayed every day—and to do it together. Pray with your heart! It was the important message. You can no longer see a person without a rosary! When parents pray, children pray, everyone prays...That was important."

Fr. Jozo explained that the communists did not know how to react to this; they were powerless.

"They asked us to stop the afternoon Mass and [prayer] program," he said. "In a strict and threatening manner, they asked me to close the church, then to go away for a few days on vacation, etc. I refused. I couldn't close the church, nor did I allow anyone to do so. I would not close the church! I did not build it, but I kept it. I had been entrusted with it and I would not close it as long as there was even one person who would come in to pray. They saw that nothing could be done about this, so it occurred to them to lock up the children in their houses—on the pretext that the parents agreed to do so—so that no one had contact with them. The children were under house arrest. The church, assembled from all over, earnestly prayed. We celebrated Holy Mass and followed the already established afternoon program. Then, the parents brought messages from the children, and I shared them in church and preached on those messages. Later, they decided to arrest me because [they assumed] another priest would come who would not dare to speak like that. However, this was not the case, and whatever move they made, it was growing better, more powerful, and stronger in Medjugorje because there was no way that it could be destroyed and stopped; that it could stop and be blocked; that we could be stopped. No way. It was in vain for any persecutor to stand up against all this and this phenomenon.

"Then they started harassing Bishop Žanić," he went on. "He was invited to Sarajevo. After five hours of conversation with UDBA, he returned to Mostar. He informed me of this conversation after midnight. It was difficult."

The visionaries were constantly surrounded by their closest neighbors, such as Ivan Ivanković, who—as he says—went to Podbrdo three times a day. They carried ropes and sticks to enclose the space where daily apparitions took place to protect the children from the crowd.

"One evening—when there was already a ban on going up the hill—my sister suggested I go to the hill, as the visionaries said that only the neighbors and they would go because Our Lady was supposed to come to Apparition Hill at 11 p.m.," Ivan Ivanković recounted. "I got dressed quickly. There was no one on the way—although, according to the ban, the police were supposed to be there. It was a beautiful summer night. We went up and there was already a little group humming and praying at the apparition site. The visionaries were there, Marinko, my wife, Janja…And then, at around 11 p.m., like a bolt from the blue, light came from the sky and descended upon us. In that moment, I 'disappeared'! Where I was and for how long, I have no idea! After I came back to reality and as I was kneeling, I just sat on my feet. We prayed, we screamed, emotions overwhelmed us…Marija said, 'Be still, Our Lady has come, we see her, and she has come to you in the light, so you will be the first to witness to the world that Our Lady has come here.'"

He also had other unusual experiences during those first days, such as seeing changes in the sun.

"One afternoon, my friend Stipe Šego and I went to the hill a little earlier," he explained. "We sat on a stone recounting those first days, and when I looked at it, I saw that it was unusual. I asked him if he saw any changes in the sun, and he said he couldn't look at the sun. And I could look at the sun normally, which cannot otherwise be done! And it looked like a host had been created inside of it, like balloons—the light and the sun was coming down toward us and then I fell on my back. He asked me what was happening, and I told him that the sun was coming down on me. That lasted maybe two or three minutes."

Ivan Ivanković reported that he saw this twice more later and then never again. He also went out once into the street and saw people in small groups kneeling and looking toward Križevac.

"I asked what they were looking at and they said 'turning of the cross,'" he remembered. "I rubbed my eyes a little and I saw that it was really rotating! It turned into a 'Tau' [a T-shape] and then rotated. I tested my cousin and asked him if it rotated to the left or to the right. He said to the left, and it was [rotating] to the left. The women around me confirmed this, as well."

Ivan Ivanković's testimony was also confirmed by neighbor Marinko Ivanković, who spent the most time with the children in those days.

"There was simply no cross on Križevac," Marinko said. "Either you saw a T-shaped cross or just the light; there was nothing else."

On that afternoon, Marinko was helping his sister and brother-in-law build their house when he saw people kneeling around the church and looking toward Podbrdo.

"'Look at Our Lady on the hill,' a woman told me," he remembered. "I stopped the car, got out, and saw exactly as if a small candle was burning and its flame was slowly rising up two meters [6.5 feet] and slowly coming down. And it did so several times. The next day, I went with a friend of mine to see where it had been burning, but we found no trace of fire there. That was exactly where the statue of Our Lady is today."

Marinko also recalled the testimony of the wife of Džudže, a butcher from Čitluk, who saw the letters written in the sky.

"She walked to the church, and when she came in front of the church, she saw—starting from Apparition Hill—the following words written in the sky: Peace, peace, peace to you," Marinko shared. "And these letters went from Apparition Hill to Križevac.

They went slowly. The letters were golden. She entered the church and said, 'Come out to see the miracle!' And whoever was in the church went out and watched. The letters moved to Križevac and from Križevac toward the church, and it gradually disappeared."

Marinko added that, at the time, they thought that the authorities "had let a plane leave a trail in the sky and to write that," but it was impossible for it to be done by a plane.

"I don't know the exact date, but it seems to me that it was July 2nd," he continued. "For the first time, Our Lady called the visionaries to come to Apparition Hill at night. Thirty to forty people went from here. We arrived exactly at 11 p.m. People had made a hole on the spot where the statue of Our Lady is now. They used to take dirt, stones; everything was dug up. My older son cut tobacco and made a cross, someone else brought flowers, another brought a plastic statue of Our Lady, and some brought rosaries and hung them [on the cross]…The visionaries began to pray. I was standing to the right of one visionary when they started making the sign of the cross, 'In the name of the Father and of the Son and of the Holy Spirit…' I stood with my head down and my eyes closed when I heard a voice say, 'Look at the sky.' You know what the sky in July in Medjugorje is like. It's without clouds, there is no moon, [just a] blue sky full of stars. And I saw—the sky was opening and light was coming toward me. I said, 'Look at the light!' A few voices behind me echoed the same. One little girl, Zdenka Jurković (12), began to cry bitterly and visionary Marija said, 'Quiet, kneel down. Our Lady will pray with us.' And everyone knelt where they were. We prayed for thirty to forty minutes. The guys from Čilići, the area below Križevac, saw the light around us and that something was happening. They came to us and found us kneeling and praying. And, at one point, the visionaries stood up and said, 'Our Lady is calling you. Whoever wants to touch her can touch her.' We all at once jumped into that hole, and they said, 'Our Lady has left! One of you stepped on Our Lady's veil and Our Lady left.'"

Marinko's house was right next to Vicka's parents' house, so the pilgrims would regularly stop by when descending from Podbrdo, as their houses were just below Apparition Hill and the path led past them.

"So, as people kept on coming down from the hill, I ran out of water in my water tank, because there was no water supply system at that time," Marinko explained. "What could we do? The communists didn't allow the firefighters to supply us with water. So, we would pretend to light a fire and they would come and pour water into our water tank. That's how they brought me fourteen tanks [of water]! Later, they regularly brought me water."

Marinko also confirmed Fr. Janko's conversation with Vicka when he asked her if it was true that Marinko charged for water.

"'What's up with you, man, he gave wine and brandy, as well, and didn't even take a dime from anybody. Our Lady will pay him!'" Marinko reported that Vicka told him.

. . .

One extremely important day in Marinko's life is also linked to that gratitude for him.

"Fr. Jozo's trial had just begun on Monday and, on Saturday, I was distilling brandy, as I am doing today," Marinko said. "Vicka said she would not attend school anymore. She and Jakov had apparitions every day. They stopped by our house because, when the brandy is being distilled, we have a little barbecue, our neighbors come. This is our custom here. At that time, we used to pray and sing Our Lady's songs and the like...They stopped by around 5 p.m. and talked with us for about ten minutes. They left, but after that, they invited me: 'Marinko, come with us for the apparition!' They invited me to come to her [Vicka's] room in their house. My shoes, clothing, and hands were dirty, but she kept insisting, saying it wouldn't bother anyone. Jakov invited me, too...They left. I kindled a fire and, two or three minutes later, I went, as well. My son Dado and his friends Mate Šego and Dražen came along with me. I just stepped on the first stair when Jakov called me to hurry up, saying that Our Lady had come. How did he know I was there? He couldn't see or hear me because he was in the house. I jumped three stairs at a time and saw them kneeling and talking to Our Lady. I also knelt down and raised my hands, 'Dear Our Lady, prove to those unbelievers that Fr. Jozo is not guilty.' I kept my hands up in the air when Vicka and Jakov told me, 'Marinko, Our Lady is smiling at you. Our Lady is coming to you! Our Lady thanks you for everything you have been doing for the pilgrims, what you have been doing for the Church, and because you firmly believe. Our Lady is blessing you and Our Lady is kissing you.'"

Sharing these words, Marinko spoke with visible excitement and tears in his eyes.

"I neither saw nor heard Our Lady, but I did feel Our Lady's blessing and Our Lady's kiss," Marinko said. "I can't forget it for the rest of my life! After that, they turned around and said, 'Fr. Jozo has come to us!' What do you mean Fr. Jozo, he is in jail?! And they said that he was listening to what they sang about him—because my wife wrote a song about him...Other people also came. Some entered Vicka's room, some stood at the door, and some stayed in the hallway. Vicka and Jakov turned and said, 'Our Lady is coming to you. Our Lady is putting her hands on each of you and is blessing you.' These were real wonders."

Marinko also recalled another unusual event from that first period.

"Fr. Jozo, who went to prison on August 17th, was replaced by Father Tomislav Vlašić from Čapljina," he began. "Fifteen days before Christmas, I was in the church and was standing, as always, in the middle of the church, where the door is now—the door was not there at the time—right where the statue of Our Lady is now.

There was silence—at that time, people didn't turn and look at anything else in the church—when, all of a sudden, I saw people looking above me somewhere in the ceiling and talking. Grgo Vasilj, a strong believer, was in church with me every night. I asked him 'what was going on?' Why did they look up and talk? He said they had seen Jesus' head in the window. It was there, he said, ten to fifteen minutes. The next day, I didn't go to the right, where I always used to go, but I went to the left. Tomislav Vlašić celebrated Mass and I looked. There was nothing. When he took and raised the chalice and the host for blessing [transubstantiation], I looked at the window: There was Jesus' head in profile. He was looking down. He had long hair, a beard, and one eye was visible. He was looking at the church. At that time, the windows were transparent, not stained glass as they are today. People were showing it to each other and discussing."

According to Marinko, this went on for several evenings. Fr. Tomislav Vlašić noticed it, as well, and raised his voice, "Why are you looking up? Jesus is here!"

"The next day, I said to him, 'Fr. Tomislav, we've known each other for a long time. You conducted marriage meetings with us. Do you think I don't know that—and, if I didn't know that, would I ever come to church and would I have this faith?' The next day, people saw and spoke about it again, but he didn't say anything this time."

Next, Marinko mentioned the event that happened at night in the field.

"We prayed all three rosaries and, at about 10 p.m., the visionaries stood up and prayed the Our Father," he began. "They knelt down and Our Lady came to them. Ivanka and Vicka were not with them. They spoke with Our Lady very briefly and then stood up. 'Our Lady is calling you. Whoever wants to touch her can touch her.' There were people from Ljubuski and Čapljina praying with us—

about 150 people. We made four lines and, as each person came to one of the visionaries, the visionary would tell that person that he had touched Our Lady's hair, her shoulder, where he touched her... Maybe 50 people had touched her. At one point, the visionaries said, 'Our Lady has gone!' They made the sign of the cross. Marija, who was three or four steps away from us, started crying bitterly."

"Marija, what happened?" Marinko asked her.

"Our Lady left all dirty!" Marija replied. "Some of you, as you were touching Our Lady's dress, it started to turn black."

"The next day, everyone went to church for confession," Marinko said.

His words were confirmed by the visionary Ivan Dragičević, who stated that, in those days, they had apparitions everywhere—not only on Podbrdo. Our Lady appeared to them in the houses, in the fields...

"In front of Đuka Ivanković's house, in the field where there is a statue now, there was a threshing floor," Ivan explained. "Wheat was always sifted there and, when the hill was blocked, we—the whole village—gathered there for prayer. We prayed all night. That's where Our Lady used to come. I remember well. We could touch her there; people wanted to touch her, then we brought their hands to her... That is when what was being discussed happened, when stains remained on her dress.

"Afterward, we had apparitions in the houses—at Jakov's mother's house, where we met and prayed, or at Vicka's house," he continued. "Later, we moved to the church, to the sacristy. Then, from the sacristy to the choir loft, from the choir loft to the bell tower, from the bell tower to the parish house, where the Mass intentions are now being recorded. We moved to these places because the previous places were banned. They [police] used to come, so we had to move."

Ivan added that these days would never be erased from his memory, no matter how difficult they were.

“I think the most difficult time was when Fr. Jozo was taken to prison,” he shared. “That day, when the police came and closed the church, people came from all over Medjugorje in long lines and they [the police] couldn’t do anything. It was a special sight. I was in Čapljina that day. We were with Fr. Tomislav Vlašić; we spent all day with him. We got away a bit. In the afternoon, as we returned to Medjugorje, reaching the post office, we saw that the police would not allow anyone to approach the place and that something was going on. Fr. Jozo was arrested and the church was closed.”

Ivan recalled the incident, which took place on August 17, when the pastor of Medjugorje—Fr. Jozo Zovko—was arrested by the police early in the morning.

“Every hour brought something new,” he remembered. “Many nights were sleepless; something was going to happen. We were most afraid of the authorities. I remember what my parents went through. Nothing was more difficult to me than watching what they were doing to my parents. I remember well when two men came to our house. I was upstairs and my mother said I was not at home. They told her, ‘Tell your son to stop talking about it and we’ll give you as much money as you want. We will give you everything.’ My mother and father, though under this intense pressure, said, ‘We cannot say this to our child. He sees, he tells us that he sees, and he is not afraid of anything.’”

Ivan explained that the visionaries and their parents would not have been able to withstand it with their human strength had it not been for Our Lady’s help.

“We would not have been able to do it all if Our Lady, from the beginning, didn’t give us strength, comfort us, encourage us, and give us everything we needed to do—how we were supposed to take our stand on many issues,” he said. “She asked us to be patient, not to be afraid of anything, and if we had to sacrifice on the way, we had to accept it. Nothing was ever difficult for us. Medical examinations began; nothing was difficult for us because, with her support and strength, we absolutely got it [the strength], as well. I was not afraid of anything and I could do anything."

Ivan had changed from withdrawn and timid to fearless and unyielding practically overnight.

"I see Our Lady as paradise is seen," he said. "Behind her, I see paradise—the beauty and light of paradise. The first sign of Our Lady coming is light. As soon as I see this light, I stop praying and that is when Our Lady comes. But, to describe it all, to describe her smile, her tenderness and her warmth...I have told pilgrims a thousand times: You have seen many paintings and statues in chapels and churches, but to convey the beauty of Our Lady in the painting and the statue is impossible. I tell people that if they saw Our Lady for just one second—no more than that—I don't know if life on earth would be interesting to them anymore."

Ivan has had daily apparitions since the first day, and yet, he testified that it is still impossible to get used to them.

"Every day, from last night until today, I would say there is an alarm within me and all I have done since yesterday is anticipate tonight's meeting," he said. "This is all I do—I wonder if Our Lady will be here tonight, have I been doing what she asks me to do. Through all these years this question has grown in me. Every day I want Our Lady to be happy with me, with what I do, and with what she asks of me. Not only that, but also with what my family does, because many today wonder why none of the visionaries became priests or nuns. God has another plan. In the time we live, we want to say that the world, through family, has a future. Therefore, we have chosen this path and, through this path, we can certainly give a lot."

Ivan's words were confirmed by the youngest visionary, Jakov Čolo, who said that, from the first moment he saw Our Lady, he experienced her love and there were no difficulties. He has not been afraid of anything since then.

“From the first moment when I saw Our Lady, I was ready to do anything for her,” Jakov said. “I always felt the power of God in my heart; that Our Lady was with me; that I should only go forward, so there were no major difficulties.”

However, Jakov said he was most concerned with how his mother would handle all of these events.

“Because I was her only son, I lived alone with her, and sometimes she didn’t even know where I was,” he explained. “That worried me the most. If you ask me if I were afraid of something, I wasn't.”

Jakov remembered an incident in which he and his uncle went to the Kravica waterfalls, ten kilometers (6.2 miles) from Medjugorje. The police intercepted them on the road, stopped the car, and took him for questioning.

“But, I never had any great fear of it,” Jakov said. “I thought that, if it was God’s plan, He would give me the strength to endure it all.”

Jakov explained that every day with Our Lady was special and interesting to him—both then and now.

“After a while, my mom died, and a year later, my dad also died,” he shared. “I was left alone and, in that, I recognized the power and the grace of God; I recognized Our Lady’s love that prepared me for all this. I never asked myself why. Through the graces I have received, I have also received the crosses that God gives, which must be carried in life. So, I always remember the first days that prepared me for all this and I remember the faith. Because it is beautiful to see Our Lady, but I realized that, through Our Lady, I received an even greater gift to meet her Son—to come to know Jesus Christ, who gave me the strength to go through my whole life.”

Jakov added that he was especially joyful that he spent his childhood with Our Lady.

“Although, sometimes, when I saw my friends playing soccer—which I used to love very much—and I was going to church, I wondered why I was not with them," he admitted. "But then, when I came to the church, I thanked Jesus that I could be there with Him. For me, this is a great grace and a great gift for which I can never thank God enough throughout my life."

The visionaries often asked themselves—and they asked Our Lady, too—why she chose them and why Medjugorje. They also asked numerous questions for people who came to Medjugorje.

"At the beginning, there were these questions that people used to tell us to ask because they wanted to see what was happening," Mirjana began. "So, they used to say: ask this, ask that...Basically, those first days, she used to give us simple answers, such as asking for faith here, that she found it here, asking for prayer...It was as if she had prepared us for all that would guide us through the years to come. At least, that is how I understood it.

"It's hard for me to talk about the early days because it was a shock for me," she continued. "Those days, it was like I was living in some kind of shock. I felt good only when I prayed. Only then did I have peace. I could not, by any means, comprehend that I had the honor to see Our Lady, to have deserved this. I was confused. It might have been easier for me if someone had prepared me and told me that it was possible; if I had heard of Lourdes or Fatima; if I had read those books and had learned that Our Lady could come to Earth. But, to see her without any foreknowledge that it was possible, as if I were in a fog all those days."

When asked how she knows when an apparition is coming, Mirjana replied that she always prepares herself for the apparition with fasting and prayer.

"It is not difficult for me," she said. "I am too excited to eat, anyway. And, in prayer, I wait for her to come. I feel it within myself...I start to feel the warmth in my heart, which gradually becomes stronger and it feels as if my heart is burning. If Our Lady would not come at that moment, I think that I would explode from the power of that beauty. It's not something ugly. It's exceedingly beautiful. And when she comes, it's as if I'm not there anymore. I don't feel myself. I neither see nor hear anything around me. I just see her. And all becomes blue. I always say that, perhaps, the best description of this feeling is this: As any mother, I would give my life for my children. But, when I am with Our Lady, they do not exist; I do not remember them. I am not even aware that I am a mother, a wife; that I have children. Absolutely nothing. I just desire that she may continue looking at me and that I may look at her, and that's all."

Mirjana explained that Our Lady leads their conversation, not her.

"I sense within myself what I can and what I cannot ask her," Mirjana shared. "She doesn't need to tell me, 'You can't ask this.' I feel what can be asked and then I ask that. She is always the one who leads the conversation. I have never touched her, nor has she touched me. And, like I said, I didn't feel the need for it, either, because when she is looking at you, you have everything; you feel that she is hugging you...Even now, tears still come to my eyes when I think of it [she wipes her tears away]. You feel that you are loved, important. That you are important to someone...I think that those who are in paradise feel like this."

Mirjana remembered an event several years ago when a man came to the door of her home in Medjugorje.

"He looked vaguely familiar, but I did not recognize him at first," she began. "He seemed reluctant to speak and he avoided eye contact."

"Can I help you?" Mirjana said she asked the man.

"Please, forgive me," the stranger replied.

"For what?"

"I'm one of the policemen who interrogated you back in 1981," Mirjana reported the man saying. "I'm really sorry for what we put you through."

Mirjana said that this was not the first time that someone had apologized to her like that, but she could never remember the specific incidents they felt guilty about. She had long since forgiven and forgotten. She prayed for her persecutors during even the worst harassments, like when they raised their batons as if to strike her or called Our Lady terrible names.

"It's ok, that was a long time ago," Mirjana reassured the man, who seemed relieved.

"I have something for you," he said to her, as he held up a cassette tape. He had saved the recording of that interrogation for all those years. Now, he came with the intention to share it with her.

"I thought you might like to hear it," he said to her. Mirjana remembered that a tape recorder had laid on the table during almost every interrogation.

"I recalled the distinct click of the record button that marked the beginning of each session," she said. "I never had the opportunity, nor the desire, to listen to any of the recordings. I worried that doing so now might resurrect some bad memories. But, I was also curious."

In that moment, Mirjana decided to invite the man into her house, and they put the tape in a cassette player.

"At first, I thought you were lying," the man said. "But, after we questioned you, I just wanted to shake your hand. I couldn't then—not in front of my colleagues—but now, I want to, and here's why..."

Then, he pressed play and a memory from the past crackled through the speakers. Mirjana could hear the interrogator saying, "You're deceiving the people," and her response, "I'm not deceiving anyone."

"Don't you see that your story is absurd?" the interrogator can be heard asking her on the tape.

"I'm telling the truth," young Mirjana replied in the recording.

"That's all I can do."

After so many years, Mirjana was hearing her teenage voice through the tape player. She said it felt like a surreal experience.

"I could hardly believe that the other voice on the tape—with all its gruffness and anger—belonged to the same meek man who was now sitting in front of me," Mirjana said. "The tape continued."

Next, the interrogator asked her again what she saw "on that hill."

"I saw Our Lady," Mirjana replied to him in the recording.

"You saw shit!" he shouted at the time.

"No. That's what I'm looking at right now," the young girl responded on the tape. Mirjana was surprised to hear herself being so bold.

"It would have been different had I been interrogated *before* I started seeing Our Lady," Mirjana said. "Fear would have overwhelmed me to the point of tears, and I never could have challenged a policeman—or any adult—in such a way. But, from June 24, 1981, onward, the timidity that had plagued me for most of my childhood had all but vanished."

Her guest stopped the tape and said, "It was your lack of fear that convinced me that you were telling the truth."

"I thanked him for bringing the recording and reassured him that I harbored no ill feelings from those days," Mirjana said. "'You were just doing your job,' I said. After he left, I sat down and tried to process all the memories that the recording had stirred up. I closed my eyes and my mind wandered back to the time when the interrogation had taken place."

That time—almost four decades ago—has not changed for the visionaries since the first day until now, as three of them (Vicka, Ivan, and Marija) still have daily apparitions.

"Even today, the feeling is the same," Marija said. "It is the feeling of

Heaven! The feeling that I'm no longer in this dimension, that I'm no longer attached to anything. Although I have family, I have children, I am a mother of four sons and I am certainly attached to them and this is the most wonderful thing God could give me. But, at the same time, my house is Heaven. My goal is paradise, and we are deeply aware of it. And we wouldn't think it over for a second. There is nothing to think over. Often, there are problems and difficulties and ups and downs, but faith is the gift that helps us go forward with Our Lady. Our Lady gives messages. Our Lady calls us. Sometimes, it is certainly difficult for us to see that Our Lady is sad and that she expects more of us; that we may not have responded the way she wants us to, and that, at the same time, we have the potential to respond better."

Marija remembered that, in those first days of the apparitions, they thought that other people around them also saw and heard what they saw, as well as their conversation with Our Lady.

"Our Lady summoned us with her hand and, when we approached her, we started talking," Marija recalled. "There were pictures and films taken during the first days. When the apparition ended, Our Lady blessed us and said, 'Go in the peace of God,' and we left. Then, people asked, 'What happened?' 'Haven't you heard? Haven't you seen?' We would answer and became aware that what we had seen, others had not seen."

Marija laughed at those confusing days and the crowd created by the people in their homes.

"My mother used to say that our house was no longer ours, but that it was like a bus station," she continued. "People came, passed by...I remember that, at one point, we had no more water in the water tank, but in the basement we had some wine, so my dad used to joke, 'There is no water, but there is wine.' There was a water tank in front of the parish office, so people who came from the city used to open the faucet and wait for cold water, not knowing that there was no cold water from the water tank."

Marija added that their greatest strength was the fact that there were six of them.

"I remember when the bishop called me to tell me, 'You know what, Marija? I had a priest who, every time he entered the bathroom to use the toilet or bath, he always saw a bathroom full of frogs,'" Marija shared. "He tried to explain to me that it was possible that I saw Our Lady that way, as well. I said to him, 'Excuse me, Father Bishop, but if I see frogs, then Vicka and Ivan and Jakov and Mirjana and Ivanka also see them, and that is not the case.' For him, I was like Bernadette of Lourdes. I really decided to tell him, he is my Bishop. But, I said that if I were sick..., but I am not sick and everyone knows I am not sick. I can't tell you that I see Our Lady because I'm sick. More than once, someone wants to put limitations on God. God has no limits and nor does Our Lady. We've seen her all these years. When asked at the outset how long she would appear, Our Lady asked us if we were tired of her and we said that we would never again ask these questions."

Marija noted that she learned a lot from Our Lady's presence in her life because Our Lady was always positive.

"The most positive person in all of this is her," she said. "She is our hope, not only the protectress and the one who inspires and encourages us...She says, 'I am with you,' 'do not be afraid,' 'do not forget, I am your mother.' More than once, Our Lady said that she is our mother and that she loves us. Today, there is a lack of love and peace. Sometimes, a person needs a hug. The mantle that Our Lady offers to mankind—even today—is the great need of man. And as Our Lady said, 'I did not get tired of man.' God is not tired of man and gives us hope and sends us His mother.

"I know that Our Lady is here," Marija continued. "From children, we became adults. We have been with Our Lady more than without her. We are here and bear witness with our lives. We really stand behind all of this as long as we breathe: Our Lady is here; God is at work here; we touch Our Lady; we embrace her; she speaks to us, and she looks at us. Not just us, but everyone else, as well.

"When they forbade us to go to the hill, where else would we go but to church?" she concluded. "We did not know that, in the church space—that was the law at the time—we could pray without any problems. Then, we wondered why Our Lady appeared to us on the hill—as it was soon forbidden—when she could appear in the church, as well. Thanks to Our Lady, we discovered the Church, faith, adoration, confession—that is the most wonderful thing we could experience. Such adoration as we have in Medjugorje does not exist in other places. Or confession in Medjugorje. I spoke with a Spanish priest who heard the confession of seventy people in only one day. He said that he had been a priest for thirty-five years, but he never saw such a deep confession and faith in people and the desire to convert and to approach God. That is Medjugorje—meeting with God through Our Lady. As Our Lady said, 'God has allowed me to be with you.' And, what has she done from the beginning? She allowed us to fall in love with her and to follow her. She led us and took the parish of Medjugorje as an example and, through it, she started sending messages throughout the world. Have we answered—and how well have we answered—God knows, and we will know it in Heaven."

FROM THE CONVERSATION OF FR. JANKO BUBALO WITH VISIONARY VICKA

FR. JANKO: "All right. And Vicka, we have somehow arrived at the eighth day from what was certainly a strange happening on Podbrdo on the 24th, that is, on the 25th of June. I don't know, but it seems to me that it was really somehow a bit easier for you."

VICKA: "Yes, a bit. But, even then, we had our share of agony and ill luck. For example, on that day, they summoned us and our parents to school, and..."

FR. JANKO: "Who summoned you?"

VICKA: "Well, you know who! Those from the Internal [Secret Police]."

FR. JANKO: "And, what did they want from your parents?"

VICKA: "The same thing they wanted from us! They tried to persuade them to forbid us to go to Podbrdo or else they would declare us sick; we wouldn't be able to go to school anywhere, and the like. A hundred things."

FR. JANKO: "And, you went—what else could you do?"

VICKA: "Our parents went, but we did not. Well, we did fail to come to an agreement with them half the night prior to this! But, our parents didn't go every time when they were summoned, either."

FR. JANKO: "It's clear that it wasn't easy for your parents, either. And, how they coped with it."

VICKA: "They did well. They defended us as much as they could. You know that it wasn't easy for them."

FR. JANKO: "Did your parents try to convince you that you needed to put all this aside, or...?"

VICKA: "Not at all! They were not afraid of anything. Just like us. Well, Our Lady was helping them, too!"

FR. JANKO: "And thus, you awaited the evening and your departure to Podbrdo?"

VICKA: "Well, I wish we did, my dear friar!"

FR. JANKO: "What else?"

VICKA: "Prior to that, two men from the municipality came to see us. They were sitting outside. They drank and chatted a little...And, when it was time to go to Podbrdo, they somehow got us in the car and took us with them..."

FR. JANKO: "Where did they take you?"

VICKA: "Well, we were told that we would go to the church, to have a drink or something like that. And, as we were debating with them, the car left."

FR. JANKO: "Whom did they take?"

VICKA: "Me, Ivanka, and Marija. They pushed little Jakov in, as well, but his mother pulled him out as they left."

FR. JANKO: "And, Ivan and Mirjana?"

VICKA: "They weren't present that time around."

FR. JANKO: "Did those two really come for you, or did they perhaps intend to make some kind of joke?"

VICKA: "How would I know? I only know how it was and that's it."

FR. JANKO: "And, what did they really tell you?"

VICKA: "Well, I already told you this: To go with them like for a ride, for some kind of questioning, for refreshments... They kind of tried to fool us, but they knew what they wanted."

FR. JANKO: "Did you try to refuse to go?"

VICKA: "Of course, we did! And, they kept trying to convince us that it was nothing. Well, let someone come with us, and the like... The car left and it was over."

FR. JANKO: "And, did you approach the church?"

VICKA: "Yes, we did. But, the car passed by it and crossed the bridge toward the post office."

FR. JANKO: "Which post office?"

VICKA: "Toward our post office. There, across the bridge. Well, you know where our post office is!"

FR. JANKO: "And then?"

VICKA: "We then began to pound inside the car and they stopped."

FR. JANKO: "And then?"

VICKA: "They brought us back to the church."

FR. JANKO: "With the same car?"

VICKA: "With the same one, what else?"

FR. JANKO: "And, how did they, in general, treat you?"

VICKA: "Well, quite nicely, except that they made fun of us like that."

FR. JANKO: "And, were any of your relatives with you?"

VICKA: "Yes, yes. My sister Zdenka was with me, and Ivanka's brother Mario was with her."

FR. JANKO: "And, what about their reaction?"

VICKA: "What could they do? They also resisted, but what could they do?"

FR. JANKO: "How could so many of you fit in one car?"

VICKA: "It was some kind of a van, or whatever they call it."

FR. JANKO: "All right, then. But, you didn't see Our Lady that day?"

VICKA: "Well, of course, we did! Very much! I'll never forget it."

FR. JANKO: "Where did you see her?"

VICKA: "Well, in the car!"

FR. JANKO: "In the car?"

VICKA: "Yes, yes. Right in the car!"

FR. JANKO: "And, how was that? Was the car in motion at the time or did it stop?"

VICKA: "I don't know that."

FR. JANKO: "And, how is that [possible], again?"

VICKA: "Quite simple! At the time, we didn't see the car at all."

FR. JANKO: "I don't understand!"

VICKA: "What do you want from me? When Our Lady appeared, there was neither a sign of the car nor of anyone else."

FR. JANKO: "Again, I don't get it."

VICKA: "Well, it is the same as if we would see Our Lady in this room now. We see Our Lady, but we don't see or feel anything else."

FR. JANKO: "And, did you also pray for Our Lady to appear?"

VICKA: "No, no. Who could even think of it at the time?"

FR. JANKO: "But, how?"

VICKA: "Well, Our Lady, as on so many other occasions, appeared among us and that was it!"

FR. JANKO: "Were you surprised, frightened, or...?"

VICKA: "Well, we didn't even have time to think of anything!"

FR. JANKO: "Nonetheless, that was strange!"

VICKA: "Well, yes, it was. They were frightened, but I wasn't at all."

FR. JANKO: "Who are they?"

VICKA: "Marija and Ivanka. They became petrified from fear. That's why those two [two officials] called them witches and everything else..."

FR. JANKO: "How long did Our Lady remain with you?"

VICKA: "Not for long. She told us something, she smiled, and left."

FR. JANKO: "What did she say to you?"

VICKA: "Nothing special. She told us not to be afraid of anything and the like...Her main concern was to appear to us; [to let us know] that she didn't forget us. Our Lady is good!"

FR. JANKO: "And, then what?"

VICKA: "They again invited us for some sort of refreshments, whatever. But, we just looked for a way to get away as soon as we could so that we could go home."

Holy Saint Anthony,

gentle and powerful in your help, your love for
God and charity for His creatures made you worthy,
when on earth, to possess miraculous powers.
Miracles waited on your word, which you were
always ready to request for those in trouble or
anxiety. Encouraged by this thought,
I implore you to obtain for me (*request*).
The answer to my prayer may require a miracle.
Even so, you are the saint of miracles.
Gentle and loving Saint Anthony,
whose heart is ever full
of human sympathy,
take my petition to the
Infant Savior for whom
you have such a great love,
and the gratitude of my
heart will ever be yours.

Amen.

In Appreciation of Your Faithful Support

FR. JANKO: "And, what did they do?"

VICKA: "They dropped us off at the church and left."

FR. JANKO: "And you?"

VICKA: "We stayed for a while in the church, a bit at the parish house, and then we went off to our own homes. We took a shortcut across the fields."

FR. JANKO: "All right, Vicka. According to this, Ivan, Mirjana, and little Jakov were not with you?"

VICKA: "No, no, they weren't."

FR. JANKO: "Did they go to Podbrdo to see Our Lady?"

VICKA: "As far as I know, they did not. They were confused, too, and what could they do?"

FR. JANKO: "Then, they didn't even see Our Lady this time?"

VICKA: "They did. I think they did. At least Ivan did. He later told me."

FR. JANKO: "Really strange. You didn't tell me this before."

VICKA: "Well, its turn just didn't come up. Who can remember it all?"

FR. JANKO: "And, that's the way it ended?"

VICKA: "Yes. We arrived home somewhere around sunset."

FR. JANKO: "And, what about the people?"

VICKA: "The poor people! They waited and prayed up there. Then, they went home. Where else?"

FR. JANKO: "Therefore, for the second day in a row, neither Our Lady nor Our Lady's children were at Podbrdo. Yet, the people did not give up."

VICKA: "They didn't. The people are strange when they follow Our Lady."

FR. JANKO: "So, the people are strange, and Our Lady, too!"

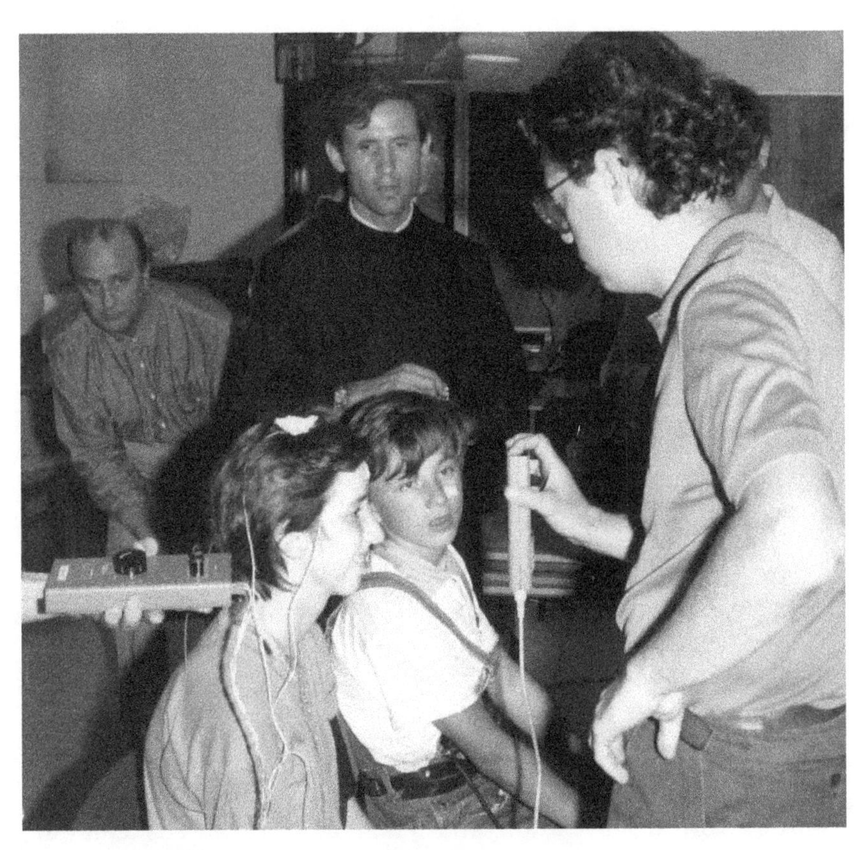

How visionaries see

A Jesuit, Father Mijo Nikić—a priest and psychologist, who was a member of the International Papal Commission for investigation of Medjugorje phenomenon—in his work "Psychological Aspects of Apparitions – Discernment of Spirits in St. Ignatius of Loyola," wrote that the philosophical principle of *Quidquid recipitur, per modum recipientis, recipitur* (whatever is received, is received in the manner of the recipient) intends to say that each of our perceptions is necessarily subjective.

"Everything that a person sees, hears, feels, experiences, comes to know, all this passes through the filter of his inner world, of his affectivity, of his past, which—to a greater or lesser extent—distorts objective reality," Fr. Mijo said. "The aforementioned truth applies not only to the messages that a person receives from this world, but also to the messages we receive from God, or from beings from the other world, such as the divine persons of the Most Holy Trinity, the Mother of God, the angels, and the saints. All that we hear from them passes through our inner world, through the 'filter of our senses,' as Cardinal Joseph Ratzinger, the current pope emeritus Benedict XVI, would say."

Fr. Mijo added that the great connoisseur of souls and renowned teacher of the spiritual life—the founder of the Jesuits, St. Ignatius Loyola—thought in a similar way. In his "Rules for Discerning of Spirits," St. Ignatius wrote that the devil can also get dressed. In other words, the devil can disguise himself as an angel of light in order to deceive a soul more effectively and take it away from God. Therefore, we need to be careful and to examine the spirits well before we completely believe them. Furthermore, Fr. Mijo said that the doctrine of the Church clearly distinguishes the public Revelation from private revelation, and remarked that there is a significant difference between them.

"Public Revelation 'refers to the revealing action of God directed to humanity as a whole, and which finds its literary expression in the two parts of the Bible: the Old and New Testaments,'" Fr. Mijo said. "God gradually made himself known to men in a way that they [could] understand him. And, most of all, he spoke to them in his son Jesus Christ, who became a man to tell people in their own language what God wants and expects from them. When talking about revelation, the Catechism of the Catholic Church makes us aware that we have not yet fully comprehended or understood God's revelation: 'Yet, even if Revelation is already complete, it has not been made completely explicit; it remains for Christian faith gradually to grasp its full significance over the course of the centuries,' (CCC, 66). Jesus himself told us that he had much more to tell us, but we cannot bear it now (compare John 16:12-14)."

Fr. Mijo interpreted this and added that, in addition to public revelation, the Church also accepts private revelation—that is, various apparitions, visions, inner locutions, and so on. He also quoted the Catechism of the Catholic Church: "Throughout the ages, there have been so-called 'private' revelations, some of which have been recognized by the authority of the Church. They do not belong, however, to the deposit of faith. It is not their role to improve or complete Christ's definitive Revelation, but to help live more fully by it in a certain period of history." (CCC, 67)

"Private revelation shows its credibility by leading us back to the definitive public Revelation," he continued. "The acceptance of the recognized private revelations should comply with the rules of prudence. A Flemish theologian, an eminent scholar in this field, states succinctly that ecclesiastical approval of a private revelation has three elements: 1) the message contains nothing contrary to faith or morals; 2) it is lawful to make it public; 3) the faithful are authorized to accept it with prudence."

Fr. Mijo added that, when speaking about private revelations, Pope Emeritus Benedict XVI applied this criterion, "The criterion for the truth and value of a private revelation is, therefore, its orientation to Christ himself. When it leads us away from him, when it becomes independent of him, or even presents itself as another and better plan of salvation more important than the Gospel, then it certainly does not come from the Holy Spirit, who guides us more deeply into the Gospel and not away from it. This does not mean that a private revelation will not offer new emphases or give rise to new devotional forms or deepen and spread older forms. But, in all of this, there must be a nurturing of faith, hope, and love, which are the unchanging path to salvation for everyone."

Fr. Mijo explained that theological anthropology distinguishes three ways of perceiving or seeing reality: 1) vision with the senses and, hence, exterior bodily perception (*visio sensibilis*); 2) interior perception (*visio imaginativa*); and 3) spiritual vision or maturing, which occurs on a higher level of mystical experience (*visio intellectualis*).

"Private revelations—that is, various visions and apparitions—are considered to be a kind of interior perception (*visio imaginativa*) since the images and figures shown in the visions do not exist in the external reality and they are 'seen' only by the visionaries, for whom the aforementioned interior perception or maturing is equivalent to an external manifestation to the senses," he said. "This means that the visionaries have the impression that they see an appearance by external bodily perception as seen by all people. The aforementioned interior perception or *visio imaginativa* is activated when the soul is touched by the impulses, the stimuli of that which is beyond senses—that is, what is not visible or noticeable to the ordinary senses, but it is noticeable to some 'interior senses.' Figures appearing to people in private revelations touch the soul in a way that it reacts to those impulses. This is why there is a need for an interior vigilance of the heart, which is usually precluded by the intense pressure of external reality and of the images and thoughts which fill the soul."

He added that, according to Cardinal Ratzinger, the privileged recipients of apparitions and private revelations are often children because their souls are still too small to be distorted and the inner capacity of perception is still intact.

"The basic truth in every perception is that we never see a pure object or take literally a sent message," Cardinal Ratzinger said. "But, at the same time, we experience both [object and message] in our own, subjective way, which means that we distort them a little or, at least, we limit them. This is true of perception or cognition by the external senses, and even more so of perception by interior perception. In experiencing and interpreting external visible and invisible reality, there is always a share of a subjective factor. In her book *Psychology and Spiritual Discernment*, Noémi Meguerditchian says, 'We are approaching, comprehending, and understanding God—whether in our Bible reading or in things that happen to us—starting from our very selves, our fears, our ideals, our mental schemes of understanding, and reactions we have accumulated during our upbringing from the very beginning of our history.' Everything we see, hear, feel, and experience passes through the strainer or filter of our senses that carry out a work of translation. In the interior vision—much more than in the external one—there is a process of translation so that the subject is the one who is even more powerfully involved in the formation of the images of what appears. He can arrive at the image only within the bounds of his own capacities and possibilities."

Fr. Mijo remarked that it essentially means that the visions and apparitions are never transmitted as photography, either visual or audio, of what the visionaries saw and heard. Rather, that the image and content were "filtered" or "percolated" through the visionary's internal psychic apparatus—that is, through their conscious and unconscious desires, fears, expectations, conflicts, and attitudes.

"The aforementioned claim can be illustrated by the following example: If a devil and an angel appear together to a black man, in the interpretation of his experience and vision, the black man will most likely say that the angel was of a black, and the devil was of a white skin color, and the visionary who is a white man would say that the angel was of a white, and the devil was of a black skin color," Fr. Mijo explained. "Which one of them is right? I think we may say both of them. None have lied, but they have spoken differently. That is the fate of our perception. Everything that is received is received in the way of the recipient."

When all of this is applied to the specific apparitions—that is, if one assumes that it is an authentic revelation and an actual apparition that is perceived by interior perception, Fr. Mijo suggests that the aforementioned interior vision is not a fantasy, but instead a real and true way of perception.

"However, the talk of the experiential revelation and the interpretation of what has been seen in one or more apparitions are already a secondary elaboration of the originally experienced reality," he continued. "This means that, from the visionaries, we get 'filtered' or 'percolated' reality. The visionaries do not do that consciously. They speak as they can and know, often themselves aware that their speaking and description is far behind what they have actually seen and experienced. In this regard, Cardinal Ratzinger says, 'Rather, the images are, in a manner of speaking, a synthesis of the impulse coming from on high and the capacity to receive this impulse in the visionaries—in this case, the children. For this reason, the figurative language of the visions is symbolic.' In describing and interpreting what they have seen and experienced, the visionaries use the images and knowledge they have learned in school and in catechism classes. This is exactly what Cardinal Ratzinger had in mind when, regarding the description of the secret given by the Fatima visionary Lucia, he said, 'The concluding part of the "secret" uses images, which Lucia may have seen in devotional books and which draw their inspiration from long-standing intuitions of faith."

Fr. Mijo concluded that Cardinal Ratzinger's statement fit perfectly with what deep psychology reveals regarding the process of perception of any person.

"In an authentic apparition, the message and image conveyed to us by the visionaries are the result of impulses from above—from God, Jesus, the Mother of God, or a saint—and the existing abilities of the person who has the apparition," he said. "This means that the same event and the same message will be transmitted differently by the visionaries, each according to their abilities and capabilities or according to their desires, fears, and expectations. In other words, personal history, affective memory—everything that the visionary has experienced in his life necessarily interferes with the message and the vision he receives from above. Accordingly, we must say that we should be careful and critical in judging what the visionaries convey to us as the message from Heaven. It is not prudent to take everything they say right away 'for granted,' but we have to check the spirits. It is necessary to keep in mind that visionaries never transmit photos of visions or a recorded text of messages, but what comes to us has already passed through their inner world, their subconscious, their past. Bearing this in mind, it becomes clear that it is necessary to introduce rules on the discerning of spirits into this reality of private revelations and apparitions. The visionary Lucia from Fatima—who, herself, pointed out that she had received the vision, but not the interpretation of the secret—was also aware of this. 'The interpretation of the secret belongs not to the visionary, but to the Church,' said former Cardinal Ratzinger, and now Pope Emeritus Benedict XVI."

Fr. Mijo stated that when visionaries talk about future events that await us—which are often dramatic and scary—we should not take them literally as a proclamation of something that will inevitably come, but rather as a threatening danger that could happen if people do not convert. He went on to quote Cardinal Ratzinger in his interpretation of the Fatima secrets: "The future is not, in fact, unchangeably set, and the image which the children saw is in no way a film preview of a future in which nothing can be changed. Indeed, the whole point of the vision is to bring freedom onto the scene and to steer freedom in a positive direction. The purpose of the vision is not to show a film of an irrevocably fixed future. Its meaning is exactly the opposite: It is meant to mobilize the forces of change in the right direction."

"Therefore, there is no immutable destiny governing this world, but there is the Providence of God, which always has the last word," Fr.

Mijo explained. "Faith and prayer are forces that can reach into human history. Commenting on the statement of Pope John Paul II, made on May 13th, 1994, that the Mother's hand directed in the other direction the deadly bullet, which was to take his life, Cardinal Ratzinger concludes 'that, in the end, prayer is more powerful than bullets and faith more powerful than armies.'"

Fr. Mijo added that the great teacher of the spiritual life, St. Ignatius of Loyola, in his booklet *Spiritual Exercises* embraced the "Rules for the Discernment of Spirits." In number 313 of the *Spiritual Exercises,* he wrote that these are the rules "for understanding, to some extent, the different movements produced in the soul and for recognizing those that are good, to admit them, and those that are bad, to reject them." To that end, Fr. Mijo stated that, in the first two rules, Ignatius says that both the good and the evil spirit can bring peace and restlessness, joy and anxiety to the soul.

"That is why we have to be careful and, above all, we need to be honest with ourselves so that we can know exactly what kind of spirit it is," he said. "In order to discern the mentioned spirits, Ignatius gives a simple rule: He says that, when a person is rising from good to better, when he strives to avoid sin, and when he wants to do the will of God, that is when the good spirit brings peace and joy to the soul by encouraging it to continue on the current path. The evil spirit, on the contrary, in this case, brings restlessness, sorrow, and anguish to the soul, upsetting the soul with false reasons in order to discourage it from the path of spiritual progress. The case is reversed in persons who accumulate mortal sin upon mortal sin, when they do not care about God or their neighbor. In this case, a good spirit pricks and bites with the inner voice of conscience. The evil spirit, in this case, regularly provides apparent pleasures, seducing the soul to imagine sensual delights and pleasures in order to hold it [the soul] in vices and sins as much as possible. In the third and fourth rule, Ignatius speaks of spiritual consolation and dryness. In the next seven rules, he talks about how to act in spiritual consolation and how [to act] in spiritual dryness. In the twelfth rule, Ignatius describes how the devil behaves and how he should be confronted."

Then, quoting St. Ignatius, Fr. Mijo continued, "The enemy acts like a woman, in being weak in strength and strong of will. Because, as it is the way of the woman when she is quarreling with some man to lose heart, taking flight when the man shows her much courage and, on the contrary, if the man, losing heart, begins to flee, the wrath, revenge, and ferocity of the woman is very great, and without bounds. In the same manner, it is the way of the enemy to weaken and lose heart, his temptations taking flight when the person who is exercising himself in spiritual things opposes a bold front against the temptations of the enemy, doing diametrically the opposite. And, on the contrary, if the person who is exercising himself commences to have fear and lose heart in suffering the temptations, there is no beast so wild on the face of the Earth as the enemy of human nature in carrying out his damnable intention with such great malice."

Furthermore, Fr. Mijo shared that, in chapter 13, St. Ignatius compares the devil with a false lover who seeks to remain hidden and unknown and, in chapter 14, he says that the devil behaves as a captain and chief of the army, pitching his camp and looking at the forces and defenses of a stronghold in order to attack it on the weakest side.

"In like manner, the enemy of human nature, roaming about, looks in turn at all our virtues—theological, cardinal, and moral—and where he finds us weakest and most in need for our eternal salvation, there he attacks us and aims at taking us," Fr. Mijo quoted.

These were the rules of the first week of the *Spiritual Exercises*. In the second week of the *Spiritual Exercises*, Ignatius provides eight rules for the same purpose so that we can learn to recognize the spirits even better. In summary: (1) It is proper for God and His angels in their movements to give true spiritual gladness and joy, and it is proper for the devil to fight against such joy and spiritual consolation. (2) It belongs to God to give consolation to the soul without preceding cause. (3) With a preceding cause, both a good angel, as well as an evil spirit, can arouse consolation in the soul, but for contrary ends: The good angel for its spiritual progress, and the evil spirit to the contrary.

"The following five rules are very important to this topic of private revelations," Fr. Mijo went on. "Here is what Ignatius says in rule four: 'It is proper for the evil angel, who forms himself into the appearance of an angel of light, to enter with the devout soul and go out alone by himself—that is to say, to bring good and holy thoughts, conformable to such a just soul, and then, little by little, he aims at coming out, drawing the soul to his convert deceits and perverse intentions.' (4) By this rule, Ignatius wants to tell us that not all good messages and holy thoughts are necessarily from a good spirit. They can also be inspired by an evil spirit. How to discern if a good or evil spirit is involved in such a case is discussed in Ignatius' rule five. He says that we ought to note well the course of the thoughts. 'And, if the beginning, middle, and end is all good, inclined to all good, it is a sign of the good angel; but, if in the course of the thoughts which he brings it ends in something bad, of a distracting tendency, or less good than what the soul had previously proposed to do, or if it weakens it or disquiets or disturbs the soul, taking away its peace, tranquility, and serenity, which it had before, it is clear sign that it proceeds from the evil spirit, the enemy of our profit [progress] and eternal salvation.' (5) In the sixth rule, Ignatius talks about what the soul needs to do when it discovers the serpent's tail—that is to say, the depraved intention of Satan. St. Ignatius of Loyola, as an experienced teacher of spiritual life, says that 'the soul must immediately examine the course of the good thoughts it received from the evil spirit, discover the beginning of those thoughts, and see when and how the devil turned the water to his mill—that is, how he drew the soul into his depraved intention.'" (6)

Fr. Mijo added that Ignatius' intuition, which he presents in the seventh rule of discernment of spirits in the second week of spiritual exercises, is interesting. St. Ignatius says that, "to those who go from good to better, the good angel touches such a soul sweetly, lightly, and gently, like a drop of water which enters into a sponge; and the evil spirit touches it sharply and with noise and alarm, as when the drop of water falls on the stone. And, the above-said spirits touch in a contrary way those who go on from bad to worse."(7)

"Finally, in the eighth rule, Ignatius gives us wise advice on what to do when we experience consolation without cause—the consolation that comes from God Himself. Ignatius says that, in this case, too, we ought—with much vigilance and attention—look at and distinguish the time itself of actual consolation while it is at work from the time which follows, in which the soul still remains warm and still feels the benefits and consequences of the past consolation. 'In this second time, through one's own course of habits and the consequences of the concepts and judgments, or through the good spirit or through the bad, he forms various resolutions and opinions, which are not given immediately by God our Lord and, therefore, they need to be very well examined before entire credit is given them, or they are put into effect.' (8). In this eighth rule of the second week of spiritual exercises, Ignatius demonstrated the excellent quality as an in-depth psychologist and master of spirituality. He ingeniously observed that even when God Himself reveals Himself to the soul, it [the soul] must be careful of the decisions it makes in such a mood. And the reason for this justifiable prudence lies in the fact that a person cannot clearly distinguish between the moment when the spirit of God withdraws and when spiritual consolation ceases. Although the soul is warmed up by God's consolation, it must be aware that whatever comes to mind in that second time does not necessarily come from God, but can be the fruit of our minds, our imagination, desires, fears, and expectations. That is why all these inspirations need to be well-tested before we can put them into action."

Fr. Mijo also affirmed that he was deeply convinced that this eighth rule for discernment of spirits could bring a lot to light and solve the larger dilemmas of ambiguity in private revelations and apparitions, which they were convinced had much that was good and acceptable. But, there was also something that bothered them and that was not entirely in line with the teaching of the Church.

"It is necessary to exclude an approach that relies on a black-and-white technique, as more sensitivity and nuance should be introduced in approaching private revelations and apparitions," he explained. "It is possible that, in an authentic private revelation or apparition, one part of the message may be from God—and, as such, acceptable to the individual as to the whole Church—such as the call to conversion and prayer, and that the second part of the message must be dismissed as something that has nothing to do with God, or that even offends Him and is contrary to the teaching of the Church. That is why spirits should be carefully examined or, in other words, the content of private revelations should be critically studied. This cannot be done by the persons themselves who have had a revelation, but by people from the Church who are competent in this field, who are experts in their profession and who know how to sympathize with the Church, who have in themselves the Spirit of God."

He added that this eighth rule of St. Ignatius for discernment of spirits also tells us that it is possible for a private revelation to be truly authentic—that is, given by God—and to also contain some unacceptable aspects that the visionary has added by himself or that the devil has been able to insert into a person's soul after God's message ceased.

"Ignatius of Loyola tells us it is possible," Fr. Mijo continued. "He experienced it himself. While studying theology and philosophy to become a priest, he began to experience great impulses to just pray and fast. Because he thought such noble desires came from the Spirit of God, he gave himself up to them completely. However, examining his conscience and reflecting on his life, he realized that he was far behind in his studies such that he would not be able to finish theology, preventing him from being ordained a priest, and he was convinced that God was calling and preparing him for priesthood. That is when he concluded these tremendous impulses for prayer—which prevented him from serious study—did not come from God. He rejected them and began to study more—not leaving prayer, but now giving it an appropriate amount of time. I think that using Ignatius' method for discernment of spirits could reconcile the currently irreconcilable sides here and everywhere in the world where not everything is so clear as to the content of the messages given in private revelations."

Fr. Mijo then cited the example of Jesus' words—that He had much more to say to His disciples, but that they were not then able to hear, understand, and accept it. He added that we may believe that God is speaking to people even today, that He calls them to conversion, and that, by His own grace, He forms in them the image of his son Jesus Christ.

"We can and we may believe that, even through private revelations, God speaks to His Church and encourages her to imitate Jesus Christ even more," Fr. Mijo stated. "However, to be sure that various private revelations have been sent from God, the Church must respond in a timely manner and give her interpretation of private revelations. St. Paul gave wise counsel for the spirits to be tested whether they were from God or not: 'Do not despise prophetic utterances. Test everything; retain what is good.'"

He quoted the First Epistle of Paul to the Thessalonians. Essentially, for a message to have come from the Spirit of God, it must be in accordance with the revealed truths of our faith.

"Furthermore, the revelation coming from God brings man closer to God and to the community of believers and encourages regular sacramental life and prayer as an encounter with God," he continued. "The message that is truly from God puts God first and strives for His glory, not our own; it happens without sensationalism and noise; it includes receiving and giving spiritual goods and help unconditionally and with no cost; it does not blackmail, impose conditions, intimidate—it is not used for manipulation of any kind."

Fr. Mijo then outlined that it is not of the Holy Spirit when it is marked by one or more of the following characteristics:

1. It is contrary to the revealed truths (Old and New Testament, apostolic tradition, Church doctrine).
2. It distances man from God and from the community of believers; it distracts from the sacraments and prayer; it brings dissension, disharmony, confusion, chaos, and/or disorder into the community.
3. It leaves the man empty or unfulfilled; it tempts man and leads him to sin; it enslaves a man and/or binds him to attachment, dependence, or possessiveness.
4. It puts itself first and strives for its glory without God; it includes sensationalism, noise, self-aggrandizement, or vulgarity; it includes charging for spiritual goods and assistance; it contains elements of relativism, rationalism, materialism, hedonism, esotericism, magic, occultism, or superstition.

Similarly, from her interview with the French theologian Arnaud Dumouch, Darija Škunca-Klanac also provides important answers to these questions. Specifically, she questioned the theologian Dumouch regarding the duration of the apparitions—which, for some, is a controversial point of the Medjugorje phenomenon.

"The objection to credibility? No way," Dumouch claimed. "It is not a canonical type of argument, but a subjective impression. The same goes for the constant repetition and the childlike nature of the messages. The nature of each apparition is specific and unique. If we look at similar judgments of recognized apparitions, here's what we find: The theologians doubted the apparitions on Bac Street in Paris (to St. Catherine of Laboure) because the Virgin seemed unable to show her heart as large as the heart of Christ; theologians doubted the apparitions at La Salette because the Virgin did/could not announce a famine or stand on a branch and cry; for the apparitions at Lourdes, they found it inappropriate for the Virgin to appear in a cave above a field with pigs. Others said that Our Lady (as a person) could not be named with a term (Immaculate Conception). In short, every apparition is surprising, it is unique."

Then, when asked about the cessation of the apparitions—that is, about the answer given by Our Lady to the children that she would stop appearing when they wanted her to stop, or in "three days," Dumouch said that this "cannot, in itself, be a criterion of judgment."

"To understand this, let's take the example of Lourdes," he began. "Our Lady said, 'I am the Immaculate Conception.' Had Lourdes not been recognized, today, we would say, 'That statement is a grave theological error. Our Lady cannot identify herself with concept.' And yet, the apparition was acknowledged. Theologians find many profound and confusing meanings in this statement. The same is true of Medjugorje: If, one day, the apparitions are acknowledged, theologians will look at that statement positively and will say, no doubt, as well as for the strange sentences from Lourdes, that they mean, for example (I am speaking approximately): That the main message will last three more days and that, afterwards, Our Lady will simply keep repeating it, as mothers do repeat. Or, that Our Lady will appear for three more symbolic days (the days of the slow testing of the Church) and until the Good Friday of the Church (her entering into suffering, in the image of her Lord). So, let's wait."

Dumouch, added that "the number of apparitions is not an objection (neither in a positive nor in a negative sense)."

"The words of the Old Testament prophets are often of these types: long texts, repetitions, mysterious meanings," he explaind. "On the contrary, sometimes, as in the book of Jonah, heaven says almost nothing. Moving apparitions to the visionaries' location also occurred many times in the Old and New Testament. For example, after His resurrection, Christ appeared everywhere, even though He had repeatedly announced that He would appear in Galilee. This is quite logical: The apparition is directed to human interaction, not to some location."

To that end, Dumouch said the phenomenon of visionaries having apparitions while they are in many different places was a "special charisma."

"It is a special charisma (appearing in multiple places simultaneously) given by God to the saints in Heaven (and, sometimes, to the saints on Earth, like to St. Martin de Porres who, though living in a convent in Central America, saved many shipwrecked in the Mediterranean)," he said. "This charisma, given by God, is very important in the hour of death, when Christ and the saints welcome many dying at the same time. It implies the direct power of God because it goes beyond the natural law that dictates that each body has only one place. In the case of Medjugorje, this charisma will not be sufficient for the Church's final decision, since it can easily be imitated by forces that do not come from God (unlike miracles, such as instant healing)."

And, regarding Our Lady asking about those who were missing when the children weren't all together, he said, "In Fatima, Mary did the same during an apparition when Lucia was late because she was detained. The answer is clear: When Heaven comes to Earth, it adjusts its language to the human one. That is how Mary asks the children—to whom she is listening—questions to which she knows the answers. To some extent, the same objection is raised by those who criticize the justification of prayer: 'Why ask something from God by prayer when Heaven knows everything?' Because Heaven gives us what we are seeking and teaches us to give thanks for the gifts."

Dumouch interprets that, for St. Thomas Aquinas (*Discussion on Prophecy*), there are three depths of apparitions:

"First, some are addressed only to the senses of the visionary (who understands nothing). It is the least deep apparition. So it was in Pontmain, where the children saw the image and movements of Our Lady, but the priests understood the hidden theological meaning. The second level reaches his imagination, as in the vision of St. John on Patmos. John did not understand everything—so much so that what he saw in the dream went in all directions. This is an intermediate level. Finally, the third type of apparition penetrates all the way to the mind and heart of the visionary. This is the deepest degree. Perhaps here we have an explanation for the duration of the apparitions in Medjugorje: The visionaries enter an ever deeper inner life. Therefore, it would be a heavenly pedagogy that makes the life of the visionaries—something like for Joan of Arc—a parable of spiritual growth in life."

As for the case of Dr. Glamuzina, who actually made a theological mistake in saying Our Lady told her that "there have always been doubting Judases," theologian Dumouch said that there was no "theological difficulty in this, especially since it is a practical answer adjusted to the thoughts of a specific person."

"If that answer refers to Dr. Glamuzina herself, and if she acknowledges that her internal behavior was, indeed, at the moment, cunning and betrayal, then these words are a good sign," Dumouch explained. "They seem to indicate that the apparition reads the doctor's thoughts directly. I think that those who, in retaliation, say, 'These words are too harsh for Our Lady,' they have no right. Love sometimes must tell the truth without embellishment. In the Gospel, Jesus uses many harsh words (Matthew 23:13): 'Woe to you, scribes and Pharisees, you hypocrites. You lock the Kingdom of Heaven before human beings. You do not enter yourselves, nor do you allow entrance to those trying to enter.' This is really Jesus speaking. In this case, Dr. Glamuzina received the mentioned grace from these words. So, that's a good sign."

However, regarding whether it could be a demonic deception when the person who appeared to the children said that she was the Blessed Virgin Mary, Dumouch said that there were three theories if this did not come from Heaven:

"First, we could imagine a demon preparing a forgery for the long-run that will eventually turn into mockery," he began. "But, the nature of some conversions, the sincere restoration of faithfulness to the Church, and miracles make this theory unsustainable because, according to Jesus, 'And, if Satan is divided against himself, how will his kingdom stand?' (Luke 11:18). Second, one could also imagine purely human, fraudulent origins. Of course, it is difficult to endure for more than 28 years [referencing the time when the interview took place]. Assuming such a conspiracy, we might think that, because of the pressure on conscience, one of the conspirators would betray a secret. Third, one could also imagine purely human and sincere origin (hallucinations); it is also unsustainable. These kids are obviously healthy. In any case, in order to completely eliminate these theories, we need to check the miracles that only allow for final judgment. Namely, it has already been seen that false visionaries imitate the first criterion (compliance with Catholic dogmas) and that the second criterion is partially present (spiritual fruits) because the Holy Spirit comes everywhere where He sees the goodwill of believers."

He added that, regarding the possibility that only the first ten days of the apparitions were authentic, "that theory is as interesting as it is impossible."

"If these children had seen Our Lady and then lied, their conscience would have stung them all the more," he said. "Let us return to another comparison. After the apparitions at Lourdes ended and after their acknowledgement, Bernadette was overcome by doubts. It was a kind of 'night of the spirit,' a doubt sent, no doubt, from God to separate her from herself. She said to her superiors, 'And, what if I didn't see anything? And, what if I lied?' Her superiors dissuaded her, reminding her of the objective criteria for judgment. But, it is obvious that Bernadette, who really saw Our Lady, became incapable of deceiving. This would be the same for the children from Medjugorje."

Dumouch also commented on another phenomenon in Medjugorje that involves Satan constantly trying to disrupt Our Lady's plans.

"If the apparitions in Medjugorje are authentic, it can be said that God, as never before, allowed the demon to agitate and interfere," he explained. "It is as if everything is surrounded by conflicts, passions, restlessness. And these allowances come from God because they are intended to create humble hearts. To create a picture of the wealth of lessons that theologians will draw from this in the future, if the apparitions are acknowledged, it is enough to see what the life, struggles, and difficulties of Joan of Arc were—magnificent images of life, struggles, and difficulties in the future of the Church."

Next, Dumouch responded to those who were angry because Mary was "too talkative":

"This is not an argument to deny (or accept) the validity of an apparition," he stated. "If the apparitions are acknowledged one day, theologians and saints will say that, in Medjugorje, Our Lady was close and familial, as she had been with Jesus in his childhood. If the apparitions are condemned, they will highlight the given argument. In short, there is nothing decisive in this."

Likewise, Herzegovinian Friar Dr. Fr. Tomislav Pervan said God can and does act in history.

"We cannot 'prescribe' what He will do," Fr. Tomislav said. "Mary appears by the power of the Holy Spirit at crucial times. I would not dare to call the Medjugorje visionaries liars. Who catapulted them out of their daily life into the hotspot [of events]? Was it their whim, volition, or will? Their childhood and normal upbringing were 'stolen' from them. They became fully involved in God's plan from the beginning. At first, everyone—both civilian and church authorities—was against them. They are mature and grown up now, and they already have grandchildren. It is irresponsible to declare them 'fraudsters' if they have undergone scientific studies to confirm the authenticity of their experience, and they have agreed to all experiments.

"*Sensus fidei fidelium*—the believer's sense tells us infallibly that God is at work," he continued. "*Lex orandi [law of prayer]* creates a *legem credenda [law of belief]*. The practice of prayer and liturgy determines what the faithful believe. Prayer in the Spirit also determines belief because, in the Church, liturgy is the place where religious truths were born. The faithful populace accepted the apparitions as fact and truth."

Next, when asked why the visionaries were reproached for their secular life—they did not become priests and nuns— Fr. Tomislav replied with Pope Francis' words: Who am I to judge and to enter into one's private life and family?

"We should first rake our own—and not someone else's—yard," he explained. "Let us remember the first days and months and all the objections, harassments, and persecutions to which they were exposed! If the battle for family—the fundamental building block of society—is waged today, is it any wonder that the visionaries have decided for family life? To show the world what it's like to live in a family, how the family should 'function.'"

To that end, regarding the Medjugorje apparitions in the context of the previous apparitions in Lourdes, Fatima, and Guadalupe, Fr. Tomislav suggested that "Mary's apparitions are regularly a response of Heaven to the needs of the Earth."

"When evangelization was impossible in 16th-century Mexico, as recorded by history, Mary brought tens of millions of Aztecs to the Church in ten years," he stated. "She appeared for four days to Juan Diego and imprinted the celestial 'water sign' on the image of Our Lady of Guadalupe. It was similar with Lourdes—when the fear of communism circulated Europe—or with Fatima in the midst of the World War and on the eve of the great October Revolution and communist upheaval in Russia. It was so in Kibeho (Rwanda) and Medjugorje, where she persistently called for conversion and peace."

Fr. Tomislav added that the message of Medjugorje to today's world is "for all time, beyond time, and evangelical."

"Christ's message from the beginning was the proclamation of the Good News in Galilee," he said. "The time has been fulfilled. The kingdom of God is near. It is necessary to convert and believe the word of Jesus. Jesus has the first and the last word in time and space. At a time when truth is being denied, His word is truth. He is the truth of our lives, and the message that *God is*!"

Critics of the first seven days

It's widely known that the Medjugorje phenomenon has its critics, and among the most persistent is the former bishop of Mostar-Duvno and Trebinje-Mrkanj dioceses Monsignor Ratko Perić. His position on the first seven days of apparitions in Medjugorje is presented in its entirety from the official diocesan website, where it appeared under the title "The First Seven Days of the 'Apparitions' in Medjugorje" on February 28, 2017. Following is the article by Msgr. Perić:

. . .

Because "the Church of the living God" is "the pillar and foundation of truth" (1 Timothy 3:15), the goal of all past research on the

"Medjugorje phenomena" has been to determine the truth: Are the apparitions authentic or not? *Constat vel non de supernaturalitate*? [Latin: Agreed or not of the supernatural?] This was the goal of the first diocesan commission in Mostar (1982-1984), the extended commission (1984-1986), the commission of the Bishops' Conference in Zagreb (1987-1990), the commission of the Congregation for the Doctrine of Faith in the Vatican (2010-2014), and the evaluation of the same Congregation (2014-2016), as designated by Pope Benedict XVI. It is all now in the hands of the Holy Father Pope Francis.

Throughout all this time, the position of this Chancery has been clear and resolute: This is not an authentic apparition of the Blessed Virgin Mary.

Although, at times, there has been talk that the apparitions during the first days might be considered true, many "additional", unreligious elements tied to these events evolved, and this Chancery has always promoted the truth regarding those first days. After copying and transcribing the audio cassettes of the conversations of the pastoral staff in the parish rectory of Medjugorje with the boys and girls who claimed to see the Virgin Mary, we bring forward with conviction and responsibility the reasons and findings regarding the inauthenticity of the alleged apparitions. And, if the real Madonna, the Mother of Jesus, did not appear as she has not, then all of these are self-proclaimed seers, ostensible messages, a so-called visible sign, and alleged secrets.

During the years of my service as bishop, first as a coadjutor bishop (1992-1993), and then as diocesan bishop, through my preaching, the publishing of books (*Prijestolje mudrosti* 1995, *Ogledalo pravde* 2001, *Isusova majka* 2015) and some fifty Marian and Mariological articles, I strived to explain the role of the Blessed Virgin Mary in the incarnation and the mission of the Son of God, and her Son, as well, as her providential intercession for the Church to which she is the Mother by grace. At the same time, I pointed out—as did my predecessor of blessed memory, Bishop Pavao Žanić—the inauthenticity of the Medjugorje apparitions that have now reached 47,000. This Chancery has always sought to inform the Holy See, especially the recent popes—Saint John Paul II, Benedict XVI, and Francis—on these events. We have, therefore, summarized some points here regarding the first days of the "apparitions," which convince us deeply of the inauthenticity of the "apparitions."

An ambiguous apparition. The woman who allegedly appeared in Medjugorje acts contrary to the real Madonna, Mother of God, in the apparitions the Church has recognized as authentic. She does not normally speak first; laugh in a strange way; disappear after certain questions and then return. She's submissive to the "seers" and the pastor: She comes down from the hill to the church (although reluctantly). She is not sure of how long she will appear; she allows some of the people present to step on her veil, which is dragging on the ground, and to touch her garments and her body. This is not the Madonna from the Gospels.

A strange quiver. One of the "seers," Ivan Dragićević, during a conversation with the chaplain Fr. Zrinko Čuvalo OFM (1936-1991), said that, during the first day of the apparitions, he noticed a "quiver" of the hands of the vision. [1] What kind of "quiver"? This cannot arouse only a suspicion, but also a deep conviction that this is not an authentic apparition of the Blessed Virgin Mary, even though the apparition apparently presents itself this way on the fourth day. [2]

A false anniversary. The alleged apparitions began on June 24, 1981. However, the directors of the "Medjugorje phenomena" decided that the anniversary should not be celebrated on the 24th, but the 25th of June. The rationale for this choice is that, on June 25, 1981, allegedly, all six "seers" were present for the "apparition"—the chosen six amongst the many who in those days bragged about having "apparitions." The real truth, which repudiates Vicka Ivanković's version, has been told by Ivan Dragićević himself: "I was there the first night, not the second." [3] Of the six usual "seers" (except for Marija Pavlović), Jakov Čolo was present at the apparition for the first time on the second day. [4] Therefore, the date of the anniversary is unfounded, inaccurate, and false.

The (in)visible child. The figure that allegedly appears as a woman was portrayed differently. Some of the "seers" saw a covered child in the hands of the woman. These were Vicka and Ivanka Ivanković [5], Mirjana Dragićević [6], and Ivanka confirmed it again [7]. Ivan, however, firmly denies seeing the child. On the contrary, he could see from a distance the "eyes" and "eyelashes" of a female figure. [8]

A deceitful sign. The "seers" have, since day two, asked the vision for a "sign" as proof of an authentic apparition. According to Ivanka, the "sign" of the apparition was a reversal of the watch on Mirjana's hand: "The watch turned around completely." "She left a sign on the watch!" [9] A most ridiculous and strange sign!

But, when frequently asked to give a visible sign, the apparition would smile and disappear on a regular basis. [10] Sometimes, she returned instantly. At one moment, a layman named Marinko, who leads the "seers," intrudes and suggests to them: If the Madonna cannot give a sign, she "should ask Jesus to help her." [11]

Ivanka is sure the apparition will leave a sign on the hill, maybe in the form of water. [12] We have been waiting for nearly four decades, and there has been no sign, no water—only fabrications!

An unexplained silence. During the first seven days, the apparition takes no initiative and never speaks first. [13] It responds to the questions of the "seers," in general, in a dubious way, nodding its head [14], postponing, promising a healing miracle, and leaving a message to the world: "The people should firmly believe as if they see me," and to the Franciscans: "They should firmly believe" [that she appeared]. [15]

Strange messages. During the first days, according to the tape-recorded conversations, no purpose for the alleged apparitions can be seen: The apparition did not justify itself and did not give any special message for the "seers" or the Franciscans—except to believe that she "appeared"—or for the faithful of the parish or the world. Yet, the private "messages" are of this nature:

Ivanka's mother, who died two months before, sends a message: "Listen to grandma because she's old."

The apparition says to Mirjana that her late "grandpa is all right" and that she "has to go to the cemetery."

Ivanka heard from the apparition that the reason the "apparitions" are in Medjugorje is "because there are a lot of faithful."

Vicka heard the apparition came so "the people would reconcile." [16]

Ivan heard it say, "You are the greatest believers." [17]

Jakov simply says, "Listen, when I ask a question, inside me, I think what she would say and then she says it the way I was thinking she would." [18] Nothing other than imaginations and fabrications!

False prophecies on false apparitions. When Ivanka asks how long it will stay and appear, the apparition answers: "As much as you want, as much as you like." [19]

Mirjana says she will ask the apparition how many days it will appear and then adds that some voice from within her says it will still appear "two to three days." She repeats that once more. [20]

When the pastor, Fr. Jozo, asked when the "apparitions" would stop, Vicka answers, "I think it is the same as if we were to say that we would never come again, but that she leave us some sort of precise sign, it would surely stop." [21] Does this mean that, because the desired "sign" has not occurred in 37 years, the "apparitions" are not stopping?

Then came a categorical statement from the apparition, which "appeared" not in Medjugorje, but in neighboring Cerno, on Tuesday afternoon, June 30, 1981, that it would appear "three more days"—on July 1, 2, and 3, 1981. In answering the pastor's question regarding how long it would appear, five of the "seers"—all except Ivan—answered unanimously, "Three days."

Then, the apparition changes its mind and "appears" non-stop for 37 years—to three "seers" every day (Ivan, Marija, and Vicka) and to the other three once a year (to Mirjana since 1982, to Ivanka since 1985, and to Jakov since 1998). In addition to that, to two of the seers of the group, the "apparition" has appeared once a month since 2007 (with "messages" for the world): To Mirjana on the 2nd and to Marija on the 25th of each month.

Different dresses. From the interviews with the "seers," the apparition is dressed in different ways. She had a dress that was, according to Ivan, "blue" on the first day [22]; according to Ivanka, "brown" on the second day [23]; and, according to the other "seers"—Jakov [24], Mirjana [25], and Ivanka—"grey" on the sixth day [26].

More anxiety than peace. Additionally, some anxious nervousness could be observed when three of the "seers"—Ivanka, Mirjana, and Vicka—"fainted" and fell on the ground on the third day, June 26th. "They fainted, but nothing happened to me," Marija courageously said of herself. [27] Vicka: "Father, I went up there and brought with me some blessed salt and holy water. And, I said, if it's not Our Lady, it will leave. We will sprinkle some and see. Really, we will see. I came and began, 'In the name of the Father, and of the Son, and of the Holy Spirit. Amen. If you are Our Lady, stay among us, if you are not, go!'" [28] There is a constant request for a visible "sign" for people to believe them. The sign is mentioned in most conversations [29] and it can be sensed that the "seers" are nervous because there is no visible sign.

Scandalous touches. Something very unusual and serious: The apparition allows someone from the crowd to step not only on her veil that extends to the ground, [30] but also to touch her body. Vicka had already touched her on the second day. "And, when you touch her, Father, your fingers bounce back like this," she said. [31] Ivanka repeats this and adds that, touching her body, she feels that "the air is something like silk, our fingers move back like this, when we touch her, they move away." [32] They also allowed a doctor to touch the apparition: "And, look, she touched her dress." [33] Those stories of touching the alleged body of the Madonna, her dress, and stepping on her veil create in us the feeling and the belief that it is something undignified, inauthentic, and scandalous. We can only say: This is not the Catholic Madonna!

Intentional manipulations. The interlocutor of the "seers," Fr. Jozo Zovko, parish priest, is nervous because the apparition does not send specific messages to the world and the Franciscans and because she does not move from the hill to the church where her statue is located. Moreover, he asks if Our Lady can be "obliged"—literally!—to come down to appear in the church. Fr. Jozo: "But, I want to know this, Mirjana: If Our Lady does not appear in the church, can you oblige her to show herself in church? Maybe she can. What do you think?" Mirjana: "I do not know. We never thought of that." Fr. Jozo repeats: "I think she can oblige: 'Our Lady, I ask of you to appear in the church.' What do you think?" And then, Mirjana gives in and thinks it would "still be better that way because the police would not look for us then..." [34] And, just like that, with manipulations, the "apparitions" move to the parish church on July 1, 1981. This "obliging" of the alleged Madonna to come down and appear in the church is playing with magic and not Christ's Gospel.

Conclusion. The work of the commission on the "Medjugorje phenomena" in Mostar was followed by a statement by Bishop Pavao

Žanić in Medjugorje on July 25,1987. The purpose of the Bishop's statement was to clearly point out that there are no supernatural apparitions and revelations in Medjugorje. After the work of the commission in Zagreb, a declaration was issued by the Bishops' Conference in Zadar on April 1, 1991. It said: On the basis of studies conducted so far, it cannot be affirmed that these matters concern supernatural apparitions or revelations.

Considering everything this Chancery studied and researched so far, including the study of the first seven days of the alleged apparitions, we can calmly claim: Our Lady did not appear in Medjugorje! That is the truth we hold on to, and we believe in the Lord's word that "the truth will set us free" (John 8:32).

+Ratko Perić, Bishop

[1] Cassette 2, conversation of Fr. Zrinko Čuvalo with Ivan Dragićević, Saturday afternoon, June 27, 1981.

[2] Cassette 7, conversation of Fr. Jozo Zovko with Mirjana Dragićević, Sunday morning, June 28, 1981.

[3] Cassette 2, conversation of Fr. Zrinko Čuvalo with Ivan Dragićević, Saturday afternoon, June 27, 1981.

[4] Cassette 1, conversation of Fr. Zrinko Čuvalo with Ivanka and Vicka Ivanković and Marija Pavlović, Saturday morning, June 27, 1981.

[5] Cassette 1, conversation of Fr. Zrinko Čuvalo with Ivanka and Vicka Ivanković and Marija Pavlović, Saturday morning, June 27, 1981.

[6] Cassette 6, conversation of Fr. Jozo Zovko with Mirjana Dragićević, Saturday afternoon, June 27, 1981.

[7] Cassette 11, conversation of Fr. Jozo Zovko with Ivanka Ivanković, Sunday evening, June 28, 1981.

[8] Cassette 2, conversation of Fr. Zrinko Čuvalo with Ivan Dragićević, Saturday afternoon, June 27, 1981.

[9] Cassette 1, conversation of Fr. Zrinko Čuvalo with Ivanka and Vicka Ivanković and Marija Pavlović, Saturday morning, June 27, 1981.

[10] Cassette 10, conversation of Fr. Jozo Zovko with Mirjana Dragićević, Sunday evening, June 28, 1981.

[11] Cassette 13, conversation of Fr. Jozo Zovko with Ivanka Ivanković, Tuesday afternoon, June 30, 1981.

[12] Cassette 13, conversation of Fr. Jozo Zovko with Ivanka Ivanković, Tuesday afternoon, June 30, 1981.

[13] Cassette 13, conversation of Fr. Jozo Zovko with Ivanka Ivanković, Tuesday afternoon, June 30, 1981.

[14] Cassette 1, conversation of Fr. Zrinko Čuvalo with Ivanka and Vicka Ivanković and Marija Pavlović, Saturday morning, June 27, 1981.

[15] Cassette 11, conversation of Fr. Jozo Zovko with Ivanka Ivanković, Sunday evening, June 28, 1981.

[16] Cassette 1, all the quotes from conversation of Fr. Zrinko Čuvalo with Ivanka and Vicka Ivanković and Marija Pavlović, Saturday morning, June 27, 1981.

[17] Cassette 2, conversation of Fr. Zrinko Čuvalo with Ivan Dragićević, Saturday afternoon, June 27, 1981.

[18] Cassette 16, conversation of Fr. Jozo Zovko with five "seers," Tuesday evening, June 30, 1981.

[19] Cassette 13, conversation of Fr. Jozo Zovko with Ivanka Ivanković, Tuesday morning, June 30, 1981.

[20] Cassette 14, conversation of Fr. Jozo Zovko with Mirjana Dragićević, Tuesday morning, June 30, 1981.

[21] Cassette 15, conversation of Fr. Jozo Zovko with Vicka Ivanković, Tuesday morning, June 3 [30], 1981.

[22] Cassette 2, conversation of Fr. Zrinko Čuvalo with Ivan Dragićević, Saturday afternoon, June 27, 1981.

[23] Cassette 1, conversation of Fr. Zrinko Čuvalo with Ivanka and Vicka Ivanković and Marija Pavlović, Saturday morning, June 27, 1981.

[24] Cassette 5, conversation of Fr. Jozo Zovko with Jakov Čolo, Saturday afternoon, June 27, 1981.

[25] Cassette 6, conversation of Fr. Jozo Zovko with Mirjana Dragićević, Saturday afternoon, June 27, 1981.

[26] Cassette 11, conversation of Fr. Jozo Zovko with Ivanka Ivanković, Sunday evening, June 28, 1981.

[27] Cassette 1, conversation of Fr. Zrinko Čuvalo with Ivanka and Vicka Ivanković and Marija Pavlović, Saturday morning, June 27, 1981.

[28] Cassette 1, conversation of Fr. Zrinko Čuvalo with Ivanka and Vicka Ivanković and Marija Pavlović, Saturday morning, June 27, 1981.

[29] Cassettes 1, 2, 5, 6, 7, 9, 10, 11, 14, 15, 16.

[30] Cassette 7, conversation of Fr. Jozo Zovko with Mirjana Dragićević, Sunday morning, June 28, 1981.

[31] Cassette 1, conversation of Fr. Zrinko Čuvalo with Ivanka and Vicka Ivanković and Marija Pavlović, Saturday morning, June 27, 1981.

[32] Cassette 11, conversation of Fr. Jozo Zovko with Ivanka Ivanković, Sunday evening, June 28, 1981.

[33] Cassette 13, conversation of Fr. Jozo Zovko with Ivanka

Ivanković, Tuesday morning, June 30, 1981.

[34] Cassette 14, conversation of Fr. Jozo Zovko with Mirjana Dragićević, Tuesday morning, June 30, 1981.

INSTEAD OF THE END...

...because the apparitions are still occurring

The apparitions in Medjugorje are still occurring, and it is unknown when they will end. We are also still awaiting a visible sign, which the visionaries begged Our Lady to leave since those first days so that people would believe that they see her. But, even though there is no such sign, the visible sign in Medjugorje is the millions of people who believed in Our Lady's messages that were conveyed to them by the visionaries and that they continue to convey up to this day. That is why this book will end with the thoughts of one of the most authentic witnesses of the Medjugorje phenomenon from its earliest days, although he is also a man who somewhat distanced himself from the eruption caused by the apparitions: Fr. Zrinko Čuvalo, the chaplain of Medjugorje who managed the parish in those early days while Fr. Jozo Zovko, the parish pastor, was in Zagreb.

"It seems to me—as far as I remember and since I carry it within myself—that the call to prayer, penance, and conversion was more like our attempt to offer the world something in place of the hill; as something more valuable; as something we assumed might be the content of a message which we didn't have yet, and because of which we were restless," he began in an interview with Fr. Svetozar Kraljević. "Even on the first Sunday—before we met the children and listened to them, when we did not yet know the message—we said that Our Lady, if she came, had a message. In our statement, Fr. Jozo put it in this way: 'We must be patient, but also know that a message can be nothing else but a call to faith and conversion.' That is why, before we received a message, we—at least I—assumed that it should contain this, because there couldn't be anything else. The Revelation is complete and we have the Revelation. Now, we can only be warned of the omissions in our attitude toward the Revelation; of our opposition to the Revelation. I understood it this way and we committed to pray and fast a little more, in doubt, because we were in crisis. We needed help. Personally, I have never been inclined to any great prayer or fasting. But, the truth is that I have also never lost the spirit of prayer. I say it, I did not fast as I should and could but, for example, I always found it hard to hear from believers that they ate meat on Fridays. Well, people work hard and the Church didn't talk much about fasting, but I still found it hard to hear that fasting was disappearing. Or, for example, when looking for fish on Fridays, they make some extraordinary 'fasting' delicacies. I often had such a lunch, because that Friday—that day of penance—would be more solemn and more abundant than other days; it was not true fasting. So, I did not lose my sense of fasting, although I did not strictly fast. Even now, I did not accept the recommendation, that of 'bread and water'; I never took it literally, but as a strong invitation to fast: Eat a little something daily and I don't mind if it's soup or regular tea."

Fr. Svetozar Kraljević told him that "this is a nice attitude" and Fr. Zrinko added that he had a similar attitude regarding other messages, too.

"As it was with fasting, I retained some freedom in accepting other messages and never took everything quite literally," Fr. Zrinko continued. "I did not take the messages as an absolute requirement, but simply as the liberating will of God. I feel that there is a spirit of penance—the expression of God's love for us that is most important. It also doesn't matter to me through whom that message was communicated, whether through the mouths of children, through the Church, or through the vote of the people spontaneously; it is not important. In fact, many things happened spontaneously: The children started to pray the seven 'Our Father' prayers on their own and Mary, in a way, only blessed it. Now, why did they start [to pray] exactly that? Why not something else? In the end, I believe that this is also the finger of God, that it is a gift from God. For example, I remember that Fr. Jozo, at the first Mass, immediately invited people to penance, to conversion, to prayer; it was at the beginning of the Mass, in the Penitential Act. The guiding principle was: One who commits himself to Christ, he goes with Him to pray, to fast; he goes with Him to the desert; he goes to wrestle with the devil and conquer him, to come back victorious. From the first day, we began to insist on values that have a tradition, not only through two thousand years of Christianity, but throughout the Revelation period—through four thousand years. I accepted that as the only path I ever knew. This was the most important thing to me: Did these children ever have an experience, did they receive anything from God through the intercession of Our Lady in any way? Did Our Lady intervene before this—perhaps only one sentence that might read, 'Tell those people down there to stop quarrelling. Let them reconcile among themselves and let them reconcile with God because it is high time?'"

Then, Fr. Svetozar asked him if he believed Our Lady had intervened there.

"Somehow, I am inclined to believe so, and not on the basis of the children's statements, however, but on the basis of what followed, what came about because of those statements," Fr. Zrinko shared. "In my opinion, we should not rely too heavily on the children at every moment and in every detail. For example, I spoke candidly to the bishop and others: 'When the children say this or say that, when they disagree, that does not surprise me. If I were in their shoes, I would not always be clear! I would be vague sometimes!' Why? How? Suppose the children did receive something. Then, it is quite natural for them to think about it and interpret it in their own way, to clothe it in their own manner, to convey some of their own thoughts as if these were Our Lady's—for they are human, after all. How many people came to them asking for this, asking for that—well-intentioned and sometimes ill-intentioned! We can't expect them to become somebody else. They convey the message in the way they understand it, so that, sometimes, it's possible, when they are asked to say what Our Lady said, reasoning simply like this: 'I am going to say what I think she said,' or 'I suppose that's how it was,' or 'As far as I remember, she said it this way.' In other words, each of them puts their own stamp on these events. Fr. Jozo called for fasting and declared Friday as a special day for penance. Fr. Tomislav continued with this upon his arrival, insisting on deeper and longer prayer, especially calling for strict fasting."

Fr. Zrinko went on to explain the way in which the pastoral direction in Medjugorje evolved.

"We remained open; we were in suspense," he said. "What was to be expected? If it's really God's messenger who is coming, then he can't bring anything else but a warning, a rebuke, or advice. What could we do then? We saw what it was. We understood the state of the parish, the world, and man, in general. We saw what was missing and what had disappeared: Prayer had vanished; fasting had practically disappeared throughout the whole Church. The world thought the Church reforms rescinded fasting. I often heard from Christians, 'What, hasn't fasting been abolished?!' Such a mentality was gaining ground. Prayer disappeared; it was banished by radio and television. Even Mass was observed more as a custom. Young people already had their different interests and preoccupations. Quite often, religious customs were only observed—the Mass and the like—while, in other situations, even the custom disappeared."

Fr. Zrinko described his own experiences from the beginning of the apparitions. But, he also had opportunities to observe people and, after the first two or three months, he said the people also experienced what he did.

"It is interesting to note that, from September onward, hardly anyone—including those who came from other areas—went to the hill or looked toward the hill during the apparition," he said. "Naturally, there were always the curious ones who had come for the first time and heard about the spinning of the cross and so they would keep staring in hopes of seeing the cross spin. Logically, staring for a long time, they would observe, 'Well, it seems to me that it did spin.' If you stare for such a long time, it has to start spinning in your head. However, most people simply sought God and experienced the presence of Our Lady in the church and in the sacraments. Indeed, most of those people came for a meeting with God, for a meeting with Our Lady, for evening service. It was not only the Mass, but also what preceded it. People came for the rosary and stayed for the prayer for the sick that followed—even those who were not ill and who did not need it. They simply stayed behind; they wanted to be together with Our Lady there. I got the impression that the people had formed an attitude similar to mine. And, in this process, it became clear to me that God was working here. I was one hundred percent convinced, and my conviction is no less today. After all, it is God's business; how and through whom God works is not relevant to me at all. What matters is that He does work! And, in this process, it became clear to me that the children were involved as instruments through which God was working."

At that point in the interview, Fr. Svetozar told Fr. Zrinko that he believed that God works both through the children and through the others.

"Yes, he worked through everybody," Fr. Zrinko agreed. "After all, it is God's business. It is not relevant to me at all, I mean, through whom God works. What matters is that He does work! And, if God is at work here, I must come and cooperate with Him, I have to join. I would like to illustrate my view with an example which Fr. Zoran Senjak shared with me. When one of his parishioners returned to Chicago from Medjugorje, he met his colleague who asked him, 'Did you see Our Lady?' Although the question was asked mockingly, the former calmly replied, 'Yes, I did. I saw both God and Our Lady.' What he meant was that he had experienced both and that he had not been deceived. And, this is exactly what people experience and what gathers and keeps them together, and that is what brings them here again and again. To many, it is strange that people gather right here, and they say that God is everywhere. Yes, God is everywhere, but He is at work here in a special way."

Fr. Zrinko continued:

"I didn't speak about some other aspects that affected me. When

I started to analyze certain acts of the authorities—starting from the communal authorities and continuing to the federal ones in Belgrade, and from the ones in Rome, as well as our local church authorities, I mean all of the authorities who had any influence and importance whatsoever—I realized that they had all acted in different ways and everybody tried—in their own way—to turn the events into a course of their own liking. No matter what move they made—and those moves were different, coming from different directions, at different times, of different intensity—never did the thing move in the direction it was tugged, but always in another, unforeseen direction. Yet, when you take it altogether, you see it was heading in one single direction that had been defined from the beginning. No matter how you tugged, it always moved in its own direction, following its own inner logic. For example, I resented that guard so much—the rude acts barring access for people, for cars, etc.! Later, in front of some officials, I said that I should invite all the militia and the whole Čitluk SUP to a barbecue because what a mess it would have been if it hadn't been for them! You can imagine what a jam it would have been if cars had been admitted. What it might have become if they had not forbidden going to the hill. Later, I thought, 'Well, folks, how shallow we are when we ask who organized all this.'

"Once, I suggested something similar to Bishop Koss when he came to Medjugorje: 'If somebody had tried to arrange this, he would have never thought of this.' We were all angry at what the adversaries were doing, and now I say, if it hadn't been for that, it seems to me that it couldn't have all come to this. Now, I conclude that God engaged them all—those in the SUP, the municipal officials, the bishop, the provincial, and those clergymen and friars who were always with us, and those who didn't even let their parishioners come here—to make this possible. For example, for the first Christmas, huge crowds of people planned to come. We were in serious trouble with respect to how we would accommodate so many people for that night; anything could happen. It was easy to assume a thief, a robber, an instigator would come. But, God solved the whole problem with a heavy rain. Those who did come had to wade through knee-deep water on the asphalt road. Those who couldn't find a place in the church went back home and everything was solved.

"We often worried about how everything was going to turn out and there were reasons for such worry every day. But, when you sum everything up, it seems as if a director had taken his position behind the stage, was watching how everything was going, and then arranging everything. You could fret as much as you wanted; everything went its own course. For me, that was a sign of God's hand, God's presence; that God managed it all because man is not that clever. I was especially fascinated by the way God thwarted man's plans, his wits, and power. Then, you can't but see God's hand here. Here, God's hand was somehow visible to me. No matter how hard they tried, the enemies failed in leaving the church without Mass for even a single day. Humanly viewed, Mass seemed impossible to celebrate. Fr. Jozo had been imprisoned. We had been put in quarantine and were not allowed to leave the house. Barricades had been erected and watched by guards. Nobody was allowed to approach the church. All the other priests had left. Yet, the Mass did start—with only ten minutes delay! So, the police let everybody go to the church and the Mass was said. It was celebrated by a priest who I didn't know at all—Father Stanko Dodig, a Capuchin, a man from the village, guardian of a monastery in Rijeka. He had been called to preach in Sarajevo and, on his return, he dropped in to see his mother. Everything that was done turned out well. Even now, all the difficulties and sufferings are words powerfully spoken and a calling to penance for all those who come here. It is a message which says: Either do not approach or do penance. The whole environment of Medjugorje leads to penance."

Fr. Zrinko also shared how he was severely affected by Fr. Jozo's arrest.

"How did I feel about it? I told the people when Fr. Jozo was taken. It was difficult, indeed," he admitted. "I could best portray this difficulty by saying that I was really sorry for having stayed behind, for not having gone myself. Later, on several occasions, I regretted that I was not in his place—not because of some 'fame,' but simply because of the maltreatment of those of us who remained. I immediately sent a report to the provincial and the bishop regarding what had happened, in which I said that it was absolutely out of the question for me to be pastor in Fr. Jozo's forced absence. In addition, I asked not to be made acting pastor, either. This was accepted and so, before the Feast of the Nativity, Father Tomislav Vlašić received a decree appointing him pastor. Life went on. Many people did not know who the acting pastor actually was. We both knew what each of us had to do and it didn't matter who the pastor was. Each time somebody came asking for the pastor, we would say, 'Well, you are asking the wrong person, the pastor is in prison.' In this way, it was clear to everyone who the pastor was and that the real pastor was not there.

"The adversaries of Medjugorje wanted me to be the pastor. First, I never led the evening service; second, the adversaries were opposed to the evening Mass, at which I never presided; third, I did not talk to the children, I did not come out on their behalf, I did not represent them; fourth, from the day that Dragica Ivanković confronted me, I was regarded as being against the apparitions. I guess the children did find me very stern, rude, not so meek as Father Jozo. This reputation preceded me. So, there was an impression that Fr. Zrinko was opposed, and it was built on the basis of an attitude that many did not understand, or they understood in a completely inaccurate way.

"From the beginning, some people thought that I would 'blow it up' because, to those who looked at the cross and said that the cross was spinning, I used to say, 'It's spinning in your head!,' or 'If you don't want it to spin in your head, turn around and listen to the Mass, and don't stare up at the cross!' Or, for example, they looked up at Apparition Hill during Mass and I yelled, 'Hey, you, Our Lady is behind you. She is in the church. Why are you looking up there?' etc. I called out everyone a little, not just pilgrims. To those in authority, I used to say, 'What have you come here for? What are you looking for here? Did you also get stuck in mysticism and superstition?!'"

Fr. Zrinko noted that, although there was an expectation that the celebration of the Mass would stop, Fr. Tomislav did not give up; he was tough. Then, in January of 1982, Church authorities decided to appoint Fr. Zrinko as acting pastor instead of Fr. Tomislav, and Fr. Zrinko remained in that position until the end of August. Regarding Fr. Jozo's imprisonment, he said that it was a "general national mourning."

"And, to make that grief even more painful, it appeared in all the media that 'the people were relieved' and that they actually drove Fr. Jozo out, and that the same people sought appropriate punishment for the atrocities he committed and for the shame he had brought to his region," Fr. Zrinko said. "Well, that was a caricature of the time and of the situation: On the one hand, there was a general mourning among the people and, on the other, [the authorities] acted on behalf of that people and Fr. Jozo's arrest was justified by the alleged demands of the people for his removal from the parish, by persecution from Medjugorje, and for punishment because—imagine—he desecrated the honor of his people and caused great harm to them."

Fr. Zrinko also organized the defense of Fr. Jozo Zovko.

"I sent an invitation to those who listened to Fr. Jozo on that day—those who remembered, as a minimum, the important things that he had said and who were ready to testify before the court—to contact the parish office as soon as possible and leave their personal information so that I could enlist them as witnesses in Fr. Jozo's defense," he explained. "From 12:30 to 10:00 p.m., 530 witnesses contacted us! And, what happened to the money that was taken from the parish office? On August 17, 1981, the day Fr. Jozo was taken away, the [parish] house was searched and all the money and all the bank books found at that time were confiscated and stored in the State Bookkeeping Office in Čitluk. From there, everything was transferred to the SUP bank account. All the money was kept in that account—both foreign currency and dinar—and, after almost a year, they returned all the money with interest. In total, converted into dinars, cash and bank accounts, there was about one hundred and twenty million [equivalent to about $30,000 USD in 1981]. Only that much. Nothing more than that 70 million dinars of that was left over from the previous pastor; we put this in the account as a deposit for a future loan with which we intended to complete rectory."

At the end of their conversation, Fr. Svetozar Kraljević asked Fr. Zrinko if there was anything he would like to say about the time he ran the parish, whether something special had happened at the time—something by which he made his own mark—thinking, above all, about the evolution of events associated with the apparitions and the arrival of pilgrims.

"There is no special mark," Fr. Zrinko said. "I was guided only by the intent to not put obstacles in God's way or to be such an obstacle myself. I let things go their way, only taking care lest something should creep in that wouldn't be in conformity with the discipline of the Church and God's Revelation. That was the only thing about which I was sensitive and watched vigilantly. The rest, I left to time and place."

Fr. Zrinko Čuvalo passed away in 1991.

Literature & sources

1. Kraljević, Fr. Svetozar. *The Apparitions of our Lady at Medjugorje.* Information Center "Mir" Medjugorje, Medjugorje 2012.

2. Čović, Sabrina. *Meetings with Fr. Jozo.* Editions Sakramento, Pariz 2006.

3. Škunca, Darija. *Understanding Medjugorje.* Klanac Information Center "Mir" Medjugorje, Medjugorje 2009.

4. Ivković, Žarko and Bubalo, Robert and Despot, Zvonimir and Hančić, Siniša. *Medjugorje – The Mystery of Our Lady's Apparitions.* Večernji list, Zagreb 2006.

5. Ivković, Žarko and Bubalo, Robert and Despot, Zvonimir and Hančić, Siniša. *The Mystery of Medjugorje – 30 Years of a Phenomenon / Documents of the Yugoslav Secret Police.* Večernji list, Zagreb 2011.

6. Rupčić, Dr. Ljudevit. *Our Lady's Apparitions in Medjugorje.* Medjugorje 1983.

7. Rupčić, Dr. Ljudevit. *Medjugorje – The Gates of Heaven and the Beginning of a Better World.* Ziral, Mostar 1999.

8. Marin, Jakov. *Queen of Peace in Medjugorje.* Rkt. Parish of St Mary – Dolac, Zagreb 1988.

9. Šego, Krešimir. *Our Lady of Whispers.* Naklada Brotnjo, Medjugorje 1988.

10. Dugandžić, Marija. *Medjugorje in the Church.* Information Center "Mir" Medjugorje, Medjugorje 2001.

11. Bubalo, Fr. Janko. *A Thausand Encounters with Our Lady in Medjugorje.* Jelsa Parish Office, Hvar 1985.

12. Soldo, Mirjana. *My Heart Will Triumph.* Matica hrvatska Čitluk, Čitluk 2016.

13. *Medjugorje – a. d. 1981. – The beginnings of Our Lady's Apparitions.* "Novelti Millenium," Zagreb 2011.

14. Audiotapes of Fr. Jozo Zovko's interviews with visionaries on June 28 and June 30, 1981.

About the author

Darko Pavičić is a journalist for Večernji list (the largest daily newspaper in Croatia).

He has been dealing exclusively with religious issues for 30 years, writing about the work and life of religious communities—especially the Catholic Church—in Croatia, and is among the leading analysts in the field in Croatia.

He also often participates in public debates, especially on television.

CPSIA information can be obtained
at www.ICGtesting.com
Printed in the USA
JSHW012230211022
31985JS00001B/1